PRAISE FOR MICHAEL PATRICK WELCH

In this wonderfully quirky music- and art-focused book, Welch concentrates on his New Orleans—the New Orleans that he and his friends know. There is plenty of information on many aspects of artsy New Orleans: Mardi Gras festivities, literary New Orleans, art galleries, burlesque clubs, theater, comedy clubs, thrift stores and costume shops, record stores, as well as a discussion of the Mardi Gras Indians, profiles of local musicians, and even a chapter on family fun.

> —*Chicago Tribune*

I've been friends with Michael Patrick Welch for a number of years, and in New Orleans he seems to have really found his place. On my first visit from New York, before the flood, he took me on an epic bike ride tour of the city. We saw everything from grand mansions to beautiful bombed-out neighborhoods, and no matter where we went that day, Michael knew someone. Michael obviously loves New Orleans very much, and on my visits there he has shown me so much that I never expected, and would have not seen otherwise.

> —Jonathan Ames, creator of HBO's *Bored to Death* and author of *The Extra Man* and *The Double Life Is Twice as Good*

Michael Patrick Welch is a true community light.

> —Chuck D, Public Enemy

Your boyfriend is very, very talented.

> —Ray Davies of The Kinks to Michael Patrick Welch's girlfriend, Jazz Fest 2003

Michael Patrick Welch is America's greatest living writer!

> —Tony Clifton to a dressing room full of burlesque dancers

D0789941

FOURTH EDITION

NEW ORLEANS
THE UNDERGROUND GUIDE

MICHAEL PATRICK WELCH
with Brian Boyles

PHOTOGRAPHS BY ZACK SMITH AND JONATHAN TRAVIESA

LOUISIANA STATE UNIVERSITY PRESS   BATON ROUGE

Published by Louisiana State University Press
Copyright © 2018 by Louisiana State University Press
First and second editions published by the University of New Orleans Press,
2009 and 2011
Third edition published by Louisiana State University Press, 2014

Designer: Barbara N. Bourgoyne
Typefaces: DubTone and Helvetica Neue, display; Ingeborg, text
Printer and binder: Sheridan Books

Maps are by Morgana King.

Library of Congress Cataloging-in-Publication Data

Names: Welch, Michael Patrick, 1974– author. | Boyles, Brian, 1977– author. |
    Smith, Zack, 1975– photographer. | Traviesa, Jonathan, photographer.
Title: New Orleans : the underground guide / Michael Patrick Welch with
    Brian Boyles ; photographs by Zack Smith and Jonathan Traviesa.
Description: Fourth edition. | Baton Rouge : Louisiana State University Press,
    [2018] | Includes index.
Identifiers: LCCN 2018018056| ISBN 978-0-8071-6990-2 (pbk. : alk. paper) |
    ISBN 978-0-8071-7041-0 (pdf) | ISBN 978-0-8071-7042-7 (epub)
Subjects: LCSH: New Orleans (La.)—Guidebooks. | New Orleans (La.)—
    Description and travel.
Classification: LCC F379.N53 W44 2018 | DDC 976.3/35—dc23
LC record available at https://lccn.loc.gov/2018018056

CONTENTS

EVERYTHING ELSE IN NEW ORLEANS

ACKNOWLEDGMENTS

We would first like to acknowledge that any attempt to comprehensively document every one of New Orleans' various music and art communities would be impossible. Further editions of this book will fill in any embarrassing holes we may have left out this fourth time around.

We also acknowledge that, while Bywater/Marigny and other recently gentrified New Orleans neighborhoods don't need more advertising, the musicians who live there and the bars they play in do. We acknowledge that it's our duty to educate tourists on this gentrification, and especially the ways in which short-term rentals and the "sharing economy" in general have damaged the city and its culture.

Thanks to **Brian Boyles**, who wrote a not-insignificant chunk of this book, and to **Alison Fensterstock**.

Big thanks to writers who donated text: Jules Bentley, Renard "Slangston Hughes" Bridgewater, Richard Campanella, Michael Martin, Daniel "Impulss" Perez, and dear Veronica Russell (R.I.Power).

Most of the book's photographs were taken by **Zack Smith** and **Jonathan Traviesa**. Equally big thanks to the photographers who graciously donated their work to benefit the artists photographed, especially **Robin Walker** and **Gary LoVerde**, but also: Amahl Abdul-Khaliq, Martin "Quickie Mart" Arcenaux, Katrina Arnold, Tad Bartlett, Tim Black, Josh Brasted, Katie Breaux, Rachel Breunlin, Mark Caesar, Paul Cheenne, Sam Deen, Ed Doskey, Geoff Douville, Cedric Ellsworth, Alleyn Evans, Zachary "Gnarbot" Gnar, Sierra Hudson, Katja Liebing, Sam Lucia, Eli Mergel, Trixie Minx, Taylor Murrow, Rick Olivier, Chana Rose Rabinovitz, Rat Bastard, Valerie Sassyfras, Matthew Seymour, Benjamin Simmons, Lamarcus Smith, Scott Stuntz, Matt "DJ Matty" Uhlman, Taslim Van Hattum, Jason Van Ness, Joe Vidrine, Josh Vine, and Kim Welsh.

Thank you, **Morgana King**, for making the neighborhood maps.

Thanks also to those who donated their time to give recommendations, favorites, and other stories: Mark Caesar, DJ

RQAway, Geoff Douville, Otis Fennell, Jonathan Ferrara, Juicy Jackson, Katey Red, Walt McClements, Leo McGovern, Alex McMurray, Paul Oswell, Justin Peake, Matt Russell, Nick Thomas, Andrew Vaught, Paul Webb, Mike IX Williams, and our dear, departed Veronica Russell.

Special thanks to **Lord David**, who protected me from physical violence after this book's first edition came out, as well as Blake and Patrick at Dirty Coast, Creighton Durrant, Edward Jackson, Bill Lavender, Katie Hunter-Lowery, Harry Cheadle at Vice.com, plus *Gambit Weekly*, *OffBeat*, and *Antigravity* magazines.

NEW ORLEANS
THE UNDERGROUND GUIDE

WELCOME TO NEW ORLEANS!

Welcome! We created this fourth edition of *New Orleans: The Underground Guide* to counter the incomplete image of the city that you have in your head. It ain't your fault. New Orleans is often marketed as its old self. They'll have you thinking you can still hop off your plane and go hit a brothel in Storyville—when really, it's a little tough to find even good, legal *music* in the French Quarter these days. The streets of New Orleans do still sound like brass bands, Mardi Gras Indians, and trad jazz, but the city that invented genres from rock 'n' roll to bounce rap continues to create and perfect new styles for the world to enjoy.

So, while most other guidebooks point you toward the old-timey, Big Easy, Crescent City jazz jambalaya goodness, of which there is plenty, this guidebook hopes to lead you to the new and unexpected (along with a nice handful of traditional favorites). We will aim you toward hundreds of hard-to-define New Orleans rock bands, rappers, and DJs—musicians who sound like New Orleans without playing the standards. New Orleans' past should be glorified and its amazing traditions kept alive, but we continue writing these books to prove that New Orleans' most important artistic days are *not* behind it!

Much has changed in the city since this book's first edition in 2009. There is more to do in New Orleans now than ever. We've added over two hundred new nightclubs, new bands, and new restaurants that host live music, plus new and unique insights from locals like author and historical geographer **Richard Campanella** (who in our family chapter describes a day of New Orleans activities with his son), songwriter and club owner **Luke Allen of Happy Talk Band** (who discusses the songwriters he loves to book at **Siberia Lounge** in Marigny), and noise music impresario **Sebastian Figueroa** aka **Proud/Father**, who has superb taste in experimental sound. In this latest edition, we've also added new sections on New Orleans photography, breweries, gumbo, oysters, snowballs, and other important categories.

This book's original premise remains intact: Having written about music for all of New Orleans' publications (*all* of them), I noticed that many of the city's nontraditional musicians got almost no press, and so I wanted to give them some attention and drum up business for the nightclubs where they regularly performed. We also wanted to help guide the many smart tourists who come to New Orleans specifically to hear live music—and that meant motivating tourists to go outside of the French Quarter to explore the city's many other amazing neighborhoods. I've since felt very conflicted about sending tourists into our neighborhoods . . .

When I say there's more to do now here than ever, I also mean gentrification has taken hold in earnest. In the big picture, Katrina only jabbed at our housing market, before the scourge of short-term rentals landed the solid right hook that has turned many of New Orleans' most historic neighborhoods into hotel

Jonathan Traviesa

districts. So, while we still believe you should respectfully bask in the cultural and artistic wonders provided by our many neighborhoods, we stress that you should make conscientious decisions. As when visiting rain forests, please take only go-cups and leave only tips—and be smart about where you lay your head. In our hotels chapter, my favorite local writer, **Jules Bentley**, details the particular problems associated with short-term rentals in New Orleans' still-sensitive post-Katrina housing market.

Fun!

No, really though, the book is still focused on the fun, and the new. We have, as always, come at this project again hoping to act as friends of yours who want you to meet our wild, artistic friends and understand the unique fun we have and why we live in New Orleans.

And that reason, mainly, is music!

Per usual, our book's writers and photographers all live here in New Orleans, participating wholeheartedly in the city's music, art, photography, journalism, and literary scenes. We will continue bringing all these smart, creative locals together for further editions of this book, hoping to prove to you that New Orleans is not what you think.

—Michael Patrick Welch

READ THIS BOOK

We have placed the names of notable locals and local businesses in bold. All of those bold names are indexed by page number. The index will help you locate all six times we mention Dragon's Den, and all five times we big up Mannie Fresh.

Each business or event entry is listed first by its neighborhood (Bywater, CBD, Uptown, etc.). The West Bank (not listed in the neighborhoods section) extends from the other side of the river in Algiers (still Orleans Parish) all the way to Los Angeles. Another way to think of the West Bank is that it's a suburb of New Orleans, just like wherever you live.

If any entry lacks a URL, try that band or business on Facebook or Twitter.

The sections detailing individual musicians were initially designed so you could walk up to a bank of flyers on say, Frenchmen Street, and be able to cross-reference the flyers with the names in this book, and decide what you're interested in hearing and seeing. But since then, in 2009, the city banned the posting of flyers. Yes, I agree, that's fascism.

EIGHT AWESOME
NEIGHBORHOODS

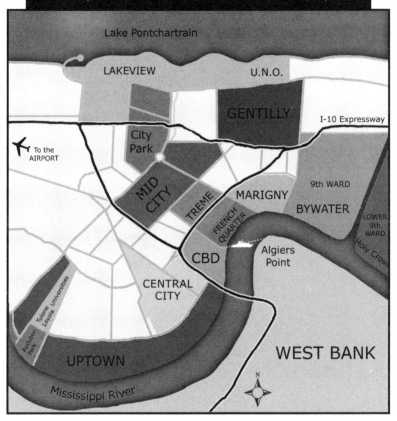

As a visitor, you will understand and enjoy New Orleans more if you think in terms of neighborhoods. New Orleans' neighborhoods are each distinctly flavored, with their own accents and styles.

This book admittedly overlooks some New Orleans neighborhoods. And because you won't meet many locals on Bourbon Street (aside from your bartender or the lady who gave you a lap dance), our book doesn't spend a lot of time in the much-hyped French Quarter either—though make sure and spend a day or two wandering the Quarter's pretty/smelly streets, for sure.

We focus on the city's current music hotspots in eight neighborhoods, starting in the east and moving upriver: 1) **Bywater**, 2) **Faubourg Marigny**, 3) the **French Quarter**, 4) **Central Business District (CBD)**, 5) **Central City**, and 6) **Uptown**. Then north of the Quarter there's 7) **Faubourg Tremé** and 8) **Mid-City**.

Note: Because New Orleans is shaped like a crescent, and seems to have been laid out geographically by a drunk person, our N/S/E/W coordinates are imprecise.

Zack Smith

BYWATER

Boundaries: Florida Ave. (N), Mississippi River (S),
Industrial Canal (E), Press St. railroad tracks (W).

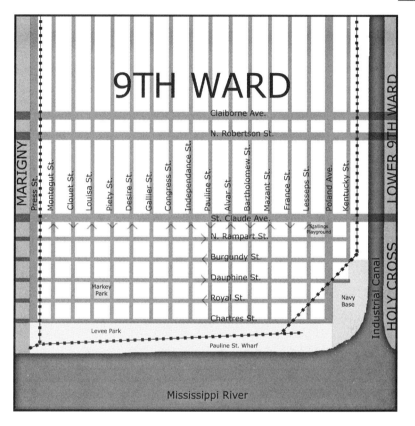

Some locals believe that real estate agents long ago coined the term "Bywater" (meaning both near the river and the Industrial Canal) to disassociate the neighborhood from the rest of the Ninth Ward. Since Katrina, Bywater has changed maybe more than any other neighborhood. Because the "sliver on the river" didn't flood, young hipsters and tech people from urban centers where housing has always been expensive began moving to New Orleans in droves, undeterred by what locals would consider ridiculous, prohibitive housing costs. While the rest of the city was rebuilding, Bywater was welcoming a slew of new coffeehouses, music clubs, and small-plate restaurants.

Many of the neighborhood's classic old Creole cottages and shotgun houses (often made of wood from the dismantled ships of long-ago Spanish and French immigrants) have recently been prettied up—making it even more of a dream for photographers and architecture enthusiasts. The new **Crescent Park** and its rusty rainbow bridge along the Mississippi River are nice, upscale editions to this already beautiful hood.

Bywater's art and music scenes remain hip but rarely pretentious. Many of the city's musicians cling to their longtime Bywater living situations, so it's still easy to find a musical party any night of the week here. The new **St. Claude streetcar line** was built since this book's last edition, and the continuing growth of the **St. Claude Arts District** means more art galleries than ever before (don't miss the **St. Claude Arts Walk** on each month's second Saturday). So, if you came to New Orleans for unique music and experiences, and if you came to follow strange new friends on adventures often involving bikes and beer and pot and music, then Bywater is your jam.

FAUBOURG MARIGNY

(FAW-borg MER-ih-nee)

Boundaries: St. Claude Ave. (N), Mississippi River (S), Franklin Ave. (E), Esplanade Ave. (W)

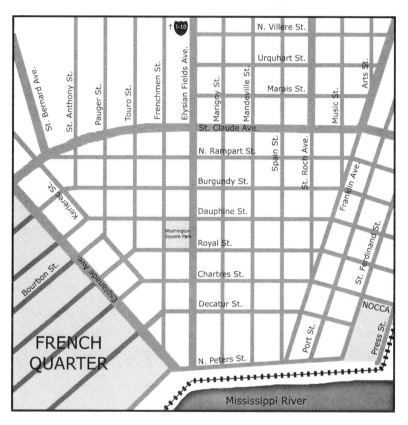

The Faubourg Marigny is a cute, clean(ish), and charmingly crammed together neighborhood of shotgun houses named after its founder, Bernard de Marigny, the guy who popularized the game "craps" (no joke!). All of the city comes to hear and play music on the Marigny's famous Frenchmen Street. Since this book's last edition, the Frenchmen Street music district has completed its transformation into a baby Bourbon Street, complete with hot dogs and cover bands. However, places like **FAB** gay book store and art gallery, the musical eatery **Three Muses**, and club **d.b.a.** make fighting the drunken crowds worth it.

Then, just up Frenchmen and around the corner on St. Claude Ave. sits the holy musical trinity of **Hi-Ho Lounge, Siberia Lounge**, and **AllWays Lounge**—all great places to catch live bands and DJs, and with a new art market, the **Art Garage**, squeezed in between.

The dollhouse cuteness of the Marigny might even make you let your guard down and wander down dimly lit, seemingly unpopulated streets after sunset. Don't do that, ever, not anywhere you haven't been, and not in New Orleans.

THE FRENCH QUARTER

Boundaries: Pretty much a big lopsided square, bordered by
Rampart St. (N), Decatur St. (S), Esplanade Ave. (E), and Canal St. (W)

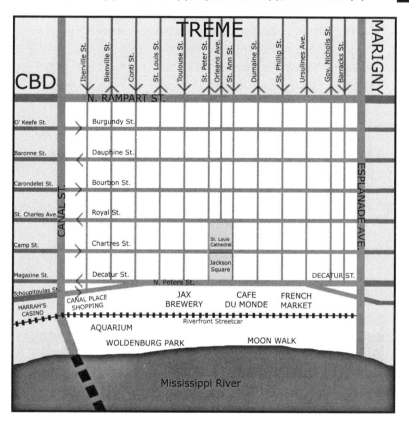

Part national landmark, part American party zone, the French Quarter remains a functioning residential/commercial neighborhood. It's also a giant open-air mall of bars, antique shopping, street performers, more bars, bad art, strip clubs, daiquiri stands, and, in its margins, old-timey New Orleans music. Modern musical standouts include nightclub **One Eyed Jacks** and famous **Preservation Hall,** which offers the standards, plus an increasing degree of progressive, mostly acoustic music.

Perfect for endless wandering and stumbling, the Quarter hosts hundreds of classic bars like my favorite, **The Chart Room** (300 Chartres St.), which allows for amazing people-watching, while charging below-market prices for stiff drinks. **Jackson Square** hosts tarot readers, "psychics," questionable artists hawking their wares, and people painted completely gold, all to the tune of bad folk music and good brass bands (many of the city's best traditional players hone their chops in the square, passing the hat). There's also the old **French Market** on lower Decatur (near the river just off Esplanade), which features a giant selection of cheesy New Orleans souvenirs, and more cool cheap sunglasses than you've ever seen (Two pairs $7! Don't pay more!).

If the weather's nice, gravitate down to the **Mississippi River** and its romantic **Moon Walk**, named for former New Orleans mayor **Moon Landrieu** (a good place to smoke pot, just watch for bike cops). We also suggest taking the **Canal Street ferry** ($2 per person each way) across the Mississippi to quaint Algiers Point on the West Bank, to take in the best view of the city. **William Burroughs** lived in Algiers at 509 Wagner Street, and was once visited there by Jack Kerouac, as documented in *On the Road*.

So, yes, make sure to spend a day wandering the French Quarter, drinking before sunset from your go-cup until you're tipping every single street performer. Just don't spend your whole vacation in the playpen.

Night or day, you'll meet all types of humans in French Quarter bars.

Zack Smith

CENTRAL BUSINESS DISTRICT (CBD)

Boundaries: S. Claiborne Ave. (N), Mississippi River (S),
Canal St. (E), Lee Circle (W)

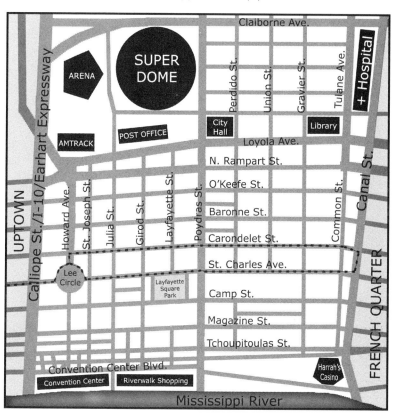

The CBD hosts all of New Orleans' tall office buildings, which would make any outsider think it's our "downtown." To locals, the CBD is the small chunk between Uptown (Garden District) and downtown (everything below Canal Street). In recent years the booming sports entertainment zone around the Superdome and New Orleans Arena has created new buzz in the area. The CBD boasts some decent New Orleans restaurants, though many are open only for weekday lunch, catering to the working stiffs.

The traditional contemporary galleries of **Julia Street Arts**

District are continually open and nice to peruse (more street-level work can be found downtown, of course). The portion of the CBD nearest the river is called the **Warehouse District**, though many of the area's old nineteenth-century warehouses have been converted into condominiums. Redeveloped around the time of the 1984 World's Fair, the Warehouse District is also home to the **Contemporary Arts Center** (CAC) (900 Camp St.) and the **Ogden Museum of Southern Art** (925 Camp St.). During the day, you can drink or lunch at restaurants including **Cochon** (930 Tchoupitoulas St.), and at night rock out at the venerable **Howlin' Wolf** (907 S. Peters St.) or at medium-sized dance music club **The Republic** (828 S. Peters St.).

CENTRAL CITY

Boundaries: S. Claiborne Ave. (N), St. Charles Ave. (S),
MLK Blvd. (E), and Louisiana Ave. (W)

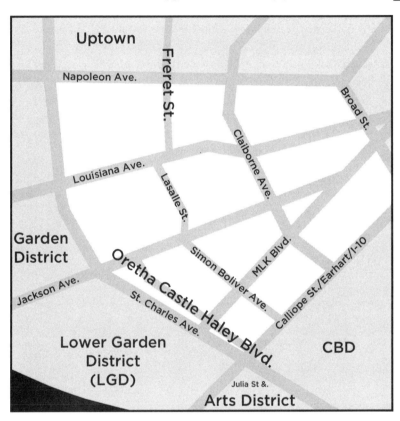

During Jim Crow, Central City and particularly Dryades Street served as the city's largest African American–patronized commercial area. In the '60s, the fact that black folks were not allowed to work at the stores they patronized eventually prompted lunch-counter protests that defeated economic segregation. The vast neighborhood was free to bloom as a hub of brass bands and Mardi Gras Indian culture (The Indians' **Super Sunday** event is held on "a Sunday soon after" St. Joseph's Day [March 19] near Lasalle Street). Even in its blighted '90s incarnation, Central City pumped out talented rappers from Soulja Slim to Juvenile, plus multimillionaire record-label moguls Birdman and Master P.

Today the area, which did not flood much during Katrina, is back to being an African American culture and entertainment hub. Central City hosts the world's best **MLK Day Parade** (King founded the Southern Christian Leadership Conference here in 1957). The neighborhood's Main Street, Oretha Castle Haley Blvd. (named after a famous lunch-counter protestor), hosts the **Ashe Cultural Center** (a constant flow of Afrocentric art, music, dance, film, and theater), the **New Orleans Jazz Market** (performing arts center with live jazz, a jazz archive, and of course a bar), **Café Reconcile** (best, cheapest gumbo in the city, served by at-risk youth), the **Southern Food and Beverage Museum**, and a new version of the famous old **Dryades Market**, serving prepared foods and specialty groceries—to name just a few.

UPTOWN

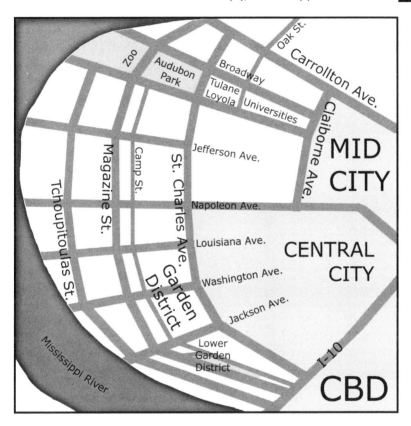

Boundaries: Carrollton Ave. (N), Mississippi River (S), Carrollton at the river bend (W), Lee Circle (E)

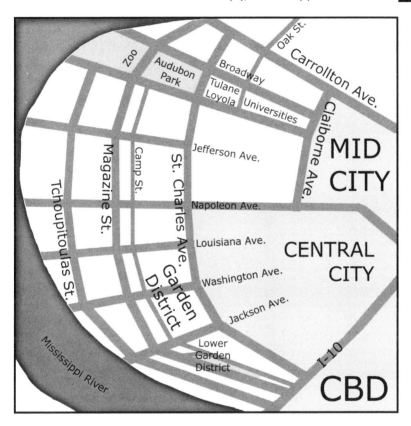

The designation "Uptown" is an umbrella term to describe several distinct areas of New Orleans west of ("above") Canal Street: When riding the streetcar, you'll enter Uptown once you roll beneath the interstate, known as the Calliope overpass. The first stretch of St. Charles features many eateries and fast-food joints, and is highly recommend when viewing Carnival parades. Get off around Jackson Avenue to explore the **Lower Garden District** (LGD) neighborhood: a slightly unkempt hood that features the dog-and-bum friendly **Coliseum Square Park** (intersection of Coliseum and Euterpe Streets), plus numerous cool dive restaurants and bars. On the river side of Magazine Street is the **Irish**

Channel and its community center/bar and restaurant, **Parasol's** (2533 Constance St.), with its definitive po'boys.

Moving upriver along St. Charles, just down from Napoleon, a lovely New Orleans moment can be had with a drink on the veranda of the **Columns Hotel** (3811 St. Charles Ave.). Across St. Charles and above Napoleon you come to the **Upper Garden District**, which is the "Uptown" you'd expect, with over-the-top grand mansions, well-manicured lawns, plus more than enough eating and shopping on St. Charles and along Magazine Street.

After passing Tulane and Loyola Universities, the streetcar turns at the Riverbend into the Carrollton section of Uptown, home of college-kid-friendly restaurants and bars. **Oak Street** offers many fun businesses including the **Live Oak Café,** which serves great breakfast, brunch, and lunch food.

FAUBOURG TREMÉ

(FAW-borg Trem-May)

Boundaries: Claiborne Ave. (N), Rampart St. (S),
Esplanade Ave. (E), Canal St. (W)

The relatively small but culturally invaluable Tremé neighborhood is famous as the first area in America where free people of color could buy and sell land, even as the country was still enmeshed in slavery. Following the neighborhood's starring run in David Simon's hit series of the same name on HBO, and an influx of gentrification (Airbnb hit Tremé hard), it remains a beautiful place where you'll always find something interesting on the streets and in the doorways. Tremé's corner bars and corner stores, churches and funeral homes, were the breeding ground for centuries of musicians to hone their horns and drums. The

Tremé's unique history and energy are the reasons why New Orleans will always be what imprisoned former mayor Ray Nagin once called "a chocolate city."

Along with a lot of gorgeous architecture, the Tremé hosts homegrown museums dedicated to celebrating African American culture, history, and art: The **Backstreet Museum** (1116 Henriette Delille St.) and the **New Orleans African American Museum** (1418 Governor Nicholls St.) make for good stops. **Armstrong Park** and the new **Congo Square** are a pretty walk from the French Quarter. Birthplace of modern musicians from **Trombone Shorty** to singer **John Boutté**, the Tremé is also where many beautiful second-line jazz funerals pop up—while regular churchgoers are welcomed at traditional musical services in the country's oldest black Catholic church, **St. Augustine** (1210 Governor Nicholls St.).

Zack Smith

MID-CITY

Boundaries: Carrollton Ave. (N), I-10 (S),
Pontchartrain Expressway (W), N. Broad St. (E)

Mid-City is a mixed-income residential neighborhood that boasts
some of New Orleans' best architecture—houses as gargantuan
as those uptown but more colorful and less uppity—plus many
small bars and restaurants. Mid-City sits midway between the
Mississippi River and Lake Pontchartrain, making it a prime area
for flooding, aside from Esplanade Ridge, one of the longest,
highest shelves in the city. This low-key but visually stunning
neighborhood was damaged by Katrina but came back strong:
The **Fair Grounds** horse-racing track hosts every **Jazz Fest**.
The **New Orleans Museum of Art** (NOMA) still represents in

vast and wondrous **City Park,** also home to the **Voodoo Music &
Arts Experience** each October. Mid-City also hosts many mini-
hoods, including Bayou St. John (good freshwater fishing both
there and inside City Park) and the Bayou Road area, home to
my favorite New Orleans–style restaurant, **Liuzza's by the Track**.
Mid-City is for chillin'.

1. MUSIC VENUES

Music, food, and drinking in the streets are the main attractions in New Orleans. The French Quarter definitely does not have the market cornered on music; great clubs thrive in every neighborhood.

ALLWAYS LOUNGE & THEATRE

Marigny, 2240 St. Claude Ave., 504-218-5778; theallwayslounge.net

The longtime home of Cowpokes, a gay bar with a rootin'-tootin' theme, this space was taken over by a punk-rock and theater-friendly, sex-positive contingent. Expect anything from acoustic country bands to erotic literature readings to jock strap lube wrestling on All-Ways's photogenic red-velvet stage. The back room serves as a community theater, hosting all manner of local, alternative performances. It's also just a friendly bar, always offering something wild and daring and fun.

BACCHANAL

Bywater, 600 Poland Ave., 504-948-9111; bacchanalwine.com

Hosts live jazz and serves up excellent creative foods in a verdant outdoor courtyard. At peak times it is absolutely overrun by bros and Beckys, so be warned.

BANKS STREET BAR

Mid-City, 4401 Banks St., 504-486-0258; banksstreetbarandgrill.com

For music ranging from rock, R&B, and electro to metal and even live reggae, there's rarely a cover at Banks Street Bar. Small enough that the bands run their own PA, the club often hosts multiple shows per day—a rarity even in New Orleans. They've also got free red beans and rice on Mondays and (often) free oysters on Thursdays. Though seemingly on a deserted island after Katrina, Banks now enjoys **Wakin' Bakin'** breakfast shop next door, **Clesi's Crawfish and Catering** nearby, and **Mid City Pizza** across the street.

BAR REDUX

Bywater, 801 Poland Ave., 504-592-7083; barredux.com

As far back as you can get in Bywater, this little bar with good food (sandwiches, burgers, gumbo, and red beans) hosts solo singer-songwriters, DJ nights, film festivals, the Music & Poetry reading series, and a local, low-key comedy open-mic night.

BJ'S LOUNGE

Bywater, 4301 Burgundy St., 504-945-9256

Charles Bukowski would have loved sitting in BJ's listening to the great jukebox with (or perhaps in spite of) the host of colorful alcoholic neighbors and musician types who call BJ's their second home. On Thanksgiving and other holidays, BJ's hosts live music and potluck dinners with smoked duck and crawfish mac-n-cheese, among dozens of other neighborhood dishes. Wednesday night is the **BloodJet Poetry Series**, co-curated by **Megan Burns** and **J. S. Makkos**. Warning: Like Vaughan's around the corner, BJ's takes *no credit cards.*

BULLET'S SPORTS BAR

Tremé, 2441 A. P. Tureaud Ave.,
504-948-4003

A robbery in his old bar gave Rollins "Bullet" Garcia Sr. his nickname, which he passed on to his bar, now two decades old. An old-man watering hole known best for amazing jazz from the likes of trumpeter **Kermit Ruffins** and the Pinettes all-female brass band,

Bullet's also serves old-school seven-ounce pony beers as well as "setups," meaning a half pint of liquor, a mixer, and ice. Bullet's hosts music several nights a week—and a great food truck always parks out front during live shows—but you better call and check beforehand, if music's what you're after.

CAFÉ ISTANBUL

Marigny, 2372 St. Claude Ave.,
504-975-0286; cafeistanbulnola.com

The 55,000-square-foot Healing Center hosts an ever-revolving cast of artsy shops, while in the back hides a 3,800-square-foot entertainment hall with a great bar. On its polished oak stage, the Café Istanbul Performance Theater offers a continuing calendar of music, dance, theater, poetry, comedy and film, while its balcony also serves as a gallery space for visual art.

The Café Istanbul nightclub and community center lives inside the Cultural Healing Center on St. Claude Ave. in Marigny.

Zack Smith

CHICKIE WAH WAH

Mid-City, 2828 Canal St.,
504-304-4714; chickiewahwah.com

Named for the song recorded by **Huey "Piano" Smith and the Clowns** in 1958 (for the French Quarter–based **Ace** label), this Mid-City joint books a cheerful grab bag of homegrown acts, from **Creole String Beans** swamp pop to **Jumpin' Johnny Sansone**'s barroom blues, with extra-late late-night gigs during Jazz Fest. They usually serve a bar-food menu, something like pizza or tacos to soak up booze. Of note: Chickie Wah Wah is the closest place to hear live music near Orleans Parish Prison.

CHRIS OWENS CLUB

French Quarter, 500 Bourbon St.,
504-523-6400; chrisowensclub.net

Bourbon Street may be the most American of alleys in our fair city, so surprises are few and primarily nipple-based. Dancer Chris Owens remains a fixture from another era, a performer and club owner who's graced her own stage from the 1960s and today appears (eerily unchanged) on weekends as a time capsule/one-woman floor show of sequins and pizzazz. If you're on Bourbon Street, check in, and if Chris isn't in, don't be surprised to find bounce music and furious dancing. Saturdays also feature a very local Latin night in a room perfect for dreams of a Puerto Rico on Mars.

CIRCLE BAR

CBD, 1032 St. Charles Ave.
at Lee Circle, 504-588-2616;
circlebarnola.com

This teeny-tiny living room-esque venue holds maybe seventy-five concert-goers, and hosts shows almost every night. The jukebox—courtesy of original owner **Kelly Keller**, a legendary underground-rock personality who passed away in 2004—boasts one of the finest collections of punk, garage rock, and Louisiana R&B and soul as ever there was. Sometimes the tiniest concert venue has the biggest parties.

DRAGON'S DEN

Marigny, 435 Esplanade Ave.,
504-940-4446; dragonsdennola.com

Up the precarious, twisty red stairwell you'll find a dim, red-lit room anchored on one end by the bar and on the other by a wrought-iron balcony overlooking the grassy Esplanade Avenue neutral

Jonathan Traviesa

Who knows what lies up the Dragon's Den's dark, mysterious staircase? Uh, check the listings.

ground and the mouth of the lower Decatur strip. With turntable booths and live music stages both upstairs and downstairs, the nonetheless tiny Dragon's Den hosts several monthly electronic music parties featuring hip-hop, jungle, reggaeton, and the like, with a smattering of rock 'n' roll bands across the calendar.

THE DRIFTER

Mid-City, 3522 Tulane Ave., 504-605-4644; thedrifterhotel.com

This new hipster hotel hosts concerts and other events by its pool (a pool being necessary to sanity during New Orleans' summers). In the mornings, the Drifter provides specialty coffees before transitioning into fresh frozen cocktails, Japanese beers and sakes, and local wines. Live shows here are sporadic, from bands to DJs to fashion shows to the occasional kooky water ballet.

ELLIS MARSALIS CENTER FOR MUSIC

Bywater (actually Upper Ninth Ward, very near Bywater), 1901 Bartholomew St., 504-940-3400; ellismarsaliscenter.org

The centerpiece of the **Musicians' Village** neighborhood in the Upper **Ninth Ward**, this 17,000-square-foot facility serves as a performance, education, and community venue. The 170-seat hall is combined with recording studios and teaching facilities for individual and group instruction, and a general community gathering place. From music to dance, theater to film, the center aims to harness the exceptional talents of the residents and students in the surrounding Musicians' Village.

NOLA MOMENT

FRENCHMEN STREET

A concentrated dose of music

Similar to Austin's famous 6th Street, **Frenchmen Street** is back-to-back clubs and funky, relatively inexpensive restaurants. Once considered the locals' alternative to Bourbon Street, it has since become a smaller version of Bourbon Street. However, in between the cover bands and the white boy funk, you'll find tons of good music—you just may have to vie with bros and Beckys for a space on the dance floor.

There are fourteen music clubs on Frenchmen Street. Frenchmen is to be enjoyed as a whole, as a casual stumble door to door. Just go down and wander and you'll find what you want. But if'n you are interested, here are some favorite spots:

Drummer Simon Lott and crew get the crowd to lie on the floor at d.b.a.

Zack Smith

BLUE NILE

532 Frenchmen St., 504-948-2583; bluenilelive.com

This very eclectic club with two nice stages and sound systems (separate door costs) hosts everything from live hip-hop MCs and DJs to dancehall nights hosted by **DJ T Roy**, lots of traditional New Orleans music (from **Kermit Ruffins** to various **Nevilles**), a marginal amount of indie rock, a few fashion shows, and even the Open Ear experimental jazz series. Their programming varies so wildly, it's advisable to make sure you know who's playing before you pay the cover.

d.b.a.

618 Frenchmen St., 504-942-3731, dbaneworleans.com

d.b.a. often books two shows a night at 6 and 10 p.m., a roster of New Orleans music—jazz vocals to rowdy funk to straight-ahead rattling blues. This is also where **Stevie Wonder** chose to pop in after **Jazz Fest**, and countless others. If you've visited d.b.a. more than a few years ago, the sound and the stage space have been much improved—and it was already pretty rad.

MAISON

508 Frenchmen St., 504-371-5543; maisonfrenchmen.com

This larger-than-it-seems concert venue features a stage in the downstairs window with early-evening jazz shows you can watch from the street, plus a big stage upstairs that hosts comedy nights and giant rap shows. Order up a plate of Jamaican ginger-beer pulled pork, or sandwiches such as steak and brie, or check out their jazz brunch every Sunday from 10 a.m. to 3 p.m., when the NOLA Jitterbugs offer swing dancing lessons.

Couples dance to small acoustic combos at small-plate restaurant Three Muses.

Zack Smith

SNUG HARBOR

626 Frenchmen St., 504-949-0696; snugjazz.com

Snug is considered the city's premier spot for big-name local and international jazz acts, with sets nightly at 8 and 10 p.m. Jazz patriarch and educator **Ellis Marsalis** plays here monthly with his quartet. The building's other half is given over to a casual-upscale supper club focusing on steaks, burgers, and gulf seafood. Tip: The often-pricey upstairs show is usually broadcast on a closed-circuit TV you can watch at the excellent downstairs bar.

SPOTTED CAT

623 Frenchmen St., 504-943-3887; 2372 St. Claude Ave. #130, 504-371-5074; spottedcatmusicclub.com

I make a lot of cracks about old-timey music throughout this book, but this place is the *spot*. One hundred percent acoustic jazz quintets and swing bands and singing groups, and reasonably priced drinks in a tiny li'l club. A newer second location provides high-quality music combined with a not-bad menu of southern comfort food, including breakfast.

THREE MUSES

536 Frenchmen St., 504-252-4801; www.3musesnola.com

The cramped seating areas are more than made up for with truly creative small plates of lamb sliders, stuffed pork tenderloin, and duck pastrami pizza. Three Muses' tiny front-window stage hosts several shows a night starting at 4:30 p.m., featuring heavy hitters like cellist **Helen Gillet** and pianist **Tom McDermott**.

Snug Harbor, with d.b.a. in the background.

Zack Smith

31

GASA GASA

Uptown, 4920 Freret St.,
504-338-3567; gasagasa.com

A main player in the revamping of Freret Street into a low-key entertainment district, Gasa Gasa is the city's nicest small club, hosting mostly touring rock, electronic, out jazz, and experimental music. Extra detail is paid to sound engineering here, both in the room's construction and the PA (almost every show is digitally recorded, and some bands are now choosing to make official recordings here). The shingled stage backdrop and cubic projection screen are nice touches, as are Gasa Gasa's modestly priced drinks.

HI-HO LOUNGE

Marigny, 2239 St. Claude Ave.,
504-945-4446; hiholounge.net

This club was once known for edgier downtown acts and the cheapest drinks ever. When the Hi-Ho fell under the control of Brian Greiner, who also runs the Dragon's Den and the Maison, both on Frenchmen St., the Hi-Ho kicked it up a notch, brightened the corners, added a space for food pop-ups, and raised the drink prices a little. The Hi-Ho has maintained its monthly Blue-grass Pickin' Party and popular **NOLA Comedy Hour**, while hosting a roster of progressive jazz and DJ nights.

HOWLIN' WOLF & HOWLIN' WOLF DEN

CBD/Warehouse District,
907 South Peters St., 504-529-5844;
thehowlinwolf.com

The Howlin' Wolf is just one sprawling room with a big stage that hosts anything from brass bands to comedy jams. The sound is pristine, and the dude who owns it—Howie Kaplan, who also manages the Grammy-winning **Rebirth Brass Band**—has championed our scene forever, not only booking local music but also throwing benefits and raising tens of thousands of dollars for charities like the **New Orleans Musicians' Clinic**. Attached to the Wolf is the much smaller **Howlin' Wolf Den**, which hosts smaller bands and regular weekly comedy nights.

KERMIT'S MOTHER-IN-LAW LOUNGE

Tremé, 1500 N. Claiborne Ave.,
504-814-1819;
kermitstrememotherinlawlounge.com

Ernie K-Doe had a hit in the '60s with the track "Mother-in-Law," and later became a beloved icon for his flamboyant presence in local bars and as a DJ on **WWOZ** and **WTUL** radio. The self-branded "Emperor of the Universe" passed away in 2001, and his wife Antoinette ran the bar until she died on Mardi Gras Day 2009. It's since been purchased by trumpeter **Kermit Ruffins**, who has yet to reopen on a permanent basis, but Kermit holds great music events here during Jazz Fest and Mardi Gras. The bar's outside walls are covered with artist **Daniel Fusilier**'s explosively colorful murals depicting K-Doe, Antoinette, and the couple's favorite local music personalities and **Mardi Gras Indians**.

A classical ensemble practices for a performance at the beautiful Marigny Opera House.

LE BON TEMPS ROULÉ

Uptown, 4801 Magazine St., 504-895-8117; lbtrnola.com

Le Bon Temps is a small, ramshackle old honky-tonk with a couple of pool tables, a great, greasy kitchen, and local music almost every night, often with no cover. The booking is generally just good-time rock 'n' roll, with a regular free weekly gig (Thursdays, at press time) from the **Soul Rebels Brass Band** and free oysters at Friday happy hours.

MAPLE LEAF BAR

Uptown, 8316 Oak St., 504-866-9359; mapleleafbar.com

This is a place everyone will tell you about; the **Rebirth Brass Band**'s every Tuesday night gig is the penultimate New Orleans experience, most would agree. Since 1974, the Maple Leaf, with its famous molded tin ceiling, has hosted famous local players from **James Booker** to **Clarence "Gatemouth" Brown** and **Walter "Wolfman" Washington**. The calendar remains

filled with the likes of former **Meters** bassist **George Porter Jr.** and the **Wild Magnolia Mardi Gras Indian Band**, to name just two. Many big national bands in town for Jazz Fest end up joining late-night jams at the Leaf. Also of note for literature lovers: the **Everette C. Maddox Memorial Prose & Poetry Reading**, held every Sunday in the Maple Leaf's outdoor courtyard, is the longest-running poetry reading series in North America.

MARIGNY OPERA HOUSE

Marigny, 725 St. Ferdinand St., 504-948-9998; marignyoperahouse.org

This gorgeous stone church was originally built in 1853 and then reopened in 2014 as a "nondenominational church of the arts." Home to the **Marigny Opera Ballet** (which performs the works of New Orleans–based choreographers and composers from October through March), the venue also hosts "Sunday Musical Meditations" as well as arts and religious events. Depeche Mode filmed its "Heaven" video here.

A live performance at the Music Box.

Robert Hannant

NOLA MOMENT

THE MUSIC BOX VILLAGE

Bywater, 557 N. Rampart St.; musicboxvillage.com

The artist collective **New Orleans Airlift** created several iterations of this popular, one-of-a-kind, artist-built sculpture garden-cum-sound art installation, in New Orleans, Tampa, even Russia. A series of interactive "musical houses," the Music Box eventually found a permanent home in Bywater right against the Industrial Canal. A dozen new musical buildings have already been completed at the site: Guests stomp on loud, creaky floors, bang on percussive walls, and tweak soundwaves that carry across the property.

The one-of-a-kind space also hosts highly unique shows by local and big-name stars alike, from **Quintron** (who often serves as a conductor at Music Box shows), the **Preservation Hall Jazz Band**, and Cash Money beatmaker **Mannie Fresh** to Arto Lindsay, Thurston Moore, and members of Wilco.

Congreso Cubano restaurant cooks affordable food (Cuban meat pies and fried plantains!) on show nights, and the sale of wine, beer, and ambitious cocktails goes to help support New Orleans Airlift. Music Box tickets are very cheap, but the weekly Saturday market gives you a free chance to check out the installation as well as dozens of visual artists, artisans, clothing makers, and the like.

The Music Box provides lots of adventurous education opportunities for local school kids and is a worthy cause for your donations.

OLD POINT BAR

Algiers (West Bank), 545 Patterson Rd., 504-364-0950; oldpointbarnola.com

The only music venue across the river in Algiers, the Old Point Bar is a low-key gem that brings the entire Algiers Point neighborhood (the city's second-oldest hood) together with ridiculously strong pours, great prices, and two live neighborhood bands most nights. The lawn chairs around the outside of Old Point provide the only place in the city where you can catch a genuine nice, cool breeze, while the view from atop the levee across the street is the best in the city. Said lawn chairs also make Old Point a great place for parents to sit and sip while playing with their little ones.

ONE EYED JACKS

French Quarter, 615 Toulouse St., 504-569-8361; oneeyedjacks.net

Downtown's premier independent rock club delicately balances punk and swank, with ornate flocked red wallpaper that evokes equal parts Storyville and '70s porn. (They've also got an excellent collection of velvet nudie paintings.) The building started life as a theater, meaning the gently raked floor of the showroom guarantees generally awesome sightlines from anywhere in the 400-capacity space. Expect big-name indie-rock as well as big local players in the bohemian scene. Jacks hosts **Trixie Minx**'s **Fleur de Tease** burlesque troupe, the wildly popular **Fast Times '80s Dance Night** (every Thursday as of this printing), plus low-key free, early shows in the front bar.

POOR BOYS

Marigny, 1328 St. Bernard Avenue, 504-603-2522

Owned and booked by local scumbag king impresario **Matt Russell**, Poor Boys is one of the few legit venues with both popcorn ceilings *and* a soundman, that hosts noise music, punk music, heavy metal, and loud-ass rock 'n' roll from all over the world—conveniently located in a strip of St. Bernard Avenue music clubs and bars.

PRESERVATION HALL

French Quarter, 726 St. Peter St. between Bourbon and Royal, 504-522-2841; preservationhall.com

For around $15, listen to real traditional jazz with an impeccable pedigree in a sparse but still charming environment with limited distractions (no booze, no smoking). From 8 p.m. to midnight the band plays several 30-minute sets, and your ticket is valid all night. But there's more to the Hall (est. 1961) than just trad jazz: under the stewardship of **Ben Jaffe**, son of Hall founders **Allan and Sandra Jaffe**, Pres Hall has kept it fresh and exciting by collaborating with well-known national artists from My Morning Jacket to John Oates, and releasing a new album of original music, *So It Is.*

THE REPUBLIC

CBD, 828 S. Peters St., 504-528-8282; republicnola.com

Young Nick Thomas got his feet wet booking bands at The Republic, starting in 2006. Early booking-career milestones included **TV on the Radio**, **Gogol Bordello**, and **Pretty Lights**. He founded the hugely popular **Throwback** concert and retro dance party series. These days Thomas says, "There are a ton of EDM [electronic dance music] promoters who are willing to work in partnership, and not as many in rock or indie, so our roster hasn't been as full of indie and rock as it used to be, which is unfortunate." Republic often hosts a younger crowd in the college demographic, but it is also a club known for growing local talent, especially in the DJ and electronic music scene. Thomas was the first to nurture **Force Feed Radio**'s big visual and sound spectacle. Republic remains a hotbed of both huge and emerging electronic and rap acts.

SANTOS

French Quarter, 1135 Decatur St., 504-605-3533; santosbar.com

Not alotta rock 'n' roll clubs in the French Quarter. **Benjamin Lee**, who, along with his brother **Chris**, form the outsized rock act **Supagroup**, opened Santos rock bar along the river in 2017 (Lee's involvement explains the giant photo of Lemmy from Motorhead dressed in papal garb behind the bar). This newish music venue is an extension of its sister joint, **The Saint**, a debaucherous late-night bar known as a place where mistakes are made nightly. Santos's calendar is populated with the type of heavy music that doesn't have many local venues in NOLA these days, plus legendary punk bands like The Queers and DRI.

The Dead Boys perform without their original front man at one of New Orleans' few rock clubs, Santos on Decatur in the Quarter.

Josh Brasted

SATURN BAR

Bywater, 3067 St. Claude Ave.,
504-949-7532; saturnbar.com

The Saturn Bar (whose awesome old-school neon sign appeared in the movie *Ray* through the miracle of CGI) is a bona fide New Orleans legend. Its irascible original owner, **O'Neil Broyard**, legendarily disliked making change, talking to customers, and running a bar in general. He filled the club to bursting with a collection of priceless New Orleans art, keepsakes, and garbage. Broyard passed away in 2006, and the bar is now run by his nephew **Eric Broyard** and his niece **Bailee Broyard**, who cleaned up the cat pee smell and most of the garbage. The Saturn now hosts any type of music from avant-garde jazz to metal to DJs. Its iconic calendars, T-shirts, and day planners are the hippest souvenirs you could hope for. Saturn is also very near to **Mr. Quintron's Spellcaster Lodge**.

SIBERIA LOUNGE

Marigny, 2227 St. Claude Ave.,
504-265-8855; siberialounge.com

Once a heavy metal bar with an amazing menu of Eastern European and Russian food served in the back, the newly revamped Siberia Lounge has cut out some of the louder music on its calendar and replaced it with the type of singer-songwriter fare performed by Siberia's owner, **Luke Allen**, in his **Happy Talk Band**.

SIDNEY'S SALOON

Tremé, 1200 St. Bernard Ave.,
504-224-2672; sidneyssaloon.com

St. Bernard was once a major neon strip, full of African American–owned and –patronized bars and music spots. In the '60s, construction of the gloomy, noisy I-10 overpass cast a pall over that hood. Still, St. Bernard remains home to a host of neighborhood bars—spaces that have been racially integrated but not necessarily gentrified since Katrina. Sidney's, once owned by **Kermit Ruffins**, still stands at the center of the St. Bernard strip, hosting rock 'n' roll shows, brass bands, DJs, and a great view of grand St. Bernard Ave. Thursday night is **Night Church** comedy (with free food and ice cream), with Friday and Saturday nights reserved for various mad dance parties.

SOUTHPORT MUSIC HALL

Jefferson Parish (aka suburbs),
200 Monticello Ave., 504-835-2903;
newsouthport.com

Over the decades, this suburban club has switched hands often, with owners including New Orleans Mafia boss Carlos Marcello, who controlled Louisiana's illegal gambling network and was once a suspect in the Kennedy assassination. Later in the 1960s, the hall was known as Farhad Grotto, a gathering spot for the Masonic group known as the Mystic Order of Veiled Prophets of the Enchanted Realm. Today it's the only 1,000-seat venue in Jefferson Parish, hosting local metal giants like **Crowbar** and **EyeHateGod**, '80s cover bands like **Chee Weez** and the **Molly Ringwalds**, and stray phenomena like Corey Feldman's all-girl live dubstep band.

The only speakeasy we are allowed to tell you about, The Pearl, located . . . somewhere in the Ninth Ward. Look for flyers.

Jonathan Traviesa

A drag show at Ace Hotel.

Tim Black/Ace Hotel

ST. ROCH TAVERN

Marigny, 1200 St. Roch Ave.,
504-945-0194

A 100 percent authentic, no-hype dive bar where you will feel charmingly unsafe while meeting some fucked-up locals and hearing music from under-the-radar local bands, ranging in styles from harmonica blues to metal. The city made the bar disallow animals, meaning St. Roch's weekly "chicken drop"

Zack Smith

St. Roch Tavern, back before city government started cracking down on flyers.

gambling event has been discontinued. But there's a piano in the corner (**Dr. John**, **Ratty Scurvics**, and others have been known to stop by and play a little), plus cheap, good bar food, and sometimes blood on the floor.

THREE KEYS (AT ACE HOTEL)

CBD, 600 Carondelet St.,
504-900-1180; threekeysnola.com

Attached to a boutique hotel, this split-level, 160-capacity venue is intimate, to say the least. On a black-and-white floor painted in woozy checkered patterns (no stage), live rock and jazz bands play, DJs spin, and salons, shops, and restaurants pop up, facilitating all types of creative collaborations. One of the best bookers of modern black music in the city. And check Three Keys' calendar if you'd like to get together and speak French at the type of special "French discussion circles" found mostly around Lafayette.

Indie rock band Rotary Downs plays at nightclub/Professor Longhair shrine, Tipitina's.

TIPITINA'S

Uptown, 501 Napoleon Ave., 504-895-8477; tipitinas.com

The creative force behind *Mardi Gras in New Orleans,* pianist Professor Longhair combined boogie-woogie, southern R&B, and blues in a way that permeates almost all New Orleans music these days. Since 1977 (with a couple of brief breaks), this Professor Longhair–themed music club (its name a reference to Fess's song about a drunk lady named Tina) has kept it real with a roster of mostly local music and the occasional mid-sized touring act. Tipitina's may be best known for its foundation, which all over Louisiana provides free music lessons, studio time, music business courses, and musical instruments (to brass bands that often do battle in the street outside the club each spring during Jazz Fest).

U.S. MINT

French Quarter, 400 Esplanade Ave., 504-568-6968; musicatthemint.org

The **New Orleans Jazz Museum** provides dynamic interactive exhibits, multigenerational educational programming, research facilities, and of course musical performances via its **Music at the Mint** series. At the intersection of the French Quarter and the Frenchmen Street live music zone, the third-floor Performing Arts Center at the Old U.S. Mint hosts recorded and streamed music and theatrical performances, lectures, symposia, oral histories, and curatorial panels. Concerts feature local music from jazz to acoustic and experimental sounds.

Maceo Parker's soundman Goat and his goat friend, outside of Vaughan's Loonge [*sic*].

Zack Smith

VAUGHAN'S LOUNGE

Bywater, 4229 Dauphine St.,
504-947-5562

An iconic Ninth Ward bar established in 1959, Vaughan's has for many decades been *the place* for live, local music on Thursday nights. The dilapidated-looking saloon deep in the Bywater has welcomed celebrities from **Will Oldham** to the **Rolling Stones**, who've all come down to see and hear Louis Armstrong facsimile **Kermit Ruffins** (who retired from Vaughan's after nineteen years of Thursday gigs), his replacement **Trumpet Black** (who was shot and killed in 2015), or current Thursday night house band **Corey Henry and the Tremé Funktet**. **DJ Black Pearl** spins during set breaks when free red beans are served. On at least one Friday each month, Vaughan's also hosts the amazing drag queen presentation **Coco Mesa and the Southern Barbitchurates**.

THE WILLOW

Uptown, 8200 Willow St.,
504-656-6563; thewillowuptown.com

This intimate venue with its large stage is located less than one mile from three major universities in uptown New Orleans. A place where many very young, collegiate live bands and DJs cut their teeth.

ZEITGEIST MULTI-DISCIPLINARY ARTS CENTER

Uptown, 1618 Oretha Castle
Haley Blvd., 504-352-1150;
zeitgeistnola.org

More a community center than a theater, Zeitgeist is the premier local venue in which to consume alternative film, dance, theater, and avant-garde music. Often, it's the only New Orleans venue to catch the more outré film festival favorites on the big screen with the added benefit of knowing you're supporting truly marginal, bohemian culture. Zeitgeist hosts everything from the annual touring Sex Workers Art Show to an expansive human rights film festival.

TIP THE PERFORMERS!

Zack Smith

New Orleans is a haven for people who can do things well—but usually just one thing, to the point where they're otherwise unemployable, despite their one great talent. Music, especially, is many New Orleanians' sole source of income. So, this may seem over-obvious—and good for you if it does!—but some people don't realize you need to tip *every* performer that you enjoy. You can stiff the weepy, terrible folk singer whose too-loud amplifiers pollute the air around Jackson Square (or anyone else you think is just *bad*), but otherwise, even that silver-painted ghost mime lady you took a quick picture of on your phone deserves your tip. The same goes for the bands you'll see in clubs on Frenchmen Street. No cover charge at the club? Tip. Only there for a drink? Tip anyway. The band has a tip bucket on stage with them because they are making a small wage from the club, like a waiter would. So, if that band makes you feel anything positive at all, then throw a couple singles into that bucket (but don't touch them or even say anything to them, because they are concentrating!).

If you listen to or take a photo of a performer and don't tip them, plan on spraining your ankle or losing your car within forty-eight hours. You wouldn't pull that in a strip club; don't pull it on Frenchmen Street.

2. MODERN BANDS AND MUSICIANS

Modern New Orleans music cannot be summed up with the words "jazz" or "funk" or "blues," or any genre tag. Many New Orleans musicians create a true sense of the city without sounding like old, traditional New Orleans music. Mardi Gras is just as big an influence on many of these bands (any rock band desiring to sound "heavy," for instance, should study New Orleans high school marching units). The true heart of New Orleans music is not jazz, funk, or blues, but rather, originality!

Here is just a slice of New Orleans music in the 2010s (apologies to those I've accidentally left out):

THERESA ANDERSSON

theresaandersson.com

Andersson came to prominence as a talented fiddle player and singer who, with the help of other songwriters, hybridized various forms of American "roots music" into something her own. With the release of *Hummingbird Go!* (produced by **Allen Toussaint**) and then *Street Parade,* Andersson began following her own unique muse, a muse who wanted her to use loop pedals and other modern instruments to create something truly unique, and very beautiful. It doesn't hurt that she's one of the best violinists in a state full of fiddle players, and that her voice is as strong as any American Idol contestant.

ASYLUM CHORUS

theasylumchorus.com

Eclectic multi-instrumentalist and soul singer **Lucas Davenport** leads this eight-piece singing group reminiscent of the Staple Singers, singing spirituals, roots covers, and their own original soul songs.

BABES

This full rock band from wild one-man band Rhodes plays O.C.-style psych punk. They often open big local shows for **Quintron**.

BANTAM FOXES

bantamfoxes.com

Brothers **Sam** and **Collin McCabe** present fierce rock with screeching guitar and heavy bass.

RICHARD BATES

richardbatesmusic.net

Singer-songwriter uses his tender voice to croon quirky songs of New Orleans.

BENNI

This mostly instrumental analogue solo project by Northshore resident and **Goner Records** artist **Benny Devine** (keyboardist of Nashville's Natural Child) takes you on an only slightly funny journey of the mind. (Also worth noting that he curates an excellent Facebook page called the Comments Section, which collects the worst racist garbage comments from our local newspapers, with photos of the commenters.)

BIPOLAROID

Bipolaroid's garage rock drips down the walls. Over the course of many years and many lineups, **Ben Glover**'s musical vision has evolved into something truly psychedelic, bent, and beautiful. The band's most recent incarnation features garage-rock icon **King Louie** on drums.

JOHN BOUTTÉ

johnboutte.com

You could write a book about this man and his legendary family of New Orleans musicians. The singer of the theme song of HBO's Katrina drama *Treme,* John Boutté possesses a quiet, almost feminine voice that can nonetheless make you dance—or more likely, make you cry. Boutté was one of the first artists in New Orleans to demand a nonsmoking environment before the smoking ban. He still performs the early show at club **d.b.a.** on Frenchmen St. every Saturday night.

BRASS-A-HOLICS

brass-a-holics.com

This multiracial brass band combines New Orleans brass and Washington D.C. go-go music, plus disparate influences from Miles Davis and Nirvana to Wham! and Kanye West. Trombonist **Winston Turner** is a former member of St. Augustine High School's **Marching 100**, plus the **Pinstripes** and **Soul Rebels** brass bands.

CADDYWHOMPUS

caddywhompusband.com

Noise/pop/experimental guitar-and-drums duo. The guitar playing is off the charts—somehow making finger-tapping absolutely acceptable. Tours regularly, amazing live shows. For fans of Lightning Bolt and Animal Collective.

CARBON POPPIES

Twee rock with vocal harmonies that are a little bit edgy, and are also able to get you sweaty.

CARDINAL SONS

cardinalsons.com

Three brothers combine to create pop rock structure with organ solos. Spoon guitar, and Ben Folds Five everything else.

TBC'S JUICY JACKSON ON BRASS BANDS

tbcbrassband.com

Edward "Juicy" Jackson plays tuba for **To Be Continued Brass Band**, a standout crew born from the Carver High School Marching Band. Originally famous for their sets at the corner of Bourbon and Canal Streets, TBC holds down a Wednesday night gig at **Celebration Hall** (1701 St. Bernard Ave.), where working folks go to buckjump into the wee hours. They also provide the pulse for many of the city's social aid and pleasure club parades, and pride themselves in a healthy social life. "Back when I first started, a lot of groups started infusing rap into the music," recalls Jackson. "These days we are remixing and rearranging the old music. TBC does it to transcribe and to help try to recreate the vibe that the original group created or made us feel when we heard their song."

When asked for tips on finding and walking in a second line, Juicy said, "**Gambit** (bestofneworleans.com) and **WWOZ** (wwoz.org) always have the best info on everything to do in New Orleans. Don't just try to roam the city for a parade or try to find the parade by word of mouth. Do your homework on what you wanna see."

In regard to brass bands, Juicy says, "I attend the **Maple Leaf** to see **Rebirth** on Tuesdays, then Thursdays with the **Soul Rebels** at **Le Bon Temps**, and if I'm not playing with my other band **Mainline** on a Sunday, I love to see **Hot 8** at the **Howlin' Wolf Den**."

Juicy Jackson and the
To Be Continued Brass Band.

© 2012 Paul Cheenne

One of Louisiana's last swamp pop bands, the Creole String Beans.

CHEF MENTEUR

chefmenteur.org

A space-rock band named after a famous, sketchy New Orleans highway. Chef Menteur (the name means "chief liar") makes drone-oriented "songs" built around guitar riffs, murky loops and samples, and a tight rhythm section.

CONSORTIUM OF GENIUS

consortiumofgenius.com

Part band, part multimedia weirdness, the C.O.G. is a gaggle of costumed mad scientists who carry on the tradition of New Orleans' famous TV host **Morgus the Magnificent** in musical form while, according to them, trying to take over the world. Their shows are highly theatrical and sometimes feature original films that include their fifth member, a cartoon robot.

COUNTRY FRIED

The best New Orleans has to offer in the way of twang, Country Fried boasts virtuosic strings and perfect vocal harmonies in the old-fashioned acoustic country string band tradition. Some of the city's soul and R&B influences have also snuck in.

COYOTES

With its alt-country milieu, this band began life in Los Angeles before settling in the New Orleans indie rock scene. Citing the Flying Burrito Brothers as inspiration, the Coyotes describe their sound as "cosmic Americana."

CREOLE STRING BEANS

creolestringbeans.com

One of the only bands left that plays swamp pop, a form of rural Cajun prom-dancing music primarily from the 1950s. For almost fifteen years the

Beans have played the old swamp pop hits from **Lloyd Price**'s "Just Because" to "Mathilda" by **Cookie and the Cupcakes**.

DASH RIP ROCK

dashriprock.net

The world's greatest cow-punk bar band for over twenty-five years (hits include "Locked inside a Liquor Store with You" and "(Let's Go) Smoke Some Pot"), DRR is also edgy enough to release albums through Jello Biafra's label, Alternative Tentacles. For fans of real guitar playing.

DEBAUCHE

debauchemusic.com

Russian-born **Yegor Romanstov**, backed by his "Russian Mafia Band," croons and bellows rocking drunken versions of Russian folk songs, some more than a century old, written by prisoners and gangsters, hooligans, orphans, and gypsies. One crowd favorite tells of lesbians who marry in jail then escape, only to be killed.

PHIL DEGRUY

guitarp.com

Phil deGruy only comes out into the light if he doesn't see the shadow of his "guitarp" on April Fool's Day—the "guitarp" being the guitar deGruy invented. A tiny, audible 11-string harp is built into a guitar body and played simultaneously or in syncopation with the other six strings. DeGruy's constant, dry, but subversive sense of humor on stage plus his otherworldly playing was described by former Zappa

and David Lee Roth axman Steve Vai as "John Coltrane meets Mel Brooks at a party for Salvador Dali." DeGruy also shares the stage with fellow hilarious guitar wizards **Jimmy Robinson** and **Cranston Clements** in the band **Twangorama**.

MIKE DILLON

mikedillonvibes.com

This tricky percussionist and vibes man has played in jam-band-friendly musical experiments including **Les Claypool's Frog Brigade** and his own **Mike Dillon's Go-Go Jungle**. In New Orleans, he's often seen in combination with **Galactic**'s **Stanton Moore**, jazz/funk drummer **Johnny Vidacovich**, and bass weirdo **James Singleton**. A big favorite of the **Bonnaroo** crowd, Dillon has lately played in the adventurous jazz trio **Nolatet**, and his own **Punk Rock Percussion Ensemble**.

DUMMY DUMPSTER

This punkish, noisy, unpredictable, anything-goes project started in Chalmette, Louisiana, in 2001. The microphone is mounted in the singer's decorated homemade shoulderpads, allowing him to rip around the room and petrify the crowd as he sings songs such as "I Don't Care Pubic Hair" and "Time to Kiss."

EARPHUNK

earphunk.com

This funk band mixes in electronic elements à la Galactic. They've served as backing band for Nola hip-hop legend **Mannie Fresh**.

Twenty-year-old brass-rock band Egg Yolk Jubilee.

EGG YOLK JUBILEE

eggyolkjubilee.com

This genreless brass-rock band has played Zappa-esque music with a sense of humor for over twenty years, both on stage and at Mardi Gras parades including **Krewe du Vieux** and **'Tit Rex**.

THE ESSENTIALS

meettheessentials.com

This 11-piece '60s soul cover band plays Motown hits and other gems from that era. Singer/songwriter **Micah McKee** of **Little Maker** leads this unit featuring six singers, go-go dancers, and sometimes burlesque.

NOLA MOMENT

FAUXBEAUX, GUTTERPUNKS, AND OTHER STREET MUSICIANS

In the 1990s, New Orleans was famous for attracting what were called "**gutterpunks**," a breed of street kid who combined the Blade Runner/Mad Max look with canned beer, stained white wife beaters, and soiled jeans. Often accompanied by sympathy-inducing dogs, the frequently aggressive gutterpunks leered at visitors and fell victim to nightstick-happy police. The gutterpunk breed came back strong on lower Decatur Street after Hurricane Katrina, begging from locals who'd just lost their homes. Luckily this was tempo-

Robin Walker

Fauxbeaux

rary. As the post-K years progressed, many mildly rebellious American kids who would have grown up to become gutter-punks instead began evolving into what Bywater locals now refer to as "**fauxbeaux**," a French Louisiana word meaning "false hobos."

These fresh-faced bards and waifs enjoy better hygiene and, from all appearances, less dependence on booze and crack than the gutterpunks. In suspenders, newsy caps, lace dresses, and clamdigger pants, they harken back in dress to an imagined Depression era. Clustered on corners and equipped with washtub basses, tubas, and plaintive voices, they draw on a musical fantasy where gypsies, slaves, and the Irish jammed in mellow slums to the works of Stephen Foster.

The Bywater and Margin fauxbeaux snowbirds arrive in town around Mardi Gras each year, stay through festival season, then fly (or hop a train, they'd have you believe) back up north. Some of them purport to live a soulful Kerouacian existence, while most have access to credit cards to buy nicer things, but just dig the look. Locals also refer to fauxbeaux as "chimney sweeps," "Depression-era paperboys," "funkballs," and a host of other names.

Also, unlike gutterpunks, fauxbeaux rarely beg. Instead they play music, often for donations—music that sometimes makes you wish they'd just beg the normal way. Often the music is imitative of an old-timey porch-stompin' sound. But some of their female vocalists perfectly mimic beautiful old phonograph-era singers, and a few of the more ambitious fauxbeaux have honed their chops in New Orleans and worked toward well-paying gigs for the **Jazz Fest** crowd.

The species' cultural contributions are too often obscured by a well-observed xenophobia; fauxbeaux come to town, dig in with the folks who dress like them, and rarely communicate with the many other interesting creatures around them. Still, if you see them on the street and they sound good, give them a buck. But just be aware of the difference between fauxbeaux and truly local street musicians trying to support themselves in their hometown.

GAL HOLIDAY AND THE HONKY TONK REVIEW

galholiday.com

Undeniably retro, and undeniably pretty, Gal Holiday presents high-quality recreations of old country music, plus moving original compositions.

GARBAGE BOY

Described as everything from "Queen covering Nirvana" to "the Ramones on ketamine," they fit well into the emerging "garage glam" genre and have opened for garage glam favorites like Sharkmuffin and Ex-Girlfriends.

HELEN GILLET

helengillet.com

You've never witnessed a cellist rock this hard. Dynamic and experimental but unpretentious and fun, Gillet plays jazz and medieval music, sings French *chansons* and "musettes" in her band **Wazozo**, uses loop stations in her wild solo act, and helps reconstruct the abstract orchestra pieces of bass wiz **James Singleton**—to name just a few of her many successes. If you came to New Orleans for music, Helen is a must-see.

GLAND

An ultra-feminist, all-female punk band that sings songs about body-positivity, intersectionality, etc. Gland's album *Neurotica* (actually a few hundred cassette tapes) was released by **Community Records** in 2016.

GOV'T MAJIK

By fusing free-form jazz and mind-melting atmospheric elements, this 10-piece Afrobeat band aims for the psychedelic majesty of Fela Kuti, while whipping up a world-groove dance frenzy.

GRAVITY A

gravitya.com

Self-described as "funktronica," this jam band quartet combines New Orleans funk, drum 'n' bass breaks, and trippy trance.

GREEN DEMONS

A straight-faced, ironic space alien surf rock band, powered by **Todd "Thunder" Voltz**, a videographer and character actor who has performed in movies beside Ryan Reynolds, among other huge movie stars, who all agreed that Voltz was the best actor they had ever worked with. Check out the Demons' album, *Outer Sex.*

DAVE GREGG

Primarily a street performer, Gregg plays New Orleans standards and other jazz and funk with one hand strumming a guitar around front, the other hand picking another guitar behind his back, while his bare feet play the bass. Close your eyes and you'd never even know.

GUITAR LIGHTNIN' LEE AND HIS THUNDER BAND

guitarlightninlee.com

Born and raised in the Lower Ninth Ward (and lifelong friends with **Fats Domino**'s son **Antoine Domino III**), Lightnin' studied blues guitar with masters like **Jimmy Reed** and **"Boogie Bill" Webb**, and has palled around with every major artist to come through New Orleans. His scrappy band of white punk rockers also make up the very loud band **Die Rotzz**. Together, they play sloppy, fuzzy, unhinged blues that will make you spill your drink and slap your mama.

Bluesman Guitar Lightnin' Lee performing at Ace Hotel.

Todd White/Ace Hotel

HAPPY TALK BAND

happytalkband.com

Happy Talk is mostly front man **Luke Allen**, whose bittersweet songwriting captures the bohemian, downtown New Orleans life where bartenders, strippers, junkies, artists, musicians, and other similar sorts live, drink, and die. Allen, a guitarist, plays in several combinations, from a raw, electric alt-country/punk combo to a gentle ensemble with **Helen Gillet** on cello.

CLIFF HINES

cliffhines.com

This young jazz guitar graduate of the **New Orleans Center for the Creative Arts (NOCCA)** tours his ass off with his own adventurous jazz-esque bands, or as sideman for percussion wildman **Mike Dillon**. You may catch him leading a group at Frenchmen's "mainstream" jazz spot, **Snug Harbor**, or doing an all-modular synth set at **Poor Boys**.

HOT CLUB OF NEW ORLEANS

The Hot Club perform the swing era music of **Duke Ellington**, plus **Django Reinhardt** and **Stéphane Grappelli** among others, yet avoid sounding like a museum piece by infusing the music with their own modern sensibilities. In keeping with the classic format of this music, Hot Club lacks a drummer—but will still make you dance.

HOT 8 BRASS BAND

hot8brassband.com

Once the city's hottest hip-hop infused underdog brass band, the Hot 8 have since been Grammy nominated, but still maintain the grimy power that gave them their initial word-of-mouth. Through Katrina and the shooting death of an important band member the Hot 8 have persevered and climbed the brass band mountain to its peak.

HURRAY FOR THE RIFF RAFF

hurrayfortheriffraff.com

Cat Poweresque singer and banjo player **Alynda Lee** learned music by participating in train-hopping culture, and as a result, Hurray for the Riff Raff uses acoustic instruments to spin 6/8 waltzes and modern country ballads about life's perils. After making her name in New Orleans, she sort of moved on from the city, but you can still catch Riff Raff here from time to time.

JERK OFFISERS

Adamcrochet.com/jerkoffisers

The Jerk Offisers is the world's biggest, dumbest conspiracy rock band. Hear some of New Orleans' finest musicians have fun playing these timeless garage rock masterpieces.

THE KID CARSONS

thekidcarsons.bandcamp.com

Country band of brothers and sisters featuring deep pedal steel guitar plus a lot of nuance and space. They tour quite a bit and have played with Shovels & Rope, as well as comedian Steve Martin's bluegrass group the Steep Canyon Rangers.

King James and the Special Men at BJ's.

Jonathan Traviesa

NOLA MOMENT

KING JAMES AND THE SPECIAL MEN
(WITH RED BEANS AND RICE)

specialmanindustries.com

Gold-toothed **Jimmy Horn** reconvened New Orleans downtown R&B group the **Special Men** to have fun and drink beer. A residual effect was that the band represented downtown R&B like no one else in town. Every Monday night somewhere in Tremé, Marigny, or Bywater, the dance floor is packed as the horn-and-piano-driven Special Men kick out nearly-forgotten New Orleans R&B hits like "Boogie at Midnight," by **Roy Brown**, and "Ice Man," by **Big Joe**—beside Horn's own original tunes, which fit right in. "We owe everything to New Orleans producer Dave Bartholomew, and everything he did at **Cosimo Matassa**'s studio," Horn says. "All that shit from the late '40s. We play 'Great Big Eyes,' by **Archibald and Dave**, 'In the Night,' by **Professor Longhair**. A lot of these New Orleans R&B cats who invented this shit are gone or they're sick and can't come out, so a lot of kids haven't heard this shit."

The original Special Men convened Mondays in the Tremé at the **Mother-in-Law Lounge** starting in 1999, with **Miss Antoinette K-Doe** and her red beans as its nucleus. So with the Special Men's return, Jimmy Horn's red beans are back too. "I make them for the audience at all of our shows in Miss Antoinette K-Doe's name," he says. "I watched. I paid attention. If I don't get them exactly like hers, my goal is to get them to taste as good as hers did." The Special Men are currently in residency at the **Saturn Bar**.

KING LOUIE

Harahan's most famous rock 'n' roller—as well known for his unpredictable behavior as his music—has played in a laundry list of revered local garage bands, from the **Missing Monuments** to the **Royal Pendletons**. Louie shifts between power pop, Thin Lizzyisms, and a one-man band where he plays double bass and guitar simultaneously. His tight circle of friends dance their asses off at even his smallest shows, so he's always a safe bet if'n you need some fun.

LITTLE FREDDIE KING

littlefreddieking.com

As far as blues goes, Little Freddie King is the genuine article—a real-deal bluesman with a hardscrabble bio, a guttural, menacing mumble, and a ferocious gutbucket guitar. King, who was shot twice on two different occasions by the same wife (and stayed married to her), has released records on Fat Possum but can still often be found playing **BJ's** bar in Bywater.

A LIVING SOUNDTRACK

Electronics-driven instrumental indie rock act that mixes cinematic, experimental sound with a video projector for live performances.

LOST BAYOU RAMBLERS

lostbayouramblers.com

Based in Lafayette, the Michot brothers are in New Orleans often enough and kick enough ass to consider them local. Want some post-punk with your Cajun music? LBR songs are marked by long drones from **Andre Michot**'s accordion that collapse back into furious two-stepping at the behest of front man **Louis Michot**. Perfect music for the humid trippiness of the south Louisiana landscape.

KELCY MAE

kelcymae.com

Poetic roots music about the American South with acoustic instrumentation that'll surely appeal to the Canadian North.

Bluesman Little Freddie King performing at Siberia.

Dan Tague

CLINT MAEDGEN

This conservatory-trained saxophonist started out fronting rock bands **Liquidrone** and **Bingo!** before landing a gig singing for Preservation Hall. When Pres Hall lost its clarinetist, Clint began filling in. He now plays lead sax in Pres Hall and has collaborated with every famous musician imaginable. On the side, he performs a solo show as **CMRadio**: a live sound collage featuring found sounds, beats, and snippets of his own original songs garnished with wicked sax accompaniment.

MARINA ORCHESTRA

marinaorchestra.com

Mellow tropicália as filtered through indie rock ("trop 'n' roll," the band calls it), with three female voices harmonizing in response to vocalist **Justin Powers**.

WALT McCLEMENTS

Among the scene's most fertile musical minds, this singer and accordionist puts his distinctive part-Balkan, part-Steinbeck stamp on any arrangement. McClements currently plays more often with the **Panorama Jazz Band** and tours with the Minneapolis-based Dark Dark Dark.

TOM McDERMOTT

mcdermottmusic.com

McDermott, a crafty and gifted pianist and genre alchemist—whose main idioms are traditional jazz and Brazilian choro—is often heard around town with clarinetist **Evan Christopher** or accompanying singer Meschiya Lake. McDermott's original work has a strong sense of humor and experimentation that smarty-pants jazz fans—including uptight, moldy-fig traditionalists—will totally enjoy.

ALEX McMURRAY

alexmcmurray.com

"They say if you can make it in New York, you can make it anywhere," Alex McMurray deadpans. "But what I say about New Orleans is, if you can't make it here, don't leave." An invaluable force on the downtown scene, McMurray offers his adopted city an essential musical voice, a prolific performance schedule, and, each May, he offers up his own backyard in the form of **ChazFest**. Whether performing solo or as a member of the **Tin Men** trio, playing guitar for **Happy Talk Band** or leading the **Valparaiso Men's Chorus**, McMurray bundles an everyman's laments and furies with a keen eye for the landscape.

METRONOME THE CITY

This instrumental band of New Orleans music scene veterans has played together since high school. With guitar, bass, drum kit, keys, and effects, they somehow sound like a DJ seamlessly mixing together dub reggae, metal, and Thrill Jockey–style indie rock.

MICROSHARDS

Usually a ferocious bass-wielding, tape-manipulating one-man band, Microshards sometimes enlists a drummer and keyboardist to enhance his over-distorted rock instrumentals. On some occasions, the band has gotten trashed, disrobed, and just thrown their instruments around the room in a way that's somehow honestly artful and engaging.

MIKRONAUT

This solo artist and DJ drinks a lot of cough syrup and makes extremely listenable minimalist, dub-influenced electronica on various Casios and a four-track cassette recorder. When performing, Mikro runs said fourtrack into effects pedals and creates live remixes like the old dub reggae masters. A snowbird, Mikro can mostly only be seen during New Orleans' winters.

MORELLA & THE WHEELS OF IF

morellamusic.com

This haunting and romantic coed cabaret shows original films, video, and photography created by musical siblings **Aeryk Laws** (pianist/composer/singer/guitarist) and **Laura Laws** (writer/singer). As much an "act" as a "band," Morella has performed at the **DramaRama** theater fest and the annual **InFringe** multimedia fest (see "Theater, Comedy, and Dance").

M.O.T.O.

Masters of the Obvious: Hooky garage rock with song titles like "2-4-6-8 Rock 'n' Roll," "Gonna Get Drunk Tonight," and "Flipping You Off with Every Finger of My Hand." The phrase "so dumb they're brilliant" can be found in several M.O.T.O. reviews. Unfortunately for New Orleans, M.O.T.O. is usually on tour.

NARCISSY

narcissy.com

This rarely seen (and thus relished) garage rock outfit possesses a startling sense of humor and a spastic yet smart stage presence (not to mention serious guitar chops). "The perfect thing for people who like this sort of thing," reads the website.

NORCO LAPALCO

norcolapalco.com

A New Orleans supergroup of sorts, this band is named after an area of the city lacking even one tourist destination. Former members of legendary local rock groups **Evil Nurse Sheila**, **Egg Yolk Jubilee**, **Lump**, and the **Black Problem** sew together new riffs nodding to Minutemen, Sonic Youth, even Van Halen. The band puts melody behind a ton of New Orleans in-jokes.

STOO ODOM

Standup bassist, standup guy, and wildly creative sideman, known for his work with Thin White Line and Grave Brothers Deluxe, among others. Currently plays bass for **R. Scully's Rough 7**, and MC Sweet Tea's band, **Malevitus**.

ONE MAN MACHINE

Alone or with a group (likely assembled that week), **Bernard Pearce** swears by a seat-of-the-pants improvisational style not seen much in rock circles. Usually based on one consistent loop and a few memorized poetic lyrics, One Man Machine's music, and the players who realize it, all vary wildly from show to show. Pearce is also an amazing chef, whose red beans are often featured at shows by **King James & the Special Men**.

PETE "SNEAKY PETE" ORR

With a stinging wit, this singer-song-writer-mandolin player-etc. sings songs of another time in Bywater's history when rents were low and life was simultaneously rough and perfect. Sneaky Pete's former life as a magazine writer shines through in his sardonic but empathetic lyrics (check out his collection of vague horror stories, *Stay Out of New Orleans*).

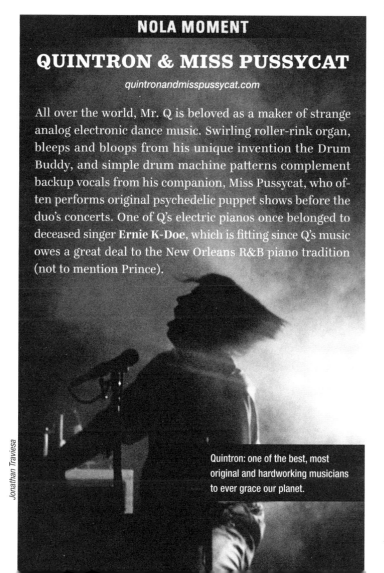

NOLA MOMENT

QUINTRON & MISS PUSSYCAT

quintronandmisspussycat.com

All over the world, Mr. Q is beloved as a maker of strange analog electronic dance music. Swirling roller-rink organ, bleeps and bloops from his unique invention the Drum Buddy, and simple drum machine patterns complement backup vocals from his companion, Miss Pussycat, who often performs original psychedelic puppet shows before the duo's concerts. One of Q's electric pianos once belonged to deceased singer **Ernie K-Doe**, which is fitting since Q's music owes a great deal to the New Orleans R&B piano tradition (not to mention Prince).

Quintron: one of the best, most original and hardworking musicians to ever grace our planet.

Jonathan Traviesa

The Rough 7 includes stars Ryan Scully and Mike Andrepont of Morning 40 Federation, noise guitarist Rob Cambre and the brilliant Ratty Scurvics on piano.

Zack Smith

PANORAMA JAZZ BAND

panoramajazzband.com

The stellar local players in Panorama often dress in traditional brass-band captain's hats and ties, but that's as far as the band's traditionalism goes. Its signature sound is classic New Orleans street parade music mixed with a healthy, exotic dose of Balkan brass and other rare forms.

NICHOLAS PAYTON

nicholaspayton.com

This progressive trumpet virtuoso refuses to call his music "jazz," a term he believes is racist (check out his excellently controversial blog, *The Cherub Speaks,* which I love even when I don't agree with Payton's POV). He instead calls it Black American Music, and urges other artists to join him under the BAM umbrella. We clearly admire his attitude, but Payton's also widely considered the city's greatest trumpet player striving for a new sound and not rehashing New Orleans' greatest hits.

PHIL THE TREMOLO KING

myspace.com/philthetremoloking

This Belgium-born guitarist who later survived New York City's infamous 13th Street squats now lives in New Orleans, mixing Velvet Underground, tropicália, gypsy punk, Casiocore, and the kitchen sink into what he calls "Tremophonic pop." Catch him at **Buffa's**, **Circle Bar**, or **AllWays Lounge**.

R. SCULLY'S ROUGH 7

Gravel-voiced former party-boy front man of the **Morning 40 Federation** (New Orleans' favorite drinking band, who still reform from time to time) wipes the smirk off and moves closer to the heart for songs he considers "garage gospel." **Rob Cambre** (lead guitar), **Ratty Scurvics** (piano), and singer **Meschiya Lake** (whose awesome backup wailing brings the group closest to their gospel goal) round out this supergroup of punk-influenced musicians as talented as any of the city's traditional bands.

RHODES

Prerecorded tracks, live drum machines, and percussion toys back this one-man band caterwauling southern electro pop, à la Britney Spears. At **Siberia** or **Saturn Bar**, Rhodes will invade your personal space. Don't attend his shows in your expensive clothes. Also see **Babes**.

RIK SLAVE

On and off since 1986, Rik Slave has been the revered front man for numerous projects—with his brother **Greg Terry** in the bent country group **Rik Slave and the Phantoms**, and then **Rock City Morgue** with White Zombie's **Sean Yseult**. Rik's most recent by-the-books rock band is the **Cons and Prose**.

ROAR! THE DUO

roartheduo.com

Trombonist, marimba player, and singer (what an awesome triumvirate!) **Carly Meyers** is a beast of a musician and an equally powerful performer, whether backing percussion god **Mike Dillon** or leading her two-piece electro duo, ROAR!, with drummer **Adam Gertner** (both of them formerly of **Yojimbo**).

ROTARY DOWNS

rotarydowns.com

Rotary Downs is one of New Orleans' few straight-up indie rock bands, not beholden to commercial aspirations and retaining a musical purity evident in its big, sweeping compositions. The band's popularity has grown as it's developed into a slightly psychedelic but even-tempered ensemble sound, featuring eclectic instrumentation.

KHRIS ROYAL

khrisroyalmusic.com

This young, local saxophone player proves that even in New Orleans, being open-minded and progressive wins the day. Leader of his own psychedelic jazz-funk band, **Khris Royal & Dark Matter**, he also serves as sideman for legendary **Meters** bassist **George Porter Jr.** in his band the **Runnin' Pardners**.

Saxophone player Khris Royal expands the boundaries of New Orleans brass music.

Sam Deen

Valerie Sassyfras puts on an amazing dance extravaganza while playing accordion and keyboard on her high-energy original songs.

Valerie Sassyfras

VALERIE SASSYFRAS

valeriesassyfras.com

An amazing one-woman band (accordion, mandolin, keyboard) who sings danceable ditties that are actually about her deepest personal feeling and hardest battles. This spiky-haired capital E entertainer is a true inspiration who can get a big room dancing all by herself.

SCARECROW SONIC BOOMBOX

Experimental punk. Guitarist **Hex Windham** also plays in **Sea Battle** and performs solo noise sets.

RATTY SCURVICS

Ratty is a unique musical artist who comes in many forms. In his one-man band **Singularity**, Scurvics's hands pound stacks of keyboards while his feet pump the snare and bass drums. In 2007, Ratty's multimedia ensemble **Black Market Butchers**—featuring Ryan Scully of **Morning 40 Federation**, plus singer **Meschiya Lake**, guitarist **Rob Cambre**, and others—released the album *In Time,* produced by multiple Grammy winner **John Porter** (an auxiliary member of Roxy Music who produced most of The Smiths' singles). These days Ratty composes a lot of music for theater productions in which he often also acts. Ratty is emblematic of how modern New Orleans music often defies categorization.

SEA BATTLE

"Deconstructivist" noise rap featuring a chorus of interpretive dancers.

SEXY DEX AND THE FRESH

A dance band blending R&B, synth pop, and raw New Orleans funk. No less than *Spin* magazine said Sexy Dex and the Fresh will appeal to "fans of '60s Motown to '80s new wave to '10s bubblegum pop."

SHARKS' TEETH

Former **Sun Hotel** members make broken, or at least bent, pop with four synthesizers. Their label, **Community Records**, claims they invoke Todd Rundgren and Orchestral Manoeuvres in the Dark (oh shit!).

SHOCK PATINA

A surprisingly rockin' spoken-word band fronted by local poet Raymond "Moose" Jackson, who describes the group as "disco goth proto-punk."

SUPAGROUP

reverbnation.com/supagroup

This established party metal group surely doesn't want to be "underground": high energy, ultra tight, big rock, never cheesy unless **Chris Lee** (husband of bassist **Sean Yseult**) and brother **Benji Lee** know you'll laugh along. Semi-retired, you may catch them at the right time of year.

Jonathan Traviesa

Singer, songwriter, producer, and multi-instrumentalist Ratty Scurvics.

JAMES SINGLETON'S JAZZ

The most amazing stand-up bassist you've ever heard or seen, the mop-haired, eternally youthful fifty-something **James Singleton** has played with everyone from **Ellis Marsalis** to **Clarence "Gatemouth" Brown** to legendary pianist **James Booker**. But unlike some of New Orleans' best-known musicians, Singleton is also original, daring, and multifaceted. "My overarching project is that I want my music to reflect two centuries," says Singleton, whose **James Singleton Orchestra** purports to perform jazz from 1913 to 2017.

Singleton is perhaps most famous for the progressive jazz outfit **Astral Project** (astralproject.com), which he's helped power since 1978 with saxophonist **Tony Dagradi**, guitarist **Steve Masakowski**, and drummer **Johnny Vidacovich**. Vidacovich and Singleton also share the band **DVS** with percussionist **Mike Dillon**—who plays in **Illuminasti** with Singleton and avant-garde saxophonist **Skerik.** The **James Singleton Quartet** finds multi-instrumentalists using punk rock textures and swing rhythms smashed together in the jazz club with acoustic piano. If the money's right, Singleton can even put together his wild concert hall string quartet.

"Part of my experience is always that someone has seen me doing my freaky shit," says Singeleton. "Then they come up to me and say, 'Weren't you the guy we just saw at **Spotted Cat**?'" Singleton plays traditional New Orleans jazz when the need arises.

Singleton doesn't like to tour, so you can almost always catch him in New Orleans. If not, he suggests you attend the weekly **Instant Opus** night of improvisational music pairing world-famous and local musicians at **SideBar NOLA**.

Exploratory bassist James Singleton can play all genres, or no genres.

Katja Liebing

Folk singer Stix Da Clown.

SWEET CRUDE'S (LOUISIANA) FRENCH REVOLUTION

Indie pop sung in Louisiana French

sweetcrudeband.com

The group's first EP, *Super Vilaine* (2012), laid the ground-work for Sweet Crude's sound, which features sparse melodic instrumentation—analog keyboards, violin, bass guitar, but no six-string—over a thick bed of drums, played simultane-ously by four drummers. One might hear shades of Arcade Fire, or Imagine Dragons, except that the lyrics are mostly in Louisiana French.

"I've seen how the last generation of people who've grown up speaking Louisiana French are getting to a point where they're passing on," says Sweet Crude's leader, Sam Craft. "We're at a critical point; when our grandparents' generation dies, that will be the last of the people really raised speaking [Louisiana French]." And so Craft set about learning this re-gional dialect, and spearheaded a French movement within his own band. The other members, including his brother Jack Craft on keyboards, are learning Cajun French by singing it.

"We were concerned at first what the reaction would be," Craft admits of his band's sound, which—apart from vocalist Alexis Marceaux belting out her words like a French Ann Wilson—does not resemble traditional Louisiana music. At times Sweet Crude's tunes almost sound like Cajun vocal tracks over instrumentals remixed by Vampire Weekend. "We worried, for one, will this alienate young people who don't know French?" admits Craft. "And two, would it alien-ate an earlier generation that think they're coming to hear zydeco music, something they can two-step to?"

But Craft's hybridized band (stablemates of **Tank and the Bangas** and bounce rapper **Big Freedia** at New Orleans' **Simple Play** booking agency) has since headlined big clubs and rocking Louisiana festivals that have put their fears to rest. "We were playing in a dancehall tent somewhere in the Acadiana region," remembers Craft, "everyone's there to jitterbug waltz and two-step. We were afraid we were gonna get crucified. But after that we were invited to play **Festival International**, and Festival Acadie [in New Brunswick, Canada], where like, you gotta play two-step and waltz music; it's strictly a zydeco and Cajun swamp pop festival. But then we were invited to play it, and that was a huge vote of confidence."

Tank and the Bangas currently rule New Orleans with their smooth, progressive Black soul experiments.

Quinn Miller-Bedell

TANK AND THE BANGAS

Tarriona "Tank" Ball pushed up from the city's burgeoning spoken-word scene to reveal a fierce singing voice and persona, influenced by Badu but packing more than a little Aretha. The Bangas include three lady backing singers who stay locked in surreal call-and-response dialogue with Tank. TatB's tight future-funk gets many locals' votes for best New Orleans band.

CHARM TAYLOR

The former singer for the **Honorable South** stretches out her soulful experi-ments in rock 'n' Afrofuturism, some-times backed by electronic artist **AF the Naysayer**.

THE TOMB OF NICK CAGE

Named for the surreal giant pyramid that actor Nicolas Cage had built in New Orleans for his future gravesite at St. Louis Cemetery No. 1 (a cem-etery famous as the final resting place of Voodoo priestess Marie Laveau, among other big local legends), this band plays deathcore, horrorcore, and "Illuminati Punk" at comics conventions and the like.

TRAMPOLINE TEAM

Fun three-piece coed pop-punk act with a front lady barking impressionistic lyrics, such as, "Paint your picture in blood / Wash it off when you get tired / Television's on." TT is the first group to release a physical 7″ record on **Space Taker Sounds** (spacetakersounds .com), formerly known as Pelican Pow Wow.

THE UNNATURALS

One of the better *AntiGravity* magazine scribes, bassist **Jenn Attaway** powers this super-tight rockabilly surf group.

US NERO

A throwback to early '90s weird rock bands, US Nero's neurotic vocals and equally neurotic grooves and time shifts will remind the middle-aged of their college days, back when music was smarter even if it was tougher to digest. US Nero's scrappy personal approach remains a rare treat on the New Orleans scene.

VOX AND THE HOUND

Psychedelic, sometimes sad, sometimes angry, folk-country.

The Trampoline Team plays pop punk that is feisty and quick.

Sam Lucia

WATER SEED

waterseedmusic.com

This progressive soul funk band has broken the Billboard Top 40 and played **Jazz Fest**, the **Essence Festival**, and other big fests countrywide. Part of a local progressive black music movement in New Orleans including **Tank and the Bangas** and **Charm Taylor**.

WHOM DO YOU WORK FOR?

whomdoyouworkfor.com

Electronic/experimental rock/noise pop band, named for an Ornette Coleman recording.

Another of New Orleans' best progressive soul bands, Water Seed.

Cedric Ellsworth

69

ZYDECO

*The music of Louisiana's rural areas
can sometimes be found in the city.*

Rockin Dopsie Jr.

Zack Smith

Sort of a Frenchified Afro-hoedown music, zydeco is a mostly fast, accordion- and washboard-driven rural Louisiana sound. Distinct from the fiddle-based tunes of neighboring Cajuns, zydeco has along the way buddied up to the electric guitar, and worn proudly its American R&B influences. First recorded for public consumption in the '50s, the music was always meant for house parties and other more intimate gatherings. Meaning, any outsider might have a truly tough time locating live zydeco way out in the sticks. Living in New Orleans, zydeco can be downright hard to find outside of French Quarter bead shops. The **New Orleans Jazz and Heritage Festival** does a great job of bringing zydeco to a bigger audience every year on its Fais-Do-Do Stage, but otherwise here are some places (mostly outside of the city) where you'll definitely catch you some zydeco howlin':

BLACKPOT FESTIVAL

Two hours away in Lafayette, La., October, 300 Fisher Rd., 337-233-4077; blackpotfestival.com

Very different than any other festival in the world, Blackpot is officially just a two-day camping festival, but for the entire week beforehand it features not only the basic music and food, but also music lessons for attendees with mega-famous Louisiana musicians, plus cooking lessons and a cook-off of dishes that can be cooked in a black iron pot. Zydeco is a major focus.

CAJUN ZYDECO FESTIVAL

Tremé, June, Louis Armstrong Park, 701 N. Rampart St.; jazzandheritage.org/cajun-zydeco

Two days of authentic, free zydeco from the likes of Grammy winner **Chubby Carrier**, **Geno Delafose**, the **Lost Bayou Ramblers**, and **Dwayne Dopsie**. Food vendors sell Italian ice, popsicles, ice cream, and other summertime treats inside a large arts market that provides handmade wares and activities for kids, plus lots of misting fans to keep everyone cool.

FESTIVALS ACADIENS ET CRÉOLES

Two hours away in Lafayette, La., October, 500 Girard Park Dr.; festivalsacadiensetcreoles.com

Really three free festivals in one: The Festival de Musique portion of the proceedings features fifty bands on four stages over three days—this paired up with the Bayou Food Festival and the Louisiana Craft Fair makes this event (with very cheap tickets!) worth the drive to Lafayette.

JOLLY INN

One hour away in Houma, La., 1507 Barrow St., 985-872-6114; thejollyinn.com

With just a few rocking chairs, some low tables and plastic lawn furniture, fluorescent lights, a small stage, and basic hardwood floors, the Jolly Inn is nonetheless one of Louisiana's last remaining Cajun cultural music centers. Along with the authentic zydeco soundtrack, enjoy a menu of gumbos, jambalaya, fresh fried seafood, and sides. A great New Orleans fieldtrip!

LEBEAU ZYDECO FESTIVAL

A little over two hours away in Lebeau, La., July, 103 Lebeau Church Road, 337-351-3902

For almost three decades now, this festival has featured live zydeco, games, and world-famous pork-backbone dinners.

MULATE'S

CBD, 201 Julia St., 504-522-1492; mulates.com

This chain restaurant is nonetheless authentic, offering bomb Cajun food and zydeco and Creole music in Louisiana's small bayou towns. In New Orleans, expect traditional Cajun groups like **Bayou DeVille** and **La Touché** to play some zydeco too.

ZYDECO EXTRAVAGANZA

Two hours away in Lafayette, La., May (Memorial Day weekend), 2330 Johnston St.; zydecoextra.com

An outgrowth of a local zydeco radio show hosted by Donald and Charles Cravins, the Zydeco Extravaganza was started in May of 1987 by the Cravins family in an effort to revive the Creole culture in St. Landry Parish. Each Memorial Day weekend, this fest features an amateur accordion contest, food and crafts booths, and of course zydeco performances by the mighty likes of **Beau Jocque**, **Keith Frank**, **Terrance Simien**, **Zydeco Force**, and **Chris Ardoin**.

ZYDECO FESTIVAL

Two-and-a-half hours away in Opelousas, La., September, Yambilee Festival Grounds, 1939 W. Landry St., 337-290-6048; zydeco.org

Nearing its fortieth year, the world's oldest zydeco festival throws down each summer in the self-proclaimed "zydeco capital of the world," Opelousas. Regulars include **Chubby Carrier**, **Lil' Nate**, and **Nathan and the Zydeco Cha-Chas**.

3. RAP

Slangston Hughes is not only a connoisseur of fine rhyme and a thrower of parties, but also a writer, who helped put together this section of the book.

As hip-hop evolved throughout the 1980s, and before bounce came along, New Orleans rap consisted of complex rhyming and true-school MCing, with lyricists such as **Tim Smooth**, **Gregory D.**, **Bustdown**, **M. C. Thick**, and **Legend Mann**. Then in 1991, "Where Dey At," allegedly the first bounce song, was recorded in two versions by **MC T Tucker** with **DJ Irv**, and then shortly after by **DJ Jimi** as "Where They At." On stage, bounce MCs demand responses regarding your ward, your school, and your project. The lyrics are often lovably dirty. Some of the zillions of pioneering bounce artists include **Partners-n-Crime**, **Ms. Tee**, **Mia X**, and **5th Ward Weebie**, whose track "F*** Katrina" captured the local sentiment after the storm.

Bounce slowly gathered the steady support of radio program directors and DJs who saw hip-hop and bounce as opposing values. Today, New Orleans DJs regularly remix R&B radio hits with bounce's signature "Triggerman" rhythm (a sample from the 1986 track "Drag Rap" by New York City's **Showboys** that turns up in most bounce). Bounce pioneer **DJ Jubilee** has earned the title "King of Bounce." In 1999, Jubilee's **Take Fo'** record label (home to artists including **Choppa**) issued *Melpomene Block Party,* the first full-length release from **Katey Red**, a gay, transvestite MC from the Melpomene projects. Other gay bounce artists have followed on Katey's (high) heels, most notably **Big Freedia** and **Sissy Nobby**.

Today, hip-hop fans of all stripes can find the culture they love represented downstairs at the **Dragon's Den** (Frenchmen St.), at **Hi-Ho Lounge** (St. Claude Ave.), and many other of the city's venues. The **Soundclash** beat battle hip-hop variety show still goes strong locally (check listings) and has evolved into outfits in both Baton Rouge and Mobile, Alabama. The growing popularity and musical appeal of hip-hop found its way into the creation of the first **Underground Hip-Hop Awards**, which now after seven years has transitioned into the **NOLA Music Awards** organized by the **Supreme Street** collective's leader **Cracktracks**, aka **Lawrence Parker.**

The following is a list of MCs suggested by local stalwarts **MC Impulss** and **Slangston Hughes** (who incidentally hosts the long-running **Uniquity** showcase, providing performance opportunities for wordy emcees, vocalists, and spoken-word artists paired with a live band):

3D NA'TEE

3dnatee.com

Beauty and bars to match, with appearances on "Sway in the Morning," a deal with Def Jam Digital, and her latest LP *The Regime* breaking the Billboard top 20, Na'Tee is one of the city's fiercest technical lyricists. Winner of the Best Lyricist Award at the NOLA Underground Hip-Hop Awards, 3D Na'Tee has recently performed at **Jazz Fest** and been praised by *XXL* mag.

10TH WARD BUCK

Upstanding entrepreneurial bounce rapper and concert promoter who got the game rolling with some of the first-ever bounce concerts at the Airline Skate Center. **New Mouth from the Dirty South Press** released a coffee-table biography called *Tenth Ward Buck: The Definition of Bounce.*

BARON AHMON

baronahmon.com

Soft-spoken Alabama native, poet, emcee, actor, impressive freestyle rhymer, and frequent collaborator with **Yung Vul** (Dominic Minix). A wordy but unpretentious MC, who one blog described as "somewhere between Mos Def and Nas."

ALLIE BABY

msalliebaby.com

An alum of groups Blak lyce (protégées of **DJ Wild Wayne**) and Gs Up, Allie Baby raps rugged and raspy about her New Orleans dreams. In the year of Katrina, Allie released her own DJ Drama–hosted mixtape, *Pre Season.* Her most recent release was 2015's *Wifey.*

ALFRED BANKS

underdogcentral.com

Using his government name now instead of his former moniker, **Lyriqs da Lyraciss**, this Uptown rapper's star continues to rise with his Billboard charting "The Beautiful," **Voodoo Fest** performances, and an award-winning VW commercial among other accolades. His *Beautiful Prelude* EP bravely tackles the subject of his brother's schizophrenia and suicide.

BILLSBERRY FLOWBOY

From Chalmette (as he will tell you, often), Billsberry Flowboy came up through the freestyle ranks in the months and years after Katrina, and legend has it he has never lost a battle. His great YouTube videos show off his deep flow and sense of humor—check out "Hip-Hop Undead" and "Yat City" (*Y'at City click / I'm keepin' these beads; / I don't wanna see your t*tt*es, b***h*).

BOYFRIEND

imyourboyfriend.com

This rap cabaret performance artist (a role she pioneered) deeply invests herself in her sex-positive housewife character (complete with rollers and bustier) as she tickles the English language with her tongue. For real: girl has bars and bars, and that's just for starters.

CHASE N. CASHE

Producer, rapper, all-around hustler waxing finessed poetics. His mixtape with DJ Drama, *The Heir Up There,* includes credits from Troy Ave, Mac Miller, Dom Kennedy, Curren$y, and more, but his first big break was a production credit on Lil Wayne's "Drop the World." Since working with Drake and Troy Ave, he's stepped up his rapping and released more solo work.

Don't underestimate this white girl in curlers; rapper Boyfriend can spit.

Michael Alford

JIMI CLEVER

jimiclever.com

This winner of the Best Rapper award from ***OffBeat*** magazine is also New Orleans' most honest lyricist. Emotion and feeling pour out in Clever's high-pitched cadence, compound rhymes, and perfect beat-riding.

CURREN$Y

currensyspitta.com

Known for buddha-blown lyrics and laid-back delivery, Spitta jumped the **Cash Money** ship to soar with his **Fly Society** crew and **Damon Dash**. His breakout album was *Pilot Talk,* but he drops constant new mixtapes. Curren$y maintains a local presence with his Wednesday night **Jet Lounge** hip-hop night at House of Blues.

DAPPA

Palmyra Street Productions rapper, singer, and producer with star appeal, these days mainly touring with **Alfred Banks** and handling his **Fresh Music Group** imprint.

Hardcore rapper Delish Da Goddess sweats her heart out to aid your catharsis. Electrifying performer.

Delish Da Goddess

DEE-1

dee1music.com

This young, creative, and real MC who doesn't curse on his albums has made serious waves since his collaboration with New Orleans beatmaster **Mannie Fresh**. Dee-1 recently turned his hit song "Sallie Mae" (where instead of owning a Maybach, Dee-1 longs to "pay Sally Mae back" and be free of student loans) into a "Knowledge for College" tour sponsored by Sallie Mae.

DEE DAY

deeday504.com

With a fan base formed through thousands of mixtape downloads, well-received music videos, and a giant billboard hovering over the I-10 as you drive into downtown, Lil Dee God's Gift has burned his brand into New Orleans' hip-hop scene.

DELISH DA GODDESS

Hardcore, bite-your-head-off MC with a huge stage presence and a fun ego that she both happily and angrily shares with her spellbound audiences. Definitely one of the best live, non-bounce rap acts in today's New Orleans.

DON FLAMINGO

rocnation.com/don-flamingo

A **Mannie Fresh** protégé from New Orleans East, formerly known as The Show. Topics include the "conscious, revolutionary, gangsta, stuntin', or everyday struggles." With the name change came signing with Jay-Z's Roc Nation management and major tours with the likes of **The Lox** in 2017.

EUPHAM

A hip-hop movement composed of **Crummy**, **DJ Mike Swift**, **Lyrikill**, and **Mercure**, giving the masses creative, quality hip-hop music that expands the genre.

K. GATES

Among his many aliases, The Wave is also called "International Gates" for good reason: the composer of "Black and Gold," the unofficial Saints' theme song, has traveled the world over from Mecca to Amsterdam, building his multi-continental hustle and honing his lyricism.

GUERILLA PUBLISHING COMPANY

Still releasing intelligent records and creating contemporary content, this clique includes **Elespee**, **Caliobzvr**, **D.O.N.**, **DJ Skratchmo**, **Private Pile**, **Suave**, **Juskwam**, and **Prospek** (providing the sonic boom-bap landscape), plus many more waving the GPC flag.

SLANGSTON HUGHES

The Connoisseur of Fine Rhyme, member of the **SuperUgly** and **Tygah Woods Crew**. Hip-hop bandleader and lyrical MC taking his reverence for old-school hip-hop and infusing it with contemporary elements. For eight years and counting, Slangston's booked and curated the hip-hop variety show **Uniquity**, a performance opportunity for rappers, singers, spoken-word artists, and bands both local and regional (check online for venue).

INFINITE I

The *I* is for *intelligence*. This freestyle king from Marrero on the West Bank and former front man of award-winning live act **Jealous Monk** gives you his news and views off-the-cuff, in real time—mind-boggling improv, both informative and funky.

KNOW ONE

An experimental MC pushing the boundaries of creativity and musicianship. Know One (aka Roan Smith) was one of the first to arrive post-Katrina and begin to rebuild not only the hip-hop scene but also the city itself, laying brick and mortar, floating sheetrock as expertly as he floats on a beat.

KOAN

koanmusic.com

This Lower Ninth Ward MC, who comes from a marching band background (sax), spits serious subject matter that has made him the perfect opener for acts like Immortal Technique, Killer Mike, and Killa Priest. He's lately been backed by live band My Theme Music. Koan's annual Summer Jam concerts at Tipitina's (usually in June) bring together great local black artists from brass bands to soul groups to rappers.

A. LEVY

The globetrotting, slick-tongued rapper and owner of the **Hut Studios** has over the years turned his Squares brand into a T-shirt line and a series of compilation LPs. Levy sometimes hosts the **Writer's Block** showcase for both local and regional emcees.

KATEY RED ON BOURBON STREET, BOUNCE RAP, AND GAY CLUBS

Katey Red

Robin Walker

With the release of her album *Melpomene Block Party* almost twenty years ago on DJ Jubilee's **Take Fo'** imprint, **Katey Red** staked her claim as the first-ever homosexual, transgender bounce rap artist. She has directly inspired the careers of other so-called punk rappers or sissy bounce artists, such as **Big Freedia** and **Sissy Nobby**. We caught up with Katey to get her advice on where you should party while in New Orleans. We also asked her which bounce rap artists you should check out, and where.

Do you have friends outside of New Orleans who come to town to visit you?

Quite a few. Mostly when my friends come to town they want to go to my shows. But if they just want to have a few drinks we either go on Bourbon Street, or else sit in **Siberia**. Ian Polk, the creator of Noah's Ark, he came down and wanted to hang out with me, so I took him to a few gay clubs out here. I brought him to one of my shows at **One Eyed Jacks** and I

Sissy Nobby performing at JazzFest with dancers.

took him to **Club Fusions** [now closed] because he wanted to see the drag show I was performing in.

Some people disparage Bourbon Street, but you're a fan?

You can never go wrong with Bourbon Street. I am not an everyday Bourbon Street kind of girl though, so when I am out there it's new to me, like going out of town somewhere. If I am on Bourbon I end up either by **Oz** (800 Bourbon St.; oznewworleans.com), or the **Bourbon Pub** (801 Bourbon St.; bourbonpub.com). They have pick-pocketers and crime but . . . after Katrina Bourbon was the first thing poppin'. That's where New Orleans make they money at the dance clubs and strip clubs and gay clubs as well as heterosexual clubs. They got bounce music, reggae music, jazz, it's all kinds of entertainment on the side street. They got people doing card tricks, they have people doing statues, people tap-dancin', people sitting on the stoop singing live and playin' keyboards. And they also have historical things. It's nice out there. Why would they talk bad about Bourbon?

Did you actually have your pocket picked on Bourbon?

Um, I had a fight on one of my birthdays on one of the side streets off Bourbon. Some guy was for some reason like, "Don't look at me." And I was like, "Don't look at me!" And he ran up on me trying to fight me and I got him off me. That was the only thing bad ever happened to me on Bourbon Street. Normally people just wanna take pictures and stuff.

RAP

Where can you hear bounce rap on Bourbon Street?

The **Bourbon Heat** (711 Bourbon St.; 711bourbonheat.com) or sometimes the **Cats Meow** (701 Bourbon St.; 701bourbon .com). Maybe it's because when I come in the club they recognize who I am and so then they start playing bounce music. If they don't play bounce music, they play it when I'm around.

Doesn't the Chris Owens Club (500 Bourbon St.; chrisowensclub.net) also play rap and bounce?

I been there before. It's real wild. I wouldn't suggest my out-of-town friends go there. Sometimes they getting wild. I seen all kinds of things going on in the bathroom—stuff you only supposed to do at home! Wow.

What about Club Caesar's on the West Bank (Gretna, 209 Monroe St., 504-368-1117)? You have always performed there quite a bit.

Most of my out-of-town friends are Caucasians, so they don't really want to go to places like Caesar's, or **Encore** (3940 Tulane Ave., 504-312-1953), 'cause it's too wild and too rough. If they want to hear bounce music all right, but they have Caucasian clubs that play bounce music. I would suggest that for them.

What's your strongest musical memory of childhood?

I grew up on bounce! Recording stuff off the radio, bounce music. **Mia X** and all them kinda people!

Who are your favorite local bounce artists?

Cheeky Blakk been in the game for almost twenty-five years. Cheeky is a legend. She needs to be heard more. [Cheeky once told me, "I see myself as a baby Millie Jackson. 'Cause she come with it raw and nasty."]. **Ha' Sizzle** had lil slight hit with "She Rode That Dick like a Soldier." He did it in concert at gay bars and stuff like that, but he never got out with it. **Walt Wiggady**, he's a big guy, he moves around real good. He don't have a hit, but with all his moves, he is perfect for a show.

LG

A Fifth Ward rapper who spits street rhymes. LG's feature with **Curren$y**, "Battlefield," premiered on BET, he went on to fill the opening slot at **Lil Weezyana Fest** in 2016, and he even rapped with **Dr. John** at **Jazz Fest**.

LUCKYLOU

This bounce-influenced, family-friendly rap artist and dancer is often accompanied by an amazing dance troupe including a Michael Jackson impersonator.

Lucky Lou is a brilliant dancer and rapper that even families can enjoy.

RAP

LYRIKILL

The creator of the important **Soundclash** beat battle (now an intermittent hip-hop talent showcase rather than a battle) is also a wordsmith, a shoe obsessive, and a member of **Eupham**'s rap crew. Chuck actually moved to Houston, but we love him too much to remove him from this book.

MADE GROCERIES

smallworldinternational.us/ madegroceries

This hardworking and passionate Baton Rouge-via-New Orleans trio persistently releases quality singles and albums, while also touring with both Robb Banks and **Curren$y**. Food lyrics abound: *"Don't try to be something you ain't; that's like tryna unfry an egg."*

MC SWEET TEA

A lady MC tackling big concepts with the help of a subtle sense of humor and a small interpretive dance troupe. She also performs as front woman for rap-rock outfit **Malevitus**, featuring noise guitarist **Rob Cambre** and other members of **R. Scully's Rough 7**.

MC TRACHIOTOMY

On the scene for two decades, Trach makes intentionally garbled psyche-delic hip-hop funk, influenced by the odd genius of bands like the Butthole Surfers and Captain Beefheart.

MERCURE

This member of the **Eupham** crew, and sometime co-host of the **Soundclash** hip-hop showcase with **El Williams**, plies his trade as a local producer, mixing synths, old-school R&B, and witty freestyles.

PELL

pellyeah.com

With a singsong flow over synth-heavy tracks—not unlike fellow native New Orleanian Frank Ocean—Pell's music has been called "dream rap." His debut full-length album, *Floating while Dreaming,* made him one of *Complex* magazine's "25 New Rappers to Watch Out For" in 2014.

NESBY PHIPS

nesbyphips.com

Hailing from **Curren$y**'s **Fly Society**, Phips is a popular beatmaker here and in NYC. He released his conscious, racially charged "Black Man 4 Sale" album while playing an integral part in the **0017th Movement**. A great-nephew of the iconic **Mahalia Jackson**, Phips has worked with **Aaron Neville**, **Trombone Shorty**, and Lil Wayne. He describes his new hip-hop supergroup **GRID** as "Frankie Beverly andMaze but on some hip-hop shit."

SESS 4-5

sess4-5.com

Appropriately known as the "Hustle God," Sess celebrated the tenth anniversary of **Nuthin but Fire Records** in 2017, and he continues to organize the annual Katrina march and second-line parade. His tracks are reminiscent of bounce, with lawn-sprinkler high-hats, but with denser lyrics—the same combo locals loved in late, great NOLA

Nesby Phips helps provide the foundation of New Orleans hip-hop.

Sierra Hudson

rapper **Soulja Slim**. Also check Sess's Nuthin but Fire mixtape CDs, featuring New Orleans' best underground rap artists.

SLEAZY

Stuntin' is a habit with this smoker-friendly and braggadocious female rapper who regularly hosts parties at **Eiffel Society** (Uptown) and has opened for Waka Flocka.

SOUL CAPITAL

Composed of **Ben Brubaker** and **DJ Miles Felix**, Soul Capital brings a fresh sound and style to the game with conscious yet entertaining lyricism and beats that move the crowd.

TRUTH UNIVERSAL

truthuniversal.com

Truth has been hustling and grinding not only in New Orleans but throughout the continental United States for decades. One of the city's most respected MCs and founder of the influential **Grassroots!** series (RIP), Truth lives up to his name on the mic, rapping about politics, the NOPD, and the game.

TYGAH WOODS CREW

New Orleans' version of the Wu-Tang Clan—at least structurally: six MCs (**Slangston Hughes**, **Mr. J'ai**, **J-Dubble**, **Blaze the Verbal Chemist**, **D. Francis**, **Alfred Banks**) unite with **DJ Mike Swift** to bring hip-hop back to its roots.

Jonathan Traviesa

Some well-dressed round-the-way girls cooling off outside a sweaty Sissy Nobby concert.

RAY WIMLEY

This transplant from Little Rock, Arkansas, has become a regular street performer who looks to inspire others to find their niche in life and go after it full force. Catch him rapping out on Royal Street in the Quarter with his backing band, Harbinger Project.

YOUNG GREATNESS

This Seventh Ward native's career launched during post-Katrina exile in Houston. He earned Mixtape of the Year honors at the fifth annual NOLA Underground Hip-Hop Awards for his project *Dollar for Hate,* which boasts features from Meek Mill, **Juvenile**, Pusha T, and others.

YOUNG RODDY

A member of **Curren$y**'s Jet Life crew, Roddy released the 11-track collaboration *Bales* with Spitta. In early 2014, Young Roddy dropped the cool-toned and laid-back solo mixtape *Route the Ruler* with features from Curren$y, Smoke DZA, and Fiend.

4. METAL AND PUNK

Club owner and loud music promoter Matt Russell (*right*) with Bywater Music store owner Paul Webb.

Believe it or not, heavy metal rock could be considered a type of New Orleans roots music. Though not invented here, New Orleans metal has a distinctly slow, low, slithery sound, with a lineage stretching as far back as bounce rap's. Since the late '80s, New Orleans has offered up legends from **Soilent Green** and **EyeHateGod** to more recent successes like **Suplecs** and the slow, grinding **DOWN**, led by Louisiana natives guitarist **Pepper Keenan (Corrosion of Conformity)** and singer **Phil Anselmo** (Pantera).

The websites **noladiy.org** and **nolaunderground.word-press.com** will teach exactly where you can "throw the goat" while in town. Or you can listen to **Paul Webb** or **Matt Russell**. Webb owns and runs **Webb's Bywater Music**, and plays guitar in mostly instrumental tech-metal combos such as **Mountain of Wizard** and **Spickle**. Matt Russell has for the last decade booked heavy bands at local bars, most recently through his Tremé club **Poor Boys**. Matt currently "sings" while Paul plays guitar in the hardcore punk band **Classhole**. "The New Orleans metal scene is like Mexican food," says Webb. "There are just a few people in many different combinations."

Knowing those combinations intimately, Webb and Russell suggest the following heavy New Orleans bands:

A HANGING

Grindcore-esque metal band that has shared the stage with everyone from D.R.I. to M.O.D.

BUCK BILOXI AND THE FUCKS

Fronted by cab driver **Joe Pestilence**, they sound like the Spits but stupider. They have stuff out on **Goner Records'** side label **Orgone Toilet**, and also local label **Pelican Pow Wow Records**.

CROWBAR

crowbarnola.com

Twenty-plus years and still heavy, these New Orleans doomcore legends were inspired by the down-tuned sludge of the Melvins and the over-the-top aggression of Carnivore. Crowbar's currently releasing new material and reissuing old records on the Housecore label.

DEMONIC DESTRUCTION

Spanish guys, transplants living in Kenner, playing death metal inspired by Slayer, Morbid Angel, and Deicide. "The band's lyrics are highly based on satanism and tyranny," states their old myspace page.

DIE RÖTZZ

dierotzz.tripod.com

A loud punk rock power trio who make a fun musical mess. Die Rötzz does double time as **Guitar Lightnin' Lee's Thunder Band**, which means they, improbably, hang out with Fats Domino sometimes, and play blues like a broken steamroller.

DISCIPLES OF THRASH

A thrash metal cover band doing '80s and early '90s stuff like Metallica, Slayer, Testament, Megadeth, Sepultura, Kreator, Death Angel. The singer's really into it.

DONKEY PUNCHER

NOLA sludge, hardcore thrash. They have a song called "Don't Drop Your Baby in the Crawfish Boil." Ridiculous.

FAT STUPID UGLY PEOPLE

Power violence. **Hollis**, the lead singer, is kinda the mascot of the scene. He might wear a coconut bra, or you never know what's gonna happen with Hollis.

GARY WRONG

jethrowrecords.blogspot.com

This Mississippi-via-New Orleans punk rock impresario heads up the Gary Wrong group, plus **Wizzard Sleeve**, while also releasing dozens of vinyl albums by the likes of Tumor Lord and True Sons of Thunder on his own **Jeth Row Records** label.

GOATWHORE

Black metal from members of Louisiana legends **Acid Bath**, **Crowbar**, and **Soilent Green**.

HAWG JAW

Hardcore music for people who don't think hardcore is interesting enough, Hawg Jaw was formed in 1996. The vocals are more expressive than in most metal, and the heavy music is twisted and brutal. This band doesn't

Jason Fischer

Gary Wrong puts the "un" in punk.

play much but is too good to kill off, so look for a reunion show while in town.

MARS

Since 2006, Mars has made slow, simple stoner doom metal for the end times. Now on tour. Always on tour.

THE PALLBEARERS

It's always Halloween for New Orleans' original sicko horror punks, who've been trafficking in loud guitars and blood since 1997. More than a couple shows have ended with the singer going to the hospital.

SPLIT()LIPS

This cool-headed punk version of multiband overlord **Jenn Attaway** mixes GG Allin, Butt Trumpet, Misfits, and Child Molesters into expert original bitch anthems such as "Get Your Rosaries Off My Ovaries" and "Vagina Dentata." Meant to be an all-girl band, they reportedly use the **Pallbearers'** drummer with a wig on.

SUNRISE: SUNSET

Wizened vets of the metal scene, including **Tom Beeman** of former Amphetamine Reptile records, stars Guzzard shredding the guitar and supernaturally tall **Ray Surinck**'s rumbling bass.

SUPLECS

Fun, heavy rock, now fifteen years strong. Suplecs's debut album, *Wrestlin' with My Lady Friend,* was released in April of 2000, and the video for the song "Rock Bottom" played on MTV's Headbangers Ball. Suplecs does an insane, free show at **Checkpoint Charlie's** each Fat Tuesday.

THOU

noladiy.org/thou

Down-tempo stoner metal featuring straight-edge front man Bryan Funk, who now also runs **Sisters in Christ** record store on Magazine St. Thou is well known in the American metal underground, because they are fucking awesome and heavy as fuck.

MIKE IX WILLIAMS OF EYEHATEGOD

eyehategod.ee

Mike IX Williams has fronted slow punk-metal band **Eye-HateGod** for almost thirty years. Williams also published the excellent dark and hilarious poetry book, *Cancer as a Social Activity* (Southern Nihilism Front). We interviewed Mike about EyeHateGod and its place in the pantheon of New Orleans metal.

First, tell me the story of EyeHateGod.

We started in 1988. Now there's different members. The cool thing at the time was thrash metal, Slayer was cool. Even I had a thrash band in New Orleans. We heard the Melvins and we were also into Black Flag, side 2 of *My War,* and obviously we were into Black Sabbath and St. Vitus and stuff like that. We weren't even 100 percent serious at the beginning; it was just something to piss off people who would play these shows, and just have fun and watch people's reaction when we'd just do feedback for fifteen minutes, and throw in three riffs as slow as we possibly could.

So you didn't have a lot of company on the scene then?

Not in New Orleans. **Soilent Green** was around. But they were more influenced by Napalm Death and they kind of started playing slower later on—I'm not sure if that's our influence. There was **HawgJaw**. And we were all friends so it wasn't like anyone was stealing from each other. EyeHateGod was like taking the Melvins even further, more filthy and dirty and with the bluesy southern feeling to it also. We were hated for a long time; people just didn't get it. We had

EyeHateGod

Gary LoVerde

a few fans who understood that it was just supposed to be heavy—in 1986 to 1988 as we were forming, people thought the faster you play the heavier you are, but that's obviously not true.

And now New Orleans is a metal capital of America!

Yeah, people have moved here from other states, man, even other countries, to be part of the scene here. It was a great time for music actually, right after Katrina, with bands starting back up, and new bands forming. The greatest thing is around 1998 and 1999 when EHG did take a sort of hiatus because of personal problems and record label trouble—during that hiatus we noticed bands were popping up in England, and Japan even—bands all over the world that were starting to kind of sound like this same exact kind of sound. That's when we noticed it was something bigger than us.

5. ELECTRONIC MUSICIANS, DJS, DANCE PARTIES, AND NOISE ARTISTS

ELECTRONIC MUSICIANS

NOLA MOMENT

AF THE NAYSAYER

afthenaysayer.com

"My stage name comes from my punk rock roots," explains AF the Naysayer. "I consider a 'naysayer' to be someone who stands up for themselves whatever the consequences; you're speaking up for yourself, and you're saying no. My music comes from that energy. AF just stands for Abstruse Function—it's like an organic math problem."

From New Orleans via Los Angeles, AF came up using the computer music program Frooty Loops, on which he still relies to create his tactile tunes. "The music I was making at first for rap group[s] was very basic boom-bap style rap, like People Under the Stairs. From there it became a matter of me not hiding in front of a vocalist but just doing instrumental music in front of a crowd." These days, AF's music blends laid-back, down-tempo electronic hip-hop, as displayed on his debut EP, the *Autodidact Instrumentals, Vol. 1*.

AF believes that, while in town, you should check out these artists:

ADAMBOMB

Experimental psychedelic, futuristic, experimental hip-hop. Slightly bent, but ultimately funk head-nod music with a subtle sense of humor.

OSCILLATION COMMUNICATION

A sort of homage to 1990s/2000s electronic music, very house music inspired, drum-n-bass influenced, encompassing a wide range of genres. OC is also one of the city's few electronic instrument repairmen.

ELIJAH SCARLETT

Sensual and meditative tracks (mostly beautiful, obscure remixes of famous songs like Shaggy's "It Wasn't Me") laced with grainy vocal samples.

ZACK VILLERE

Formerly known by the much better name **Froyo Ma**, Villere conjures everything from mellow, clicky hip-hop to emphatically emotional instrumental synth arrangements—soulful, sometimes with a light jazz influence.

BEAUTIFUL BELLS

articulatedworks.com

Instrumentalist, improviser, composer, and jazz drummer, Justin Peake also performs original, electronic future jazz made from homemade samples and improvised melodies fused with rich synthesized textures. His albums boast influences as disparate as Fela Kuti, Autechre, and John Cage. In 2012, Peake started **Articulated Works**, an art hub focusing on music. The site's

podcast, Parlour, features musician interviews and performances.

COMPUTA GAMES

computagames.com

An "'80s boogie funk throwback" side project of musician and DJ **Quickie Mart** and his partner **Chris Arenas** (incidentally, the bassist for **Eric Lindell**). Check out their singles on Austin Boogie Crew Records.

Talented multi-instrumentalist and synth-builder Naughty Palace sings electro R&B like a cross between Justin Timberlake and a-ha.

CONTEXT KILLER

Solo project from eclectic dresser and monster drummer **Simon Lott**—who boasts the ability to play passionately in any type of band, from jazz to funk—this time helming synthesizers and whatever other toys he chooses on a given night for flights of noisy improvisation.

FORCE FEED RADIO

Starting as a DJ-and-production duo in high school (not terribly long ago), **Kid Kamillion (Bryan Normand)** and **Money P. (Patrick Bowden)** grew up manning the decks at anything-goes open-format electronic music parties, mashing together southern hip-hop, techno, punk rock, plus their own original songs, edits, and remixes. When in town, they can be caught at **The Republic** and various bottle-service clubs that can accommodate the cut-and-paste digital video show that accompanies FFR's set.

ISIDRO

Post-pop, post-folk, raw tribal essence. Vocals, guitar, drums, beat box, keyboards, live looped vocals. He also performs with **Whom Do You Work For?**

THE MONOCLE

auroranealand.bandcamp.com

Saxophonist/composer **Aurora Nealand**'s solo performance project: Vocals, accordion, drums, computer, and other niceties.

MONOPOL (AKA CHRISTOPH ANDERSSON)

This young New Orleans transplant made his international name with funk-influenced electro-pop and his world-touring monthly dance music party, **TKVR**. Prior to his success, Andersson attended the **New Orleans Center for Creative Arts (NOCCA)** and once worked as a recording assistant for **Dr. John**. His original music now combines contemporary indie electro and French house music. He also remixes many **G-Easy** raps.

NAUGHTY PALACE

Markus Davis is an underground experimental R&B artist somewhere between New Orleans' Frank Ocean and fellow Caucasian Justin Timberlake, with just the slightest hint of irony in falsetto-crooned songs like "Beach Body." The devil is in the sensual backing tracks, made on home-made synths which Davis tickles live.

SETEC ASTRONOMY

Pensive and profound textures from saxophonist **David Polk** and visual artist **Everett DiNapoli.**

TRANSMUTEO

Lush and tranquil sounds improvised by mixing analog tape and digital sounds, often accompanied by video.

DJS

New Orleans has many working DJs spinning bounce and hip-hop, plus a wide variety of other forms and niches that make the world of New Orleans turntablism (digital or vinyl) an interesting landscape to explore while you're visiting.

DJ BRICE NICE

Many claim Brice Nice owns the most records in New Orleans. He also hosts "The Block Party" on 90.7 FM each Saturday from 6 to 8 p.m., a show designed to fuel an actual block party with heavy funk, brass band music, disco, dancehall and other reggae, soul, afro-beat, and Latin. Brice also cofounded **Sinking City Records** (sinkingcityrecords.com), which has released work by singer **Charm Taylor**, **Stooges Brass Band**, and the **79rs Gang** Mardi Gras Indians.

DJ CARMINE P. FILTHY

all types of electronic; carminepfilthy.com

Originally from Miami, a drum and bass and jungle capital, Filthy moved to New York City in 2005, where he spun house, techno, and Italian disco. These days, expect all of that in one set.

DJ CHICKEN

hip-hop; 504bounce.com

Best known for the **"Chicken and Waffle Mix,"** on **Power 102.9**, and often the throwback lunch mix as well, DJ Chicken has forever spun old and new hip-hop, bounce rap, and brass band music as part of the Definition crew of DJs and MCs.

Thomas Edwards

The youngest godfather of New Orleans' hip-hop DJing, E. F. Cuttin can be seen and heard at Curren$y's Jet Lounge night every Wednesday at House of Blues.

DJ E. F. CUTTIN

hip-hop; djefcuttin.com

As a member of **Go DJ's**, E. F. plays to the crowd and breaks quality records on the daily. He heads up the **Industry Influence** parties for Louisiana rap and R&B artists, and also puts together the **Nuthin but Fire** mixtape series for the record store of the same name (see "Shopping"). He currently DJs for rapper **Curren$y's Jet Lounge** night at House of Blues each Wednesday.

DJ ED MAXMILLION

hip-hop

An OG of New Orleans hip-hop who continues to open for national acts and special events, spinning classics as well as R&B and funk. If you're here to purchase vinyl, track down one of the city's preeminent purveyors of rare groove.

DJ FRENZI

lounge hip-hop

Frenzi DJs hip-hop and house DVDs and records simultaneously, most notably on Friday nights at **Omni Royal Orleans Hotel** (French Quarter, 621 St. Louis St., 504-529-5333).

DJ JUBILEE

bounce/hip-hop

Rapper, DJ, football coach, and king of New Orleans bounce music for decades now, Jubilee pops up everywhere, from the biggest block parties to the **Essence Festival** and **Jazz Fest**. His '90s tracks like "West Bank Thang" and "Do the Jubilee All" are still hot club jams today.

DJ KARO

Scratch DJ with roots in punk and new wave, Karo ended up a hip-hop DJ, who also spins exotic tunes from Bollywood to bounce to dub reggae.

DJ OTTO

A purveyor of all styles who has performed at every club and festival one could name, spinning techno, funk, disco, soul, Latin, global, house, and experimental. Lately he's been dominating the hotel rooftop pool residencies at Ace Hotel, The Drifter, Troubadour, and Tsunami/Shaw Center for the Arts in Baton Rouge. He's also helped open Techno Club, hosting Spektrum Fridays (house, disco, nu disco, electro, garage) and Nola Saturdays, featuring collaborations with live musicians.

DJ PASTA

swamp pop, classic country, undefined

Pasta is the kind of insane record savant who can play four hours' worth of your favorite songs you've never heard before, mostly on 45s. He soundtracks rock and punk nights, Louisiana swamp pop nights, even weepy country nights where, if prodded, he will whip out his massive collection of bizarre '60s country novelty songs.

DJ POPPA

hip-hop; djpoppa.com

A member of the worldwide **Core DJ** clique, one of the city's best bounce mixers, and live DJ for bounce artists. Between intermittent spots at **Jazz Fest** or **Voodoo Fest**, Poppa holds it down at various local clubs. Check his website for dates and times.

DJ PRINCE PAUPER

reggae; dominosoundrecords.com

Reggae, dub, dancehall, and world music dominate sets by selector DJ Prince Pauper, just like at his Mid-City record store, **Domino Sound Record Shack**. Pauper also spins world music on **WWOZ** (90.7 FM).

DJ Q

hip-hop

Spins hip-hop, bounce, trap. Also runs tracks for genre-bending bounce rap and dance troupe **NOLA Fam** and **Que Hefner**. Heard most recently at his "Honey Dipped" Friday soul nights at **Sidney's Saloon** (Marigny) and random weekend gigs at **The Saint**, uptown.

QUICKIE MART

hip-hop, dubstep, boogie; djquickiemart.com

After representing the hip-hop/rap scene in New Orleans for many fruitful years, Quickie Mart has become a real touring national act. Luckily, we still hear him a lot around New Orleans at both small clubs and large festivals. Quickie has spun backing rappers Devin the Dude, **The Knux**, and the late, great New Orleans **Bionik Brown** among many others. He's also released many big, stomping electro singles of his own.

Quickie Mart does not put DJ in front of his name, but he does DJ a lot: electro, boogie, bounce, traditional New Orleans funk, whatever you need. He also makes original tracks.

Brianna Sage

DJ RAJ SMOOVE

hip-hop; rajsmoove.com

A local legend, this hip-hop and reggae DJ and producer has appeared on Rap City and Showtime at the Apollo, toured with **Cash Money Records** and **Mannie Fresh**, and has done production for **Lil Wayne** ("I Miss My Dawgs," "Heat," "Who Wanna"). Raj currently holds residencies at the **Foundation Room**, on **WYLD**'s (98.5 FM) Saturday Night Live, and at **New Orleans Pelicans** basketball events.

DJ RIK DUCCI

hip-hop

A vinyl enthusiast and soul music fanatic who has backed rappers including KRS-One, EPMD, Busta Rhymes, Lost Boyz, Camp Lo, Naughty by Nature, and the late Big Pun.

DJ ROTTEN MILK

experimental

Longtime experimental and noise DJ heard most often on **WTUL** (91.5 FM), though Milk does come outside to make weird, beautiful sounds at downtown clubs like **Poor Boys** and **Siberia**.

DJ RQ AWAY

hip-hop; whatisawayteam.com

RQ Away holds down decks at several spots, keeping us abreast of what the coolest hip-hop kids are up to. His Friday "Tipping Point" parties at **Dragon's Den** are made for dancing all night.

DJ RUSTY LAZER

bounce, obscure but fun international dance music

Once the official DJ for bounce artist **Big Freedia** and **Nikki da B** (RIP), Rusty now mostly helps run the mindblowing **Music Box** art installation,

DJ Rusty Lazer receiving a smooch from Delish Da Goddess.

Delish Da Goddess

Slick Leo, who helped shape New Orleans radio in the wake of civil rights, now spins weekly at Circle Bar.

Slick Leo Coakley

but still gets back behind the decks for punk and fauxbeaux crowds in the Bywater and Marigny neighborhoods, especially at his favorite haunt, **St. Roch Tavern**.

DJ SLICK LEO

Now sixty years old, Slick Leo has influenced every New Orleans disk jockey and radio personality from **DJ Chicken** to the king, **Mannie Fresh**. Starting out at house parties in the '70s, then moving on to work at **Allen Toussaint**'s **Sea-Saint Studios**, Leo comes from live music. He's partly responsible for some local artists selling millions of records, including **Master P** and **No Limit Records**. As this book goes to press, Leo holds down regular gigs at

Paradise NOLA, the **St. Roch Tavern**, **Circle Bar**, **Legends Café**, and **Sportsman's Corner** (a club owned by rapper **Mia X**).

DJ SOUL SISTER

vintage soul; djsoulsister.com

Soul Sister's purview is deep funk, rare groove, and disco from the late '60s to early '80s, and she's been known to throw parties that pay specific tribute to Prince, Michael Jackson, and early hip-hop. Though slowing down in her forties, she still sometimes spins two to three times a week, plus sets at **Jazz Fest**, **Voodoo**, and **Essence**. Her long-running "Soul Power" radio show airs from 8 to 10 p.m. Saturday nights on **WWOZ** (90.7 FM).

DJ T-ROY

reggae

For years and years, DJ T-Roy's **Bayou International Soundsystem** has shaken the **Dragon's Den** (currently on Wednesdays) with the deepest dub and dancehall reggae. T-Roy also holds down Thursday from 2 to 4 p.m. on **WHIV** (102.3 FM) as well as Thursday nights at **Blue Nile** on Frenchmen Street.

DJ TONY SKRATCHERE

turntablist

Besides being an intelligent, experienced hip-hop DJ, Tony Skratchere—his name a pun on the Creole seasoning Tony Chachere's—is the turntablist who invented yacht bounce, a genre that puts a "Triggerman" beat behind famous smooth rock songs such as Toto's "Africa." Catch Skratchere anywhere from **The Saint** to the **Dragon's Den**, to main event shows at **The Republic** and **Voodoo Fest**.

DJ UNICORN FUKR

EDM; unicornfukr.com

A dynamic EDM DJ also known for converting junglists into house music fans. Expect vinyl from this "DJ's DJ," music producer, dance party promoter, and label co-owner (**Versed Recordings**) at dance nights like **Church** and **Kompression** (both at **Dragon's Den**).

DANCE NIGHTS

CHURCH

Dragon's Den, Marigny,
435 Esplanade Ave., 504-940-4446;
dragonsdennola.com

DJs Carmine P. Filthy, **Unicorn Fukr**, and **Rekanize** drag their own PA up the stairs of the Den every Sunday for their Church residency, where they play electro-disco, dubstep, and other bass music until way past when you would otherwise be in bed.

CURREN$Y'S JET LOUNGE

every Wednesday, French Quarter,
House of Blues, 225 Decatur St.,
504-310-4999; currensyspitta.com

The local MC with the most national shine since Dwayne Carter, Spitta delivers gauzy weed rap with effortless flow that masks his serious work ethic. A mixtape machine, he maintains a presence in his hometown with his weekly Jet Lounge at the House of Blues Parish Room: a hazy, smoke-filled environment filled with contemporary hip-hop orchestrated by **DJ E. F. Cuttin**.

FONTAINE PALACE NOLA

CBD, 218 S. Robertson St.,
504-525-9775

Formerly Handsome Willy's, this music and food oasis in the middle of the medical district has DJs almost every night, from hip-hop heroes **Rik Ducci** and **Maxmillion** to **Swamp Boogie** and **Itchy and Scratchy**.

DJs Matty and Kristen, founders of Mod Dance Party.

Matt Uhlman

INDUSTRY INFLUENCE

monthly, Howlin' Wolf, CBD, 907 S. Peters St.; industryinfluence.blogspot.com

Q93 radio personality **Wild Wayne** and MC **Sess 4-5** (CEO of **Nuthin but Fire Records**), both mainstays of the local hip-hop scene, hold down this long-running open-mic and showcase, where you'll catch the rawest aspirants, plus meet record execs and community activists. The performances are understandably hit-or-miss, but still a good source for the latest street sounds. Nothing is realer.

KOMPRESSION

house and techno; check listings

Dance to house and techno all night, then watch the sun rise from the **Drag-** on's **Den**'s lace iron balcony, then keep on dancing. Resident DJs are **Unicorn Fukr**, **Herb Christopher**, and **Ryan Deffes** (of **Junkyard Rhythm Section**). Once a more regular event, Kompression now happens intermittently, so check the Dragon's Den calendar.

MOD DANCE PARTY

old rock and soul; check listings

A monthly New Orleans tradition for over fifteen years, the Mod Dance Party features **DJs Matty and Kristen**'s hundreds of pre-1970 vinyl dance records from New Orleans and beyond. Cut loose and dance to the kind of upbeat '60s soul that the loose moniker "mod" implies. The party, which routinely rages till dawn (attendance skews young), has returned to its original home, the **Circle Bar**.

THE SAINT

Uptown, Garden District,
961 St. Mary St., 504-523-0050;
thesaintneworleans.com

Walk beneath the neon halo sign into a venue that hosts DJs and often gets blessed with sets from major names like Diplo, **Force Feed Radio**, and **DJ Musa**, plus a heavy rotation of underground locals.

TECHNO CLUB

CBD, 810 S. Peters St.;
technoclubnola.com

The description's in the title! New Orleans has needed one of these for a while now. Populated by the city's best EDM DJs including our man **Otto**, the Techno Club sits near **The Republic** in the CBD (perhaps New Orleans has an "Electronic Music District" in its future?). Only open Friday and Saturday from 11 p.m. to 5 a.m.

NOISE

Clearly, it's the end of the world. In these apocalyptic times, noise is widely accepted as music. In 2004, **Deacon Johnson** began **NOizeFest** (always last Sunday of **Jazz Fest** in April; location changes) to showcase dozens of musicians who would never be asked to play Jazz Fest. NOizeFest has always featured many electronic artists, DJs, and other weirdoes who almost never play shows otherwise. But in the last few years, New Orleans clubs have begun booking a lot more noise artists (and actually paying them to perform. I know, crazy!).

WTUL DJ **Sebastian Figueroa** (known by his stage name **Proud/Father**) books a ton of experimental and noise shows, mostly at the **Mudlark** (Bywater, 1200 Port St), some generator shows in secret spots like **The End of the World** (ask around), or at the **Parisite DIY Skate Park**. We asked Sebastian, as well as young noise artist and promoter **Corey Cruse**, which artists you should allow to melt your brain while you're visiting:

BONGOLOIDS

bongoloids.com

Actually from the town of Lafitte, Louisiana, Ray's as close to a Hunter Thompsonesque character as anyone you'll ever meet (even in New Orleans): a drug-freak psychedelic-noise musi-

cian who has attained guru status. Ray can be seen live rarely, along with partner **Suzy Creamcheese**, pounding away like a caveman on totally unrecognizable analog gear (the Tri-Wave Generator, the Coron, the Superstar 3000 toy guitar).

COREY CRUSE

Aggressive, vocal-based harsh noise. When not booking shows (or helping us with this section of our book), Cruse performs with the intensity of a young Henry Rollins both as a solo artist and in ambient metal band **Young Bathory**.

FATPLASTIK

Their work has gotten more and more freeform, which sometimes means sets of droning distorted keyboards for like ten minutes and all these loops and delay sounds. It's sort of overwhelming—you feel like you're inside of it. And though it's loud and abrasive it's really pleasant, this big ol' wash of sound. Plus the song themes discuss queer identity, isolation, and other things that are very relevant to a lot of artists here in New Orleans.

F(R)IGID

It's not just the music—**Simon Severe** plays harsh noise but puts on a full visual performance with a lot of ideas and imagery.

POCKETS MCCOY

He just overdoes it. He creates a wall of modular noise with this synth called the Surge, from a famous synth company founded in Berkley in the '70s. Pockets really understands synthesis, he understands equipment, but he's also a totally freeform person.

DONALD MILLER

The guitarist for famous New York noise ensemble **Borbetomagus** moved to New Orleans and has since collaborated often with like-minded guitarist **Rob Cambre** in **Death Posture**. Miller is as underground famous as he is reclusive, but you can catch him selling used books at **Piety Street Market** on the second Saturday of each month.

PROUD/FATHER

Ambient music often made with guitar and pedals that, without words, evokes the sensual and spiritual.

PSYCHIC HOTLINE

Sort of a one-person Throbbing Gristle industrial throwback, with themes of queer identity and fringe culture.

ROTTEN MILK

Milk moved here from Chicago, where he was a member of a band called Cave on Drag City Records. Now he does solo sets, droning analog like in Cave, but he does mix it up. He's openminded and connected with everyone that I know who is doing noise in the United States. He books stuff, he's a big part of **WTUL** (91.5 FM), a great facilitator of other people doing stuff. He is also always trying to open the noise scene up more to people who aren't straight white guys, and he brings in a perspective from outside the city.

ANXIOUS SOUND PRODUCTIONS AND NOISE GUITARIST ROB CAMBRE

Since 1997, guitarist **Rob Cambre's Anxious Sound Productions** has been the first name in adventurous modern music booking, with shows usually pairing international cult musicians with some hot New Orleans cats—including Cambre, who fits himself into almost every show he books. Luckily his "Sonic Youth meets Japanese-noise freeform guitar work" is often worth it. Often standing on stage alone, Cambre is also a member of several off-the-cuff groups, particularly **Death Posture**, featuring **Borbetomagus** guitarist **Donald Miller** and butoh dancer **Vanessa Skantze**, and in **Malevitus** with MC Sweet Tea. He also sets aflame "garage gospel" purveyors **R. Scully's Rough 7**.

Cambre hosts shows once or twice a month. There are also a few Anxious Sound events you can mark on your calendars. In particular, on January 30 each year, Cambre hosts the Anxious Sound Holiday HO-Down at the **Hi-Ho Lounge** (Marigny, 2239 St. Claude Ave., 504-945-4446; hiholounge.net): a blowout of adventurous improvisers from New Orleans, Baton Rouge, and Mississippi.

In short, if you enjoy difficult and/or complicated listening, look for the Anxious Sound label on the product. Also check out the **Instant Opus** improvised music series at **SideBar NOLA** (Mid-City, 611 S. White St., 504-324-3838; sidebarnola.com). There's also **Andy Durta's Scatterjazz** series (scatterjazz.com) of wild improvisation, free jazz, and other freaky music in a cocktail lounge setting with bar food. Billed as "intense original music to soothe the stormy mind," it happens almost every night at **SideBar**.

Rob Cambre

Jonathan Traviesa

STAR OF KAOS

Michael Bevis and **Karl DeMolay** are New Orleans harsh-noise originals. Bevis is a world-class screamer and, if you can understand him, a world-class lyricist as well.

THREE BRAINED ROBOT

A performance artist who does weird, noisy songs—self-deprecating songs about being a weirdo in this modern age. It has a comedic edge, but some of it is just very real. He's been booking noise shows here forever.

TRASHLIGHT

A group of five younger musicians from Baton Rouge that have somehow, in their short amount of time, cultivated an impressive appreciation and knowledge of goth culture. They can improvise noise, but they do have a series of songs they've written and they're a band. They're very in touch with what their idea is, and that's pretty inspiring to me.

VOLCE

She transplanted here from Minneapolis three or so years ago, plays harsh noise, no vocals, very loud, abrasive— and the way this plays off her personality, which is *very* different from the music, it makes you feel like she's getting out the hidden part of her personality, which I love to witness.

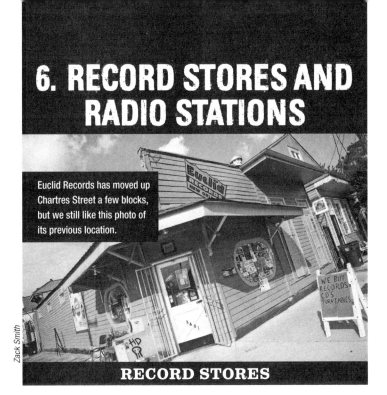

6. RECORD STORES AND RADIO STATIONS

Euclid Records has moved up Chartres Street a few blocks, but we still like this photo of its previous location.

Zack Smith

RECORD STORES

For a city that loves its music, New Orleans doesn't boast a real abundance of record stores the way, say, Austin does. Sadly, a few good record stores in the city have closed since this book's last edition. The remaining stores (including one new one, **Sisters in Christ** on Magazine St.) are of course deep and funky.

DOMINO SOUND RECORD SHACK

Mid-City, 2557 Bayou Rd., 504-309-0871; dominosoundrecords.com

In a small Rasta corner of Mid-City near Esplanade and Broad, Domino Sound houses a well-curated selection of old LPs, cassette tapes, and local bands' releases. The owner is **DJ Prince Pauper**, one of the city's best dub reggae selectors. Domino Sound has even pressed vinyl records of obscure reggae artists as well as local groups like **Why Are We Building Such a Big Ship?**

EUCLID RECORDS

Bywater, 3301 Chartres St., 504-947-4348; euclidnola.com

This sister store to the famous shop in St. Louis boasts an extensive, well-curated, and well-organized collection of pretty much every type of music. New and used vinyl, gorgeous hand-screened posters, a good selection of music books, and a stage in the corner for free in-store performances by great local bands (and sometimes secret afternoon shows by whoever's playing a big venue that night) make this one of the best record stores in town—even if the employees act like characters cut from the movie *High Fidelity* because they were too boring.

LOUISIANA MUSIC FACTORY

Marigny, 421 Frenchmen St.,
504-586-1094;
louisianamusicfactory.com

Though they do have a metal section, they don't sell rap, and mostly don't allow any of the nontraditional bands featured in this book to play the store's very fun, free, afternoon in-store concerts. But somehow we still love Louisiana Music Factory for its vast collection of (almost) all things Louisiana. Really though, don't visit Frenchmen without hitting this place.

THE MUSHROOM

Uptown, 1037 Broadway St.,
504-866-6065;
mushroomneworleans.com

Not just the obligatory funky college record store with bongs and black-light posters and a fun selection of new and used music, the Mushroom offers a deep selection of vinyl and local music.

MUSICA LATINA DISCOTECA

Uptown, 1522 Magazine St.,
504-299-4227

This jam-packed, one-room shop sells all things Latin, from the musical traditions of Cuba to Argentina, to mambo greats, plus mariachi and salsa artists.

NUTHIN BUT FIRE RECORDS

Marigny, 1840 N. Claiborne Ave.,
504-940-5680

Proprietor **Sess 4-5**, also a rapper, got his start rhyming with 504 boys like the **L.O.G.** and **Shine Baby** back in junior high. He graduated to slinging burned CDs out of his trunk and after Katrina opened his bona fide storefront across from the N. Claiborne Ave. exit ramp. Nuthin but Fire burns its own series of local rap CD compilations featuring everything from vintage bounce to the latest hits on the urban charts. It's also a great spot to pick up flyers for relatively underadvertised New Orleans hip-hop shows. Sess is also the promoter behind the **Industry Influence** (industryinfluence.blogspot.com), a hip-hop networking concert series.

PEACHES RECORDS & TAPES

Uptown, 4318 Magazine St.,
504-282-3322;
peachesrecordsandtapes.com

Store owner **Shirani Rea** was instrumental in the New Orleans rap and hip-hop scene beginning in 1975 when she opened her original Peaches record store (once a branch of the now-defunct national chain; the Nola outpost, which keeps the original sign, is now indie and, as far as we know, the only one left). Apart from a store, Peaches functioned almost as an office and community center for everyone from **Soulja Slim** to the **Cash Money Crew**. The '90s queen of **No Limit Records**, **Mia X**, was supposedly discovered while working at Peaches. Definitely not the cheapest place, but always worth a visit.

Skully'z Recordz is one of the few great things about modern-day Bourbon St.

Zack Smith

SISTERS IN CHRIST

Uptown, 5206 Magazine St.,
504-510-4379; sistersinchrist.space

A punk rock, noise, metal, ambient, etc., record store owned by lead singer of Thou, **Bryan Funk,** who hires the best local DJs and other music scene denizens to work behind the counter.

SKULLY'Z RECORDZ

French Quarter, 907 Bourbon St.,
504-592-4666

The only worthwhile attraction of Bourbon Street that doesn't serve booze, tiny little Skully'z stocks a mountain of new and used vinyl, and is a great place to pick up releases by New Orleans' alternative musicians. **Michael Bevis** from noise-music OGs **Star of Kaos** often works the counter, as does **Corey Cruse**.

NEW ORLEANS RADIO STATIONS

Here are the numbers to dial on your car radio while driving around the Big Easy.

POWER 102.9

modern urban; power1029.com

For fans of modern black music, a good alternative to the highly repetitive local Clear Channel urban-top 40 format, 102.9 has actual human DJs curating their own shows. The Powermix at 5 p.m. with **DJ Mike Swift** is a daily special, and bounce legend **DJ Chicken** seems to pop up multiple times every day (Shout out to *Posse Waaaaaaaaaa!*).

THROWBACK 96.3

You really *don't* need to be listening to Clear Channel radio while in New Orleans (we have several great community-run stations!), but I just have a soft spot for this "old school" rap station that plays music by Public Enemy, Rakim, Nas, plus local heroes like **Soulja Slim** and **Mia X**—all those types of rappers who actually rap.

WHIV (102.3 FM)

whivfm.org

Community radio station with host anything and anyone. Every day begins with an hour of protest music starting at 6 a.m. **AntiGravity** alternative music magazine has its own show here, as does comic **Chris Lane**, who gets serious, discussing the day's pressing issues with important on-air guests.

WTUL (91.5 FM)

eclectic modern; wtulneworleans.com

Tulane University's legendary radio station is the best in town, spinning anything and everything from indie rock to hip-hop, metal, noise, squalling punk, and vintage country, with requisite attention to all local bands working outside the brass/jazz/funk box. WTUL plays **Quintron and Miss Pussycat** multiple times a day, and also publishes the satiric but musically informative coffee-shop zine *The Vox.*

WWOZ (90.7 FM)

New Orleans/world/roots; wwoz.org

New Orleans' community radio station started around thirty years ago in a studio above **Tipitina's** club uptown, and now resides in the French Quarter. OZ routinely wins awards, and is an icon for roots and jazz fans worldwide, who listen on their streaming webcast. With a 24-hour schedule of volunteer show hosts, all kinds of weirdness can happen; listen in the early mornings for trad jazz and New Orleans music, and afternoon and early evening for blues and R&B. For real on-air weirdness, listen after 10 p.m., when under-supervised hosts spin everything from Ennio Morricone to Sun Ra to tapes of the late legendary oddball **Ernie K-Doe** hosting his own WWOZ show in the '90s.

FOOD & DRINK

7. FOOD, DRINKS, AND MORE MUSIC

Jonathan Traviesa

Coed jazz combo, Some Like it Hot, perform in the red room at Buffa's.

RESTAURANTS WITH LIVE LOCAL MUSIC

BAR REDUX

Bywater, 801 Poland Ave.,
504-592-7083

As far back as you can get in Bywater, this little bar with good food (sandwiches, burgers, gumbo, and red beans) hosts solo singer-songwriters, DJ nights, film festivals, the Music & Poetry reading series, and a local, low-key comedy open-mic night.

BUFFA'S

Marigny, 1001 Esplanade Ave.,
504-949-0038; buffasbar.com

Like some odd cross between the **Palm Court Jazz Café** and **Checkpoint Charlie's**, Buffa's is a dive bar in front, where you can bring your dog—but not your kids—while the back area around Buffa's very red stage is a kid-friendly, sit-down restaurant where Fido's not allowed. Seafood, giant sandwiches, and Sunday morning cocktails mark the menu while jazz artists like **Aurora Nealand** take the stage, or the eight-member singing group**, the Asylum Chorus**.

CAFÉ NEGRIL

Marigny, 606 Frenchmen St.,
504-944-4744; cafenegrilnola.com

Funk, blues, and reggae populate the music menu at this ground-level concert venue, its stage backdropped by a Bob Marley mural. Since there's never a cover, Café Negril is also the perfect place to pop in for affordable, late-night chow from Ruben's Taco Truck, serving meat and vegetarian tacos and gorditas, dishes like barbacoa, plus American street food like crawfish pies and pizza. **Soul Project** and the **Royal Blues Band** play regularly on the Negril stage, as does blues-rock singer **Dana Abbott**.

CASA BORREGA

Central City, 1719 Oretha Castle Haley Blvd., 504-427-0654;
casaborrega.com

Though Latinos pretty much rebuilt New Orleans, Latin music is still scarce here—aside from Casa Borrega, one of the city's only Latin music destinations. The renovated 1891 Greek Revival home is an art piece in itself, and its every wall is also hung with colorful Mexican art. The bar features over 100 tequilas and mezcals, while the creative kitchen cranks out Mexico City street food from tacos and quesadillas to original dishes like the "Borrego de Oro" entrée: tequila-marinated lamb, grilled nopalitos, cebollitas, and lamb consommé, all served with corn tortillas. Thursdays through Saturdays, from 7 to 10 p.m., dine while enjoying regular Latin music jams featuring **Fredy Omar** and others.

Jonathan Freilich and James Singleton play at Casa Borega, one of the few places to catch live Latin music. Great food and drinks, also.

Bob Freilich

CHECKPOINT CHARLIE'S

Marigny, 501 Esplanade Ave.,
504-281-4847

This definitive dive music club seems held together by band stickers. Checkpoint's has everything, from blues to rock to bulk burger patties (with a side of tater tots), two pool tables, pinball, even laundry machines. One of the last places in town to still serve free red beans on Mondays, Checkpoint's (open 24 hours) also hosts metal band **Suplecs'** annual sublime and tripped-out Mardi Gras show. The rest of the year the music is decidedly gruff and gutter. Karaoke every Monday night at 10 p.m. Don't sing with your mouth full!

ESTRELLA STEAK & LOBSTER

French Quarter, 237 Decatur St.,
504-525-6151;
estrellasteakandlobsternola.com

The steak and seafood here is just good enough (the special of two live lobsters, two sides, and one dessert all for $50 is hard to beat!), but the real treat while eating crab cakes and grilled oysters is one-man band **James Dee** (Wed. through Sun., 6 to 10 p.m.), who, with his truly original music, plus his pompadour, reverb-heavy saxophone, Casio beats, and mellow baritone voice, will never leave your memory of New Orleans—imagine Tom Waits as a cruise ship entertainer.

FONTAINE PALACE NOLA

CBD, 218 S. Robertson St.,
504-525-9775

Scarf late-night wraps, tacos, barbecue, grilled sandwiches, burgers, and healthy greens, all while listening to some of the city's best, most well established DJs from **Ed Maxmillion** to **Rik Ducci** (who spin both types of music: hip *and* hop).

HOWLIN' WOLF DEN

CBD, corner of St. Joseph and
S. Peters St., 504-529-5844;
thehowlinwolf.com/the-den.html

The Wolf Den is the smaller counterpart to the veteran Howlin' Wolf music venue. The Den not only exponentially increases the number of shows in the CBD, but also provides top-shelf bar grub until the wee hours. Chow on a Cuban sandwich, various po'boys, crawfish or meat pies, tacos, or jambalaya while catching the club's famous Brass Band Sundays, now helmed by the aptly named **Hot 8**.

LIVE OAK CAFÉ

Uptown, 8140 Oak St.,
504-265-0050; liveoakcafenola.com

Live Oak serves good breakfast/brunch food like shrimp-n-grits and huevos rancheros—plus Bloody Marys!

LE BON TEMPS ROULÉ

Uptown, 4801 Magazine St.,
504-895-8117; lbtrnola.com

Oh, the late, loud nights you can have at this musically important little hole in the wall. The menu includes basic bar food: burgers, French fries, po'boys, and quesadillas. Le Bon Temps still hosts **Soul Rebels Brass Band** every Thursday night, and organ player **Joe Krown** every Friday with . . . don't tell anyone . . . free oysters on Le Bon Temps' much-beloved back patio!

MAISON

Marigny, 508 Frenchmen St.,
504-371-5543;
maisonfrenchmen.com

This larger-than-it-seems concert venue features a stage in the downstairs window with early-evening jazz shows you can watch from the street, plus a big stage upstairs that hosts comedy nights and giant rap shows. Order up a plate of Jamaican ginger-beer pulled pork, or sandwiches such as steak and brie, or check out the jzz brunch every Sunday from 10 a.m. to 3 p.m., when the NOLA Jitterbugs offer swing dancing lessons.

PALM COURT JAZZ CAFÉ

French Quarter, 1204 Decatur St.,
504-525-0200;
palmcourtjazzcafe.com

Open since the night **Topsy Chapman** first took the stage here in 1989, the Palm Court showcases New Orleans–style traditional jazz and a French Creole menu featuring things like Shrimp Ambrosia sautéed in a light fennel and Pernod cream sauce over pasta, and the café's famous oysters bordelaise. Proprietor **Nina Buck** still greets and entertains her guests.

PORTSIDE LOUNGE

Central City, 3000 Dryades St.,
504-503-0990; portsidenola.com

Owned by **Danny Nick**, front man and guitarist of beloved local metal band **Suplecs**, this tiki bar offers Caribbean-inspired drinks and over a dozen beers. The kitchen hosts a rotating roster of various Caribbean pop-up chefs with some Asian nights mixed in. The stage offers fairly frequent, smart punk and metal shows and the occasional island star like Yelloman. The bar is also home to the **Wild Red Flames Mardi Gras Indians**, and is dog friendly.

Guitarist Danny Nick of metal group Suplecs makes himself a drink at the bar he owns, Portside Lounge.

Danny Nick

SIBERIA LOUNGE OWNER LUKE ALLEN SUGGESTS LOCAL SINGER-SONGWRITERS

A few years ago, Mayor Landrieu's administration was cracking down hard on clubs that didn't have their sound ordinance paperwork in order. "Now no one's cracking down on music at all and everyone's booking shows in every possible venue on St. Claude Ave.," reports Luke Allen, head bard of the **Happy Talk Band** and part owner of **Siberia Lounge** (Marigny, 2227 St. Claude Ave., 504-265-8855; siberialounge.com). "A lot of us are booking the same bands, but the thing we have is a kitchen that serves Eastern European food that no one else serves."

Since former Siberia partner **Matt Russell** took his heavy metal and noise music calendar to **Poor Boys** up around the corner on glorious St. Bernard in Tremé, Luke's patrons at Siberia have more air space to talk while eating and drinking—hence the recent addition of "Lounge" to the club's name. "My family's Ukrainian, so I learned a few things from [my] grandma and great-aunts," says **Matt the Hat**, whose kitchen cooks pierogi, kielbasa, blini, cabbage rolls, and other Slavic foods at Siberia until midnight, daily.

With both early and late concerts, Siberia's music calendar veers all over the map from local to national acts, with a preference for singer-songwriters. Siberia's food and music combine each Thursday night for the club's free "Eastern Block Party," which features a revolving cast of local, Eastern European–style bands like the Panorama Brass Band, Klezmer All Stars, and Salt Wives, along with a corresponding roster of special Eastern bloc food.

Though Luke grew up on metal and punk, he tends to book his fellow singer-songwriters at Siberia these days—meaning, men and women with acoustic guitars and earnest intentions. Here are a few of his favorites:

CHRIS ACKER AND THE GROWING BOYS

Young guy, plays country Americana. He has a great song called "ReRuns" that has a great lyric: "Feeling like a little kid in a T-shirt in the shallow end of a pool."

MAX BIEN-KAHN

His band Max and the Martians is almost Americana, but more like if Buddy Holly hadn't gotten on that plane. I especially love his song "Jealousy." He employs girl backup singers for the *oohs* and *ahs*.

TASCHE DE LA ROCHA AND THE PSYCHEDELIC ROSES

Another someone who's spent a lot of time playing on the streets and put together a really great band, a bunch of great musicians who really love her stuff, and they really make her shine and it's special.

JACKSON LYNCH

Good songwriter and arranger, fronts Jackson and the Janks, which plays Americana, soul, almost church music.

JULIE O'DELL

A great songwriter with an ethereal voice, beautiful lyrics, great imagery, really dreamy music.

PETER "SNEAKY PETE" ORR

Witty multi-instrumentalist, sings original songs of another time in Bywater's history when rents were low and life was simultaneously rough and perfect. A professional journalist and author in a former life, Sneaky Pete's lyrics are great.

ESTHER ROSE

Love her voice, writes really solid songs, good presence, country Americana.

SHANE SAYERS

He's from that **United Bakery Records** scene, writes devastatingly beautiful exploratory songs, like "Nobody Knows Where I Sleep." He's really tall so he always plays sitting down.

RARE FORM

Marigny, 437 Esplanade Ave.,
504-402-3285;
rareformfrenchmen.com

Red meat is on the menu, but Rare Form specializes in seafood-oriented dishes like blackened or fried shrimp sandwiches on a bun, and the redfish with couscous entrée. Saturday means either seafood boils or BBQ, and jazz brunch is always Sunday from 11 a.m. to 5 p.m. All this, plus nightly live music from the likes of **Nervous Dwayne**, **Steve Mignano**, and more.

SNUG HARBOR

Marigny, 626 Frenchmen St.,
504-949-0696; snugjazz.com

Eat Louisiana-style steaks and seafood (like Fish Marigny, topped with shrimp in a Creole cream sauce) on a cozy balcony overlooking concerts by jazz modernists, including members of the Marsalis family. Or just lounge in the quieter front bar where you can watch the music stage on television.

SPOTTED CAT

Marigny, 623 Frenchmen St.,
504-943-3887; 2372 St. Claude Ave.
#130, 504-371-5074;
spottedcatmusicclub.com

I make a lot of cracks about old-timey music throughout this book, but this place is the *spot.* One hundred percent acoustic jazz quintets and swing bands and singing groups, and reasonably priced drinks in a tiny li'l club. A newer second location provides high-quality music combined with a not-bad menu of southern comfort food, including breakfast.

ST. ROCH TAVERN

Marigny/St. Roch, 1200 St. Roch
Ave., 504-945-0194

An interesting, thoroughly authentic dive bar that usually serves good tacos, sandwiches, and other food truck–type fare, except served by crust punks. Everything from garage bands to blues acts and DJs make music on the bare black floor.

SWEET LORRAINE'S

Marigny, 1931 St. Claude Ave.,
504-945-9654

For almost four decades, this dressy but unassuming Marigny eatery and club has featured artists as diverse as smooth jazz violinist **Michael Ward** and free jazz titan **Pharoah Sanders**. The dinner menu boasts Creole cuisine: seafood, gumbo, wings, and pastas. Sunday brunch features singer **Danon Smith**. There's even a late-night breakfast buffet with omelet and waffle stations every Friday and Saturday from midnight to 4 a.m.

VAUGHAN'S LOUNGE

Bywater, 4229 Dauphine St.,
504-947-5562

This classic New Orleans bar doesn't have a menu but is extremely generous with random food, including reality-bending red beans during the band's set breaks on Thursday nights, free boiled seafood on most Friday nights, and amazing potluck spreads during Saints games and on most New Orleans holidays.

8. MORE FOODS THAT NEW ORLEANS DOES WELL (AND WHERE TO EAT THEM)

PO'BOYS

The po'boy is a simple thing. Fried seafood or else roast beef, turkey, or hot cooked sausage on French bread, "dressed" if you like, with mayo, tomato, and lettuce, maybe some pickles. No more. No mustard even. Given its simplicity, most po'boys you'll eat in New Orleans will be pretty damn good. As long as the bread is crunchy, the shrimp medium sized, and afterwards you're stuffed and there are still a few shrimp/oysters/hunks of roast beef left on the big white butcher paper in which your sandwich came wrapped, then that's a wrap. Out of thousands of good po'boy opportunities, these are just the first few that come to mind:

COOP'S PLACE

French Quarter, 1109 Decatur St., 504-525-9053; coopsplace.net

We'd like to tell you only about on-the-corner down-low po'boy joints, but if you're in the Quarter and want New Orleans food late into the night, Coop's is the absolute best, even though it's popular and loud. Big fat fried oysters on French bread or a bun are sublime, but we also love the blackened redfish po'boy.

FRADY'S

Bywater, 3231 Dauphine St., 504-949-9688

This unassuming yellow store with crazy painting on the outside has been a hipster secret for years, though Frady's is about as unhip as could be (I guess that's how hipness works). Just a regular corner store, the counter is usually stocked with all sorts of pralines, mini sweet potato pies, and other homemade treats. Frady's also serves the quintessential neighborhood lunch-break po'boy—and yet somehow it's like, never busy.

OAK STREET PO-BOY FESTIVAL

Uptown, November, 8100–8800 Oak St., 504-228-3349; poboyfest.com

Local art, local music (lesser-known neighborhood blues and brass bands), and a thousand variations on the po'boy sandwich.

PARASOL'S BAR & RESTAURANT

Uptown, 2533 Constance St., 504-899-2054

Part dive bar, part po'boy shop, part community center, Parasol's is the anchor of the Irish Channel neighborhood and a great place to catch a football game and an oyster po'boy. It is also the epicenter of all St. Patrick's Day activities. 7 days, 12 p.m. till.

PARKWAY BAKERY

Mid-City, 538 Hagan Ave., 504-482-3047; parkwaypoorboys.com

Considered by many po'boy experts to have the absolute best roast beef po'boy smothered in "debris" gravy that you could possibly ever have, ever (maybe tied with famous **Mother's** in the CBD, where the po'boy was allegedly invented), Parkway is also a very nice family bar with a view of the water on Bayou St. John, just outside City Park.

YOUR AVERAGE NEW ORLEANS GAS STATION

any neighborhood, anywhere in the city; no need to call ahead

A not remarkably clean gas station can nonetheless blow your mind with over-over-stuffed shrimp, hot sausage, and other 12- to 16-inch po'boys. You should be able to get lunch and dinner in one sandwich for $10 to $15 at almost any gas station. Some places skimp and use the tiniest possible shrimp, while others maybe don't keep their iceberg fresh enough, but for the most part, a po'boy is hard to screw up.

NOLA MOMENT

OFFICIAL SNACKS OF NEW ORLEANS

Zapp's are the official (and officially perfect) potato chips of New Orleans. Our beer is the flavorful **Abita** (which comes in all types from Christmas ale to a satsuma-flavored brew), while kids and adults alike enjoy **Barq's Root Beer** or **Big Shot** red drink. **Boiled shrimp** are a decadent (and messy) snack, just like **boiled crawfish** (see section below)—sniff around and you'll probably be able to find a bar serving up the crustaceans for free at happy hour. During summer, a giant Styrofoam cup full of frozen **daiquiri** to-go from one of our many local daiquiri stands (we suggest **Gene's**, the big pink building in Marigny) may mark the highlight of your vacation. During the weeks of Carnival season, there is also

king cake to be scarfed, but if your piece (or one of your pieces) has a lil' plastic baby hidden in it then, assuming you don't choke, you must buy the next king cake for your subjects. Sorry, them's the rules.

Our photographer Zack Smith and friends at a traditional crawfish boil.

Zack Smith

GUMBO

I don't even want to really get into this. . . . There are hundreds of places to get great gumbo, and I really quit keeping track after I learned to make gumbo myself (gumbobrag!), but here are a few quick suggestions. (*Note: Also order a side of potato salad and drop it right into your gumbo.*)

CAFÉ RECONCILE

Central City, 1631 Oretha Castle Haley Blvd., 504-568-1157; cafereconcile.org

Café Reconcile was founded by famous NOLA chef Emeril Lagasse to employ at-risk teens and teach them about the restaurant industry. It also serves the best restaurant gumbo I have eaten in forever, and for $6. Great gumbo for a great cause.

GUMBO SHOP

French Quarter, 630 St. Peter St., 504-525-1486; gumboshop.com

Any restaurant worth its salt in the French Quarter serves a gumbo, and I definitely cannot promise this is the best, but they do have *gumbo* in their name, so theirs must at least be competitive!

LIUZZA'S BY THE TRACK

Mid-City, 1518 N. Lopez St.,
504-218-7888; liuzzasnola.com

The first gumbo I ever ate in New Orleans! It's more like a spicy tomato and rice soup with shrimp and sausage than a traditional gumbo. Locals do not take kindly to gumbo experimentation, but this obscure gumbo recipe gets a pass, and still remains my favorite in town.

LIUZZA'S RESTAURANT AND BAR

Mid-City, 3636 Bienville St.,
504-482-9120; liuzzas.com

This other Liuzza's, in the same neighborhood as the Liuzza's I just described, has nothing to do with that Liuzza's. Weird, huh? They even both serve beer in giant frozen schooners. But this Liuzza's serves seafood gumbo with traditional gooey okra, shrimp, and small oysters.

CRAWFISH

You can get this boiled, spicy poor-man's shrimp all year round somewhere in the city. Crawfish are biggest and best during the chillier months—all through New Orleans' festival season, coincidentally or not. Prior to Katrina, $1.50/lb crawfish weren't unusual, while nowadays you're looking at twice that. In restaurants they can cost $5/lb, which is insane. But somehow, some way, splurge on some crawfish while visiting. Here are some crawdaddy options:

BIG FISHERMAN

Uptown, 3301 Magazine St.,
504-897-9907;
bigfishermanseafood.com

Have always charged a bit more for their mudbugs, but Big Fisherman certainly know what they doin' in regards to spice (they gotta make your nose run just the tiniest bit).

CAPT. SAL'S SEAFOOD AND CHICKEN

Bywater, 3168 St. Claude Ave.,
504-948-9990;
captsalseafoodandchicken.com

If you're in Bywater/Marigny, Captain Sal's is the place. A big hot-deli counter with everything from egg rolls to crawfish pies to boiled shrimp and soft-shelled crabs. Grab a cheap beer and sit down, cover the dirty table with newspaper, dump out the crawdads, figure out how to crack 'em open, get into the rhythm, stare out the window onto crazy-ass St. Claude Ave., and you just may understand New Orleans.

OYSTERS

Simultaneously gross and divine, but mostly divine. It's said you should only eat oysters in months that contain an R, though there are those who eat them only on days ending in Y. Here are just a few of the million places to eat live, raw oysters (that's right, they are alive when you eat them!)

CASAMENTO'S

Uptown, 4330 Magazine St., 504-895-9761; casamentosrestaurant.com

This old man's oyster bar is only open for lunch, so get down there early for your raw oyster fix. For a group lunch, check out the Big Easy Platter, which combines over a dozen fried oysters, a pound of crab claws, a dozen pieces of fish, and three dozen shrimp plus French fries, all for $85.

FELIX'S

French Quarter, 739 Iberville St., 504-522-4440; felixs.com

Across the street from Felix's is another oyster bar that doesn't need anyone's advertising: tourists often line up for it down the block. We urge you to go sit instead across the street, inside Felix's mellow, non-touristy oyster bar where you can look out the window at the line across the street, and laugh. You will get better service at Felix's, the prices are a little lower, and because it's less busy you'll get personal time with the oyster shucker—plus some of the best raw oysters you'll find anywhere.

SAMUEL'S BLIND PELICAN

Uptown, 1628 St. Charles Ave., 504-558-9399

This place has pretty good bar food and big fat drinks all around, but I'm burying the lead: $3-per-dozen raw oyster happy hour every single day of the year. Now, a deal like that attracts people. So be warned: sometimes the service is . . . slow, to say the least. But if you hit a slower night when everything is working right, this is a great deal at a good place.

ST. ROCH MARKET

Marigny, 2381 St. Claude Ave., 504-609-3813; strochmarket.com

Much controversy swirled around the newly revamped St. Roch Market, which received tax money to build a promised grocery store for the neighborhood but ended up with a fancy-ish food court hosting a dozen individual pop-up restaurants selling interesting small plate dishes, lattes, cupcakes, and other things white people love. Now that the negative hype has died down, people are starting to appreciate the good, reasonably priced food at St. Roch Market. You can't buy groceries there, but you can always count on fresh raw oysters provided by **Elysian Oyster Bar** or **Curious Oyster Company.**

VIETNAMESE FOOD

Trying to eat healthy while on vacation and still eat New Orleansy food? Well, lucky for you the city hosts a huge Vietnamese population, many concentrated in a "Little Vietnam" out in New Orleans East (not very far if you drive Chef Menteur Highway east until you smell coffee in the air and see the Vietnamese strip malls on your left). The West Bank, on the other side of the Mississippi River, is also a haven for excellent Asian chefs. Beyond Vietnamese, New Orleans hosts every Asian possibility from cheap buffets to bougie sushi. In fact, Asian cultures have so influenced New Orleans that many of our rickety corner stores and gas stations sell fried rice dishes with their po'boys, and crawfish pies alongside (often greasily amazing) egg rolls. And of course there is the Vietnamese po'boy, called banh mi, the cheapest, best sandwich you will ever eat.

EAT-WELL FOOD MART

Mid-City, 2700 Canal St.,
504-821-7730

Get off the streetcar at Broad Street and you'll see what looks like a mini-mart (they have incredibly large selections of booze, too). In the rear, you'll find a full lunch counter that offers the largest, tastiest banh mi on this side of the river. Buy a tall boy and a newspaper and still get change on a $10 bill. Jump back on the streetcar and picnic in City Park.

HONG KONG FOOD MARKET

all Asian; West Bank, 925 Behrman Hwy. #3, 504-394-7075;
hongkongmarketnola.com

A super local mega-mart of fresh Asian food ingredients, with a concentration on Vietnamese. A vast produce section, live seafood tanks (lobsters etc. at least $2 less per pound than anywhere else), and a deli preparing and serving everything from pho (rice noodle soup with vegetables and meat) to banh mi. Several small Viet restaurants and a bubble tea stand populate the grocery store's entrance.

MAGASIN

Uptown, 4201 Magazine St.,
504-896-7611; magasincafe.com

The difference between the West Bank and the East Bank is the presence of dark meat in your pho. We recommend the former, but if you're looking for Vietnamese uptown, Magasin does a fair job and offers outside seating.

NINE ROSES

Gretna (West Bank),
1100 Stephens St., 504-366-7665;
ninerosesrestaurant.com

Nice ambiance and very affordable, with a full Vietnamese menu plus a sampling of food from other Asian cultures. Grill beef, shrimp, and/or chicken at your table yourself, then wrap in rice paper, and easily feed two to three people for around $15.

PHO BANG

Gretna (West Bank), 932 Westbank Expwy., 504-872-9002; phobangnola.com

Pho Bang serves pho and other Vietnamese soups almost exclusively. Pho is served a number of ways: tendon, tripe, beef balls, fresh eye of round, brisket, navel . . . you can get pretty much any part of the cow or pig in your bowl.

PHO TAU BAY

Mid-City, 1565 Tulane Ave., 504-368-9846; photaubayrestaurant.com

A lunch counter in the old style, Pho Tau Bay serves pho, of course, but also amazing fresh spring rolls, as well as Vietnamese-style iced coffee: New Orleans chicory coffee French-dripped over super-sweet condensed milk, to be mixed up and poured over ice. The drink's French-Asian roots make it perfect for New Orleans, especially in the summer.

TAN DINH

Gretna (West Bank), 1705 Lafayette St., 504-361-8008

Cheap, delicious, and straightforward, Tan Dinh occupies an unadorned space next to a gas station, but it may have the best variety on the West Bank. The pho is superb, yes, but the alligator, the goat, and the Korean short ribs are out of this world. Bubble tea and a friendly staff lighten things up.

VIETNAMESE KITCHEN AT LOST LOVE LOUNGE

Marigny, 2529 Dauphine St., 504-949-2009

This charming and familial dive bar up the street from **Mimi's** hosts a do-able little Vietnamese kitchen in back—perfect when combined with the Lost Love's comedy nights and other fun events.

FROZEN DAIQUIRIS

Daiquiri stands are another option that locals utilize daily. During New Orleans' hot summer, especially if you're riding your bike, a frozen daiquiri to-go can save your life. Drive-thru daiquiri stands unfortunately went extinct inside New Orleans proper after Katrina, though several still exist on the West Bank and in other suburbs (the drive-thru worker hands the lidded drink down into your car, with the straw sitting across the lid, trusting you won't poke it in when you drive off, because *that* would be illegal). French Quarter daiquiris do taste good, but they're

Ryelene "Jazz" Jasmine lets New Orleans Rum promoter Jeremy Thompson behind the counter at Gene's Daiquiris in the Marigny (our choice for #1 daiq shop in the city).

hella expensive (a medium, enough for a good buzz, should cost around $6), and they're never as potent. Find yourself a good, generous neighborhood daiquiri stand, and the only thing you'll have to worry about is drinking just one. (*Warning*: Drink one early in the day and you may survive till nighttime, maybe, but if you drink two, between the alcohol and the sugar, you will crash hard before sundown.) Man, do we love daiquiris, though.

GENE'S PO-BOYS AND DAIQUIRIS

Marigny, 1040 Elysian Fields Ave., 504-943-3861

In the hood, this is the spot. Bounce music on the radio, video poker in back, extra-sweet older folks workin' the counter, and frozen to-go drinks. Make sure and ask to see the menu, featuring crazily named daiquiri combos made up by the neighborhood such as the Good Joog, What the Fuck, Slim Shady (all the white liquors), and our favorite, Sweet Pussy (peach mixed with white Russian).

NEW ORLEANS ORIGINAL DAIQUIRIS

10 locations; 504-524-9504

The local chain that started it all. In a pinch, still excellent for chillin' outside somewhere. If you really want a buzz, you'll have to pay a buck for an extra shot.

QUEENIE'S ON ST. CLAUDE

Bywater, 3200 St. Claude Ave., Ste. B, 504-558-4085; queenies-on-st-claude.business.site

Queenie's daiqs are made from the best ingredients, but remain unpretentious. Queenie's also serves burgers, steaks, and other dinner-sized foods.

Parleaux, far back in the Bywater, is one of New Orleans' many new breweries—a kid-friendly place to quaff a massive mug of tasty beer.

BREWERIES

As seems to be the case in every city worth its salt, New Orleans has seen a huge uptick in microbreweries. Since 2009, nearly two dozen new breweries have opened in Louisiana, many of them in New Orleans. They've been a nice addition to our already established drinking culture. Here are a few places to grab a locally made brew:

COURTYARD BREWERY

Uptown, 1020 Erato St.; courtyardbrewing.com

Specializes in IPAs and saisons—26, all told. Various food trucks roll up in the late afternoons.

NOLA BREWING COMPANY

Uptown, 3001 Tchoupitoulas St., 504-896-9996; nolabrewing.com

Over a dozen NOLA beers in cans and another 23 on tap. Beautiful rooftop bar. Brewery tours on the weekends.

NOLA ON TAP BEER FEST

Mid-City, September, City Park, 1 Palm Dr.; nolaontap.org

Bro bar **The Bulldog** brings together over 400 beers from large-scale breweries, microbreweries, and home brewers. All proceeds from the event are donated to local animal shelters through the LASPCA.

PARLEAUX BEER LAB

Bywater, 634 Lesseps St., 504-702-8433; parleauxbeerlab.com

Taproom and microbrewery crafting high-quality, small-batch, locally produced beers. Bonus: It's around the corner from **Bacchanal** wine patio; bars including **Vaughan's**, **Redux**, and **BJ's**; and Jack Dempsey's seafood.

PORT ORLEANS

Uptown, 4124 Tchoupitoulas St., 504-266-2332; portorleansbrewingco.com

This place aims to get you to drink three pints: all three special, homemade beers they have on tap.

SECOND LINE BREWING

Mid-City, 433 N. Bernadotte St., 504-248-8979; secondlinebrewing.com

A handful of great homemade beers in an outdoor courtyard with good local music playing over the system. Food trucks on many occasions, and movie nights on the big screen on the first Wednesday of every month. Pet friendly!

URBAN SOUTH BREWERY

Uptown, 1645 Tchoupitoulas St., 504-267-4852; urbansouthbrewery.com

The owner, a New Orleans native, traveled overseas to learn the secrets of European beers and bring them back to his hometown. Restaurants pop up whenever food isn't being served in the Taproom. "We've set the table for a pretty serious party," the website brags, "honoring modern Southern values with worthy and daring beers."

NOLA MOMENT

INDIAN FOOD

When it comes to Indian food, New Orleanians really have only **Nirvana** (Uptown, 4308 Magazine St., 504-894-9797; insidenirvana.com) with its great location and serviceable lunch buffet daily (plus dinner buffet on Thursday and Sunday).

But those in the know also speak well of the vegan Indian cuisine at the **Hare Krishna House** (Mid-City, 2936 Esplanade Ave., 504-486-3583; iskconnola.org). Every Sunday evening these Krishnas host a free meal of Indian food. A "Love Feast," to be exact, with *kirtan* beginning at 5:30 p.m., followed by a special *arati* at 6, a discourse from 6:45 to 7:30 p.m., then the aforementioned Krishna *prasadam* (spiritual food) served free of charge to everyone (tips much appreciated). We wouldn't suggest you go here and eat great free vegan Indian food if you were going to be set upon by cultists; New Orleans' Krishnas are mostly non-American, very kind and sweet, and not the least bit pushy, making this a great casual environment in which to check out a different way of life while having good food—a bit of a ritual for New Orleanians who are low on cash and want some healthy dining. Plus, it's a very pretty early-evening bike ride down Esplanade Avenue.

PIZZA

Pizza in New Orleans is meant to be eaten by the slice from various windows during Mardi Gras, or all year round anywhere near Bourbon Street. But if you really need a whole pie (and we certainly understand that need), here are our suggestions:

MID CITY PIZZA

Mid-City, 4400 Banks St., 504-483-8609; midcitypizza.com

Across from the Banks Street Bar live music venue, this no-frills pizza joint (with a great bar) serves the usual with a few adventurous choices like red beans and rice pizza and the taco pizza.

PIZZA DELICIOUS

Bywater, 617 Piety St., 504-676-8482; pizzadelicious.com

Charmingly cramped cafeteria seating, delicious artisan pizza made with Louisiana-grown ingredients, plus salads, pasta dishes, seafood, small plates, icy draft beers, and nice wines. Bike delivery available from 4 to 10 p.m. every day.

SLICE

Uptown, 1513 St. Charles Ave., 504-525-PIES; slicepizzeria.com

The yin to **Juan's Flying Burrito**'s yang, Slice is run by the same people, though it doesn't quite follow the punk aesthetic of its older brother. Whether pizza by the slice or a whole pie, Slice offers better fare than most of the city's pizza joints, including special salads and small plates.

SUGAR PARK

Bywater, 3054 St. Claude Ave., 504-942-2047; sugarparknola.com

Some call Sugar Park's thin cornmeal-crust pizza the best in the city (count me as one), while others are weirded out by it. The restaurant also has two nice bars and a relaxing back patio where movies are often shown.

SNOWBALLS AND ICE CREAM

New Orleanians go crazy for super-sweet snowballs in the summer. Even in the sleepiest areas of town, you'll come across a snowball stand every few blocks. On the other hand, you'll need us to lead you to ice cream:

BIG CHIEF SNOBALLS

Central City, 1701, 1799 Old Galvez St.

In the hood you will find soft ice and generous syrup. Also serving frozen yogurt.

ANGELO BROCATO (BROCATO'S)

Mid-City, 214 N. Carrollton Ave., 504-486-0078; angelobrocatoicecream.com

This Italian ice cream hot spot is old-fashioned and thoroughly local. Besides incredible ice cream, Brocato's has gelato, canolis, fresh dessert pastries, and tables so you can sit down and focus on the best dessert experience in the city. Did we mention canolis?

CREOLE CREAMERY

Uptown, 4924 Prytania St., 504-894-8680; creolecreamery.com

This kid-friendly "ice cream experience" specializes in unique flavors, from carmel chicory chocolate to cucumber sorbet. The street it's on, Prytania, is a great shopping and restaurant street.

FREEZY STREET

Bywater, 2633 St. Claude Ave., 504-228-4149; freezystreetnola.com

Interesting rolled ice cream that is handcrafted while you watch (I love the sweet & salty topped with pretzels).

HANSEN'S SNO-BLIZ

Uptown, 4801 Tchoupitoulas St., 504-891-9788; snobliz.com

Since 1939 the city's most famous snowball stand has boasted a line up the block every summer. The website explains why: "The combination of fluffy ice and homemade syrups demand that each Sno-Bliz be made in layers—ice, syrup, ice, syrup, and so forth—so that the final product is fully saturated."

IMPERIAL WOODPECKER

CBD, 3511 Magazine St., 251-366-7777; iwsnoballs.com

The Caucasian version of the snowball, with all-natural juices, served in Chinese food cartons by cheery wait staff.

Our favorite New Orleans coffee shops offer so much more than coffee:

BLACK STAR BOOKS AND CAFFE

Algiers (West Bank), 800 Belleville St., 504-710-7398

This Afrocentric coffee shop in Algiers doesn't open until 10 a.m., but offers great coffee and a healthy menu from jerk chicken to vegan sandwiches. Baakir Tyehimba, Black Star's owner, collects and displays both African and local art and books, and always plays great soul, R&B, and hip-hop in his shop.

BYRDIE'S POTTERY STUDIO

Bywater, 2402 St. Claude Ave., 504-656-6794; byrdiespottery.org

This tea and coffee shop, which features sandwiches and other limited lunch fare, doubles as an official St. Claude Arts District art gallery and as a ceramics studio offering classes, as well as memberships for anyone just needing a kiln. A new gallery show opens on the second Saturday night of each month.

CAFÉ DU MONDE

French Quarter, 800 Decatur St., 504-525-4544; cafedumonde.com

Every visiting tourist simply must stop in the outside courtyard of Café Du Monde, across from beautiful Jackson Square, for the only thing they serve: fried and powdered beignets and chicory coffee (a wonderfully rich, almost dirty-tasting New Orleans version of joe). The live musicians who play to the courtyard for tips will never let you forget you're a tourist, but we are not snobby enough to guide you away from this wonderful experience.

CAFÉ ENVIE

French Quarter, 1241 Decatur St., 504-524-3689; cafeenvie.com

When you imagine sitting in a coffee shop in New Orleans—or France, for that matter—idly sipping espresso, watching the world go by, you are picturing Envie. This open-air café is perfectly situated on a bustling corner of lower Decatur, for tourists who'd just like to read or people-watch from the café's many French doors. You never know what you'll see; I once watched a runaway mule carriage toss off its passengers as it ran the wrong way down Decatur. They also serve great basic breakfasts (if you're in a rush, grab Envie's famous "Breakfast in a Cup") and tasty panini sandwiches.

CAFÉ ROSE NICAUD

Marigny, 632 Frenchmen St.,
504-949-3300; caferosenicaud.com

"Healthy sustainable food" aren't yet words dear to New Orleans' clogged heart, but you can find that here. During the day, before the live music starts, when Frenchmen still belongs to the neighborhood, Rose Nicaud is a popular local spot for coffee, laptop work, and lazing with a newspaper by the big picture windows. One of the few places you can order a "breakfast salad" or a quinoa bowl, Rose Nicaud also serves biscuits and other southern breakfasts.

CHERRY ESPRESSO BAR

Uptown, 4877 Laurel St.,
504-875-3699; cherryespresso.com

This newish place for slow-roasted espresso snobs started as a pop-up in glorious Stein's sandwich shop, then moved to this old firehouse uptown. The food is breakfast and lunch fare— from French toast to sandwiches like the Devil's Mattress: house-made sausage, fried egg, cheddar, and maple butter—plus pastries made by restaurant Lilette.

NOLA MOMENT

COMMUNITY RECORDS AND THE HEY! CAFÉ

Uptown, 4332 Magazine St., 504-891-8682; heycafe.biz

A great spot for getting news on indie shows, reading in relative peace, or watching the traffic on Magazine Street. The café's neighbors are a costume shop, an oyster joint, and the 24/7 bar **Ms. Mae's,** and the police station is across the street, so you pretty much have all you need for an interesting day on one block. The servers all help roast the coffee beans, and the in-house stereo is always eclectic and killer.

Hey! Café is also home base for **Community Records,** a This DIY record label collective started in 2008 by **Daniel Ray** and **Greg Rodrigue** that has released dozens of records on vinyl, CD, and cassette, and many more records in digital formats. They regularly host all-ages DIY shows for New Orleans artists and touring acts.

The label has also converted a diesel engine tour van to run on waste vegetable oil so that their artists can tour without heavy reliance on fossil fuels. While in town—or once you're back in your town—check out Community Records'

COFFEE

131

bands like **All People** (punk/dub reggae), **Donovan Wolfington** (emo), and **Whom Do You Work For?** (experimental electronic).

Hey! Café is the headquarters for the Community Records label.

Zack Smith

CROISSANT D'OR PATISSERIE

French Quarter, 617 Ursulines Ave., 504-524-4663, croissantdornola.com

This airy bakery, with its azure walls, white tile, and flooding sunlight, evokes casual Euro chic à la the South of France. Homemade French pastries are sweet or savory, and the baguettes are golden, chewy, and light. Plus, it's really cheap. Beware, though: it closes at 3 p.m.

FAIR GRINDS

Mid-City, 3133 Ponce De Leon St., 504-913-9072; and Marigny, 2221 St. Claude Ave.; fairgrinds.com

Serving coffee, fresh juices, muffins, bagels and quiche, Fair Grinds' two locations also host everything from art films to yoga to book releases to folk music to potluck dinners to avant-garde concerts.

FLORA GALLERY & COFFEE SHOP

Marigny, 2600 Royal St., 504-947-8358

Flora's is New Orleans' quintessential bohemian coffee shop, located on a great little local corner of bars and restaurants. Tons of interesting flyers and other local ads decorate its front door, and someone's often tinkling the piano inside, or strumming a banjo on the benches outside next to grizzled old hippies playing chess. Flora's coffee drinks are cheap, as are its Mediterranean and breakfast foods. And Flora's smells much nicer now that you can't smoke inside.

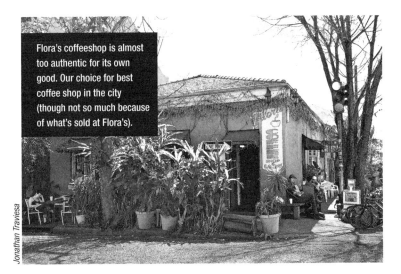

Flora's coffeeshop is almost too authentic for its own good. Our choice for best coffee shop in the city (though not so much because of what's sold at Flora's).

Jonathan Traviesa

JUJU BAG CAFÉ

Gentilly (north of Marigny),
5363 Franklin Ave., 504-872-0969

The JuJu Bag Café serves omelets, turkey burgers, and a healthier version of nachos, plus coffees and specialty teas. The big sundeck out back hosts many community events including book signings, a popular Sunday brunch, plus the weekly "Word Connections" open mic for actors, comedians, rappers, and poets.

MOJO

Uptown, 1500 Magazine St.,
504-525-2244; and 4700 Freret St.,
504-875-2243

Both of Mojo's locations provide good coffee and pastries. Plus, if you're looking for flyers, zines, and free papers, they have stacks. The fresh-made lemonade is slightly orgasmic on a summer day, and on a cooler day the fountain at nearby **Coliseum Square** is a fine place to enjoy a to-go joe cup.

ORANGE COUCH

Marigny, 2339 Royal St.,
504-267-7327;
theorangecouchcoffee.com

An upscale yet still comfy coffee shop located on a funky corner in the Marigny. Italian sodas to Vietnamese sweet iced coffees, plus mochi (Japanese ice cream rice balls). Orange Couch shows local artists and photographers, and sometimes hosts community performances, such as students from nearby **NOCCA** performing arts school.

RUE DE LA COURSE

Uptown, 1140 S. Carrollton Ave.,
504-861-4343; and 3121 Magazine St.;
ruedelacourse.com

Rue serves bagel sandwiches such as the Marigny (sundried tomato cream cheese, avocado, sprouts, dressed with lettuce and tomato) and the Tremé (roast beef, provolone, red onion, and horseradish sauce, dressed) all day. The converted bank on Oak Street is

COFFEE

a great place to read and sip, while the Magazine St. shop with its massive picture window is one of the world's best people-watching spots—both are located in charming commercial food and shopping districts. Outdoor seating available.

SATSUMA

Bywater, 3218 Dauphine St., 504-304-5962; and Uptown, 7901 Maple St., 504-309-5557; satsumacafe.com

Healthy breakfasts and excellent cold-pressed organic juices keep Satsuma's Bywater location packed most mornings—luckily the **Bargain Center** thrift store next door makes it worth it. From bacon and eggs, to avocado toast, to Vegan Curry Scramble (quinoa or tofu with roasted cauliflower, kale, sweet potatoes, and a coconut ginger curry). Sandwiches include a Cuban, and a black bean burger. If the lines are too long, you can always get the city's best po'boy from **Frady's** across the street.

ST. COFFEE

Marigny, 2709 St. Claude Ave., 504-872-9798

St. Coffee serves up the usual (exceptional iced coffee) plus Jarritos Mexican sodas, excellent doughnuts, and fresh pastries. Tables out front provide a perfect spot from which to watch the beautifully sketchy goings-on of St. Claude Ave.

TOUT DE SUITE

Algiers (West Bank), 347 Verret St., 504-362-2264; toutdesuitecafe.com

Breakfast at Tout de Suite consists of filling dishes like over-the-top biscuits and gravy served in a hot skittle, and the Atchafalaya crawfish étouffée served over creamy stone-ground grits with two eggs. The lunch menu offers great fresh salads, soups (the French onion here is amazing), and sandwiches like the rotisserie chicken with pecans, celery, apples, and baby greens drenched in honey-basil vinaigrette. For parents, **Confetti Kids Park** is just around the corner at 451 Pelican Ave.

Z'OTZ

Uptown, 8210 Oak St., 504-861-2224

Named for a Mayan glyph, Z'otz's sign doesn't bear its name—just a giant question mark. Still, it's hard to miss. The 24-hour shop is big with students, goth kids, and bohemian sorts who enjoy the unusual candies, vegan pastries, and offerings like bubble tea and yerba mate. Z'otz hosts a semiregular "night market" after-dark crafts bazaar, plus occasional DJ nights, open-mic events, and acoustic performances.

EVERYTHING ELSE IN NEW ORLEANS

10. GALLERIES AND ART MUSEUMS

New Orleans' visual art scene has long played second fiddle to attractions like music and food, but the same playful, liberated, indulgent attitudes that created the conditions for those local pleasures have also encouraged a vibrant arts community, especially since Katrina.

The city's art can sometimes be too self-referential, pandering to touristy notions of "outsider art," but following the international art biennial **Prospect.1**, which called New Orleans home in 2008, the city's underground art scene has come out fighting.

ST. CLAUDE ARTS DISTRICT

The many new high-quality, big-personality galleries in Bywater/Marigny call themselves the **St. Claude Arts District**, and provide a much welcome complement to the already existing **Julia Street** galleries in the CBD, which are nice, but maybe a li'l too "professional." Between the two districts, though, New Orleans can now proudly brag on its art scene. The St. Claude Arts District hosts many concurrent show openings on the second Saturday of each month.

ANTENNA

Bywater, 3718 St. Claude Ave., 504-298-3161; antenna.works

Via its 501c3 literary and visual arts umbrella Press Street, Antenna produces an array of risk-taking solo and group exhibitions, special events, educational programming, and artist talks. Press Street also hosts the 24-hour arts education extravaganza **Draw-a-Thon** (each December); **Room 220**, a blog dedicated to the literary life of New Orleans; free public film screenings; and the publication of books focusing on the relationship between the visual and literary arts.

ART GARAGE

Marigny, 2231 St. Claude Ave., 504-717-0750; artgarage.events

The old Frenchmen Street Art Market moved up the street when Frenchmen

Street became another Bourbon Street. Artisans from all over the city offer paintings, jewelry, and other creations in a living room setting decorated with a telephone booth, an indoor gazebo, and soft strings of Christmas lights. Open on weekend nights, the Art Garage sits between clubs **Siberia, Hi-Ho,** and **AllWays**.

BARRISTER'S GALLERY

Bywater, 2331 St. Claude Ave., 504-525-2767/504-710-4506; barristersgallery.com

Barrister's maintains a permanent collection of strange folk, outsider, and ethnographic art from Africa, Haiti, and Asia. The gallery also brings in a monthly featured contemporary exhibit in keeping with its focus on the eclectic and unorthodox.

BYRDIE'S POTTERY STUDIO

Bywater, 2402 St. Claude Ave., 504-656-6794; byrdiespottery.org

This tea and coffee shop doubles as an official St. Claude Arts District art gallery and as a ceramics studio offering classes, as well as memberships for anyone just needing to use a kiln. A new art show opens on the second Saturday night of each month.

THE FRONT

Bywater, 4100 St. Claude Ave., 504-301-8654; nolafront.org

This talented collective of modern-leaning artists can get wacky, but The Front is the most meticulous high-quality gallery in the SCAD. Open noon to 5 p.m. Saturday and Sunday. Expect installation work, and experimental movies (and beers) in the backyard.

The Front is one of the tighter galleries in the scrappy St. Claude's Arts District.

Jonathan Traviesa

GALLERY CO-OP AT THE NEW ORLEANS HEALING CENTER

Marigny, 2372 St. Claude Ave.,
504-940-1130;
neworleanshealingcenter.org

This collective of roughly a dozen artists hosts rotating local and national exhibits in the New Orleans Healing Center, home to **Café Istanbul**, the new **Spotted Cat**, and the health food co-op.

GOOD CHILDREN GALLERY

Bywater, 4037 St. Claude Ave.,
504-975-1557;
goodchildrengallery.com

This laid-back space features high art with personality, and often a sense of humor. The Good Children collective includes the duo **Generic Art Solutions (GAS)**, who continually enact a performance piece called "Art Cops," where they roam the more highfalutin' local art world arenas in cop uniforms, handing out tickets for bad art and other offenses. Saturday and Sunday, 12 to 5 p.m., and special nighttime events.

NEW ORLEANS ART CENTER

Bywater, 3330 St. Claude Ave.,
707-383-4765;
theneworleansartcenter.com

Monthly shows feature art in every medium (with a good deal of jewelry and other crafts thrown in). Live figure-drawing classes on Mondays.

NEW ORLEANS COMMUNITY PRINTSHOP & DARKROOM

Bywater, 1201 Mazant St.;
nolacommunityprintshop.org

This print-making collective provides public access to affordable equipment, training, and services. Designed to help independent artists and entrepreneurs grow their business through screen printing, the Community Printshop also provides adult education, youth education, and outreach. And it shows new work by local artists. Open Tuesday and Thursday evenings, 6 to 10 p.m.

STAPLE GOODS

St. Roch, 1340 St. Roch Ave.,
504-908-7331

Located in a former corner grocery in the St. Roch neighborhood, Staple Goods is an artists' collective dedicated to innovative programming of contemporary visual art by its members and invited guests from the United States and abroad. Open weekends noon to 5 p.m.

UNO GALLERY

Lakefront, 2429 St. Claude Ave.,
504-948-6939; unostclaudegallery.
wordpress.com

An exhibition space dedicated to showing the work of University of New Orleans MFA candidates and faculty as well as exhibitions in conjunction with district and community events. Open Fridays, Saturdays, and Sundays from 12:00 p.m. to 5:00 p.m. and by appointment.

NOLA MOMENT

Artist and gallery owner Jonathan Ferrara in the Julia St. Arts District.

ARTIST JONATHAN FERRARA ON THE JULIA STREET ARTS DISTRICT

Julia Street is the more established local arts district, featuring slick, higher-dollar contemporary work. The street hosts multiple art show debuts on the first Saturday of every month, plus huge events like the **White Linen Night** art walk (first Saturday of August).

A fan of more contemporary, cutting-edge work, gallery owner **Jonathan Ferrara** sees the bright side of Julia Street, where he moved his long-running gallery in 2007 (400A Julia St., 504-522-5471; jonathanferraragallery.com). "Julia Street has really turned around in the last ten years," Ferrara told me in 2009. "When I moved to the Warehouse District in 2000, Julia was a lot of designer-esque stuff. And with my moving here and spicing things up, shaking things up, the market has definitely changed to a more contemporary, less designer, more artistic-driven emphasis, which is a good thing. Before it was boring. Now it's much more exciting. It's not as exciting as St. Claude," he adds. "The edgier stuff is not gonna take place on Julia Street, but the work here is overall better, presented better."

Ferrara took us on a tour of Julia Street and attempted to describe each gallery in his own words:

LEMIEUX GALLERIES

332 Julia St., 504-522-5988; lemieuxgalleries.com

Started over twenty years ago by **Denise Berthiaume**, a local who does great things, focuses on a lot of colorful work, landscapes, still lifes, a lot of craft-based works as well. Very good local content.

SØREN CHRISTENSEN GALLERY

400 Julia St., 504-569-9501; sorengallery.com

Specializes in local artists. Mainly sells work to designers and stuff that will go over your couch. A lot of animals and things like that.

ARTHUR ROGER GALLERY

432–434 Julia St., 504-522-1999; arthurrogergallery.com

He is the grand-daddy, the old standard bearer, a mixture of older and younger artists, some exciting, some not so exciting, very much engages with the designer world. He also has his project space at 434 Julia Street, where he showcases younger artists.

BLAKE BOYD SATELLITE

440 Julia St., 504-581-2440; boydsatellitegallery.com

Not sure what he's doing here, no one is really sure. His first show was called "Megalomania" and it was all images of him, so that tells you how that starts. If you look at the letters on the building it says "Boyd Satellite" and the initials on the door are "B.S." Something might be up with that. He likes to operate in the shocking end of things.

CALLAN CONTEMPORARY

518 Julia St., 504-525-0518; callancontemporary.com

Formerly Bienvenue, this one's run by **Boris Slava** and **Steve Callan**, who also have a gallery in the Quarter, both specializing in works that are ethereal and vary from sculpture to painting and everything in between. They have a very clean and precise aesthetic, stuff you can hang in your house as well, and fit into the aesthetic you're looking for.

GALLERIES

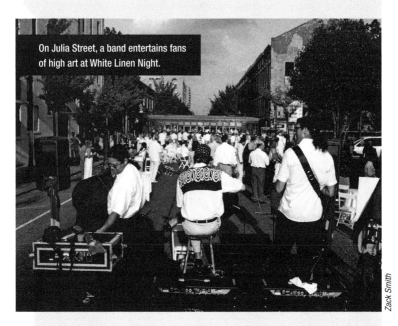

On Julia Street, a band entertains fans of high art at White Linen Night.

ARIODANTE CONTEMPORARY CRAFT GALLERY

535 Julia St., 504-524-3233; ariodantegallery.com

Contemporary crafts, a lot of great glass, and jewelry, not necessarily the fine art end of things.

STEVE MARTIN FINE ART

624 Julia St., 504-566-1390; stevemartinfineart.com

He shows his own work more than other artists, though he does incorporate others. A lot of bright-colored works, sculptures. He's been on Julia Street for over ten years and had a gallery in Miami for a while after Katrina.

GEORGE SCHMIDT GALLERY

626 Julia St., 504-592-0206; georgeschmidt.com

Schmidt's the quintessential artist-in-residence painter, jack-of-all-trades, renaissance man. He is one to speak his mind continually. He's "The Sheik of Julia Street." And he will be the one to tell you not to build or change anything on Julia Street.

ALGIERS FOLK ART ZONE AND BLUES MUSEUM

Algiers (West Bank), 207 Leboeuf St., 504-261-6231; folkartzone.org

Charles Gillam has painted all the rocks and trees outside his home along the Algiers levee to look like famous New Orleans R&B stars. In back, the faces of Lil Walter, James Booker, and others protrude from the stone walls of the Blues Room. Another wall is dedicated to the women of blues from **Ma Rainey** to **Eve Taylor**. In the second room of his homemade museum, guests are confronted with a pile of original wood sculptures and flat paintings by outsider artist **Gregory Womack**, best known for his work with bottlecaps (i.e. the bar at House of Blues). In the far back of his home-turned-museum Gillam keeps pieces given to him by fellow artists, including prison rodeo hero Edward Butler's carving of Elijah Mohammed, and the late Roy Ferdinand's supposed last pencil-and-marker drawing on poster board, depicting a "Last Supper" in the ghetto.

AMISTAD RESEARCH CENTER

Uptown, Tulane University, 6823 St. Charles Ave., 504-862-3222; amistadresearchcenter.org

Though not an art museum, the Amistad meticulously chronicles African American history and accomplishments especially in the worlds of music and art. For example, Amistad is where you can access the entire **NOLA HipHop and Bounce Archive** by musicologist

Holly Hobbs with rappers **Truth Universal** and **Nesby Phips**.

BACKSTREET CULTURAL MUSEUM

Tremé, 1116 Henriette Delille St., 504-657-6700; backstreetmuseum.org

Do not expect Roman columns at this museum. Located in the Seventh Ward just a hop from the Quarter, the colorful and amazing Backstreet Cultural Museum is curated by "self-motivated historian" **Sylvester Francis**. His overflowing repository of artifacts documenting New Orleans' African American urban cultural traditions are also shown each year on the grounds of **Jazz Fest**, but it's better to dig them in their historic Tremé home. Like the **House of Dance and Feathers**, Backstreet provides a unique, personal window into the worlds of Mardi Gras Indians, social aid and pleasure clubs, traditional jazz funerals, and Carnival groups like the **Northside Skull and Bones Gang** and the **Baby Dolls**. On Mardi Gras day, it's a good place to spot some downtown Mardi Gras Indians out showing off their pretty, handmade suits.

CLAIRE ELIZABETH GALLERY

French Quarter, 131 Decatur St., 504-309-4063; claireelizabethgallery.com

Showcasing a variety of original contemporary artworks from emerging and midcareer artists since 2014, the gallery's "Amy's Art Cart" charity—which provides art therapy for children undergoing treatments—has raised over $22,000 for Children's Hospital of New Orleans.

CONTEMPORARY ARTS CENTER (CAC)

CBD, 900 Camp St., 504-528-3805; cacno.org

Formed in 1976, this four-story, 10,000-square-foot visual and performance art mecca hosts a cool, eclectic year-round program of huge gallery shows, films, music, and other events, amid their fine permanent collection. Directly across the street from the Ogden Museum of Southern Art.

DR. BOB'S ART GALLERY

Bywater, 3027 Chartres St., 504-945-2225; drbobart.net

If, during the course of your visit to New Orleans, you do something like eat in a restaurant, drink in a bar, or shop in a store, the odds are you'll see a quaint, hand-painted sign with a bottle-cap frame that says "Be Nice or Leave." These are the work of Dr. Bob, a local character and self-styled folk artist whose Ninth Ward warehouse is almost always open to the public. Visit as much for his personality as for the color-splashed, rough-hewn art.

HOUSE OF DANCE AND FEATHERS

Lower Ninth Ward, 1317 Tupelo St., 504-957-2678; houseofdanceandfeathers.org

This tribute to New Orleans' urban cultural groups presents the social history of the Lower Ninth Ward through sto-

ries and artifacts from Mardi Gras Indians and social aid and pleasure clubs. The museum began as a personal archive (and barbershop) in the backyard shed of **Ronald Lewis**, a former streetcar repairman. His collection was completely rebuilt after Hurricane Katrina and now does double duty as a meeting spot for community organizers. In 2009, Lewis and the excellent documentary/education group **Neighborhood Story Project** (see "Literary New Orleans") published a full photo catalog and history of the House of Dance and Feathers. Call for an appointment.

MICHALOPOULOS GALLERY

French Quarter, 617 Bienville St., 504-558-0505; michalopoulos.com

This is not underground in the slightest. Michalopoulis's fish-eye paintings of New Orleans' architecture have made him world famous, and ubiquitous, and much imitated. But he is a genuinely amazing painter. This gallery represents a small taste of his work.

MUSEUM OF DEATH

French Quarter, 227 Dauphine St., 504-593-3968; museumofdeath.net

The California version of this museum was so popular this second location recently opened in the French Quarter. You have your Jack Kevorkian assisted suicide machine (the actual one!), an area dedicated to morticians, bones and skeletons, a cannibalism exhibit, a huge collection of artwork made by famous serial killers. The experience is deeply morbid, but the collection is genuinely impressive.

The Ogden after Hours music series at the Ogden Museum of Southern Art in the CBD is always more than just a concert.

NEW ORLEANS HISTORIC VOODOO MUSEUM

French Quarter, 724 Dumaine St., 504-680-0128

Again not an art gallery, but we encourage you to indulge your fantasies and worries about the Voodoo religion here, and buy a nutria paw or alligator claw keychain. Learn about real zombies, gris-gris, and Voodoo queens.

NEW ORLEANS MUSEUM OF ART (NOMA)

Mid-City, Esplanade Ave. at City Park, 504-658-4100; noma.org

Presenting international exhibits and cultural festivals, plus an amazing outdoor sculpture garden, NOMA holds its own against any national museum, with the added benefit of being in City Park, with its beautiful lakes, bayous, playgrounds, beignet shop, and bar. . . . A trip to NOMA is always worth it for many reasons.

OGDEN MUSEUM OF SOUTHERN ART

CBD/Warehouse District, 925 Camp St., 504-539-9650; ogdenmuseum.org

The Ogden rotates an amazing collection of contemporary and classically important pieces from below the Mason-Dixon, from modernist work to outsider folk art. The museum also hosts **Ogden after Hours** (every Thursday from 6 to 8 p.m.), a popular concert series with the after-work, white-wine-in-plastic-cups crowd. Southern musicians play two short sets broken up by a twenty-minute interview conducted by a local music writer. Best place to see a ninety-year-old blues or soul legend sharing some amazing life stories. Directly across the street from the 10,000-square-foot **Contemporary Arts Center (CAC)**.

GALLERIES

PERFECT PEACE ART GALLERY AND STUDIO

Central City, 1228 Oretha Castle Haley Blvd., 504-931-1915; indigopaintedprayers.com

African American art gallery in the bustling arts and commerce area along Oretha Castle Haley in Central City. Art lessons and "creativity spas" also offered.

PHOTOGRAPHER ZACK SMITH ON WHERE TO SEE GREAT PHOTOGRAPHY AND WHERE TO TAKE GREAT PHOTOS

Our man Zack Smith outside of his photo gallery on Magazine St., Uptown.

Matthew Seymour

PHOTO GALLERIES

FRANK RELLE

*French Quarter, 910 Royal St.,
504-265-8564; frankrelle.com*

Relle creates massive prints of specific, often swampy Louisiana landscapes, often photographed at night with meticulous lighting. Highly recommended.

A GALLERY FOR FINE PHOTOGRAPHY

*French Quarter, 241 Chartres St.,
504-568-1313; agallery.com*

A collection of 5,000 photographs spanning the history of photography from its origins to the present day.

NEW ORLEANS PHOTO ALLIANCE

*Uptown, 1111 St. Mary St.,
504-513-8030;
neworleansphotoalliance.org*

Monthly gallery shows, photography events, and portfolio reviews, plus exhibitions, opportunities, and educational programs for photographers of all skill levels.

ZACK SMITH PHOTOGRAPHY STUDIO

*Uptown, 4514 Magazine St.,
504-251-7745; zacksmith.com*

Zack has photographed the culture, music, and art of Louisiana and New Orleans for over twenty years. His studio provides business headshots, photography workshops, fine art photography, mentorships, and group courses in the technical aspects of photography. The shop displays his newest fine art, from classic cultural scenes of New Orleans to nature to portraits. Hours vary, so call for an appointment.

WHERE TO TAKE PHOTOS

COUTURIE FOREST, CITY PARK

*Mid-City, 1009 Harrison Ave.;
neworleanscitypark.com*

The last great vestige of privacy in the rustic-turned-golf-course haven of City Park.

SHRIMP AND OYSTER COMMUNITIES OF SHELL BEACH AND YSCLOSKEY

The end of New Orleans East

Dare to photograph on the other side of "The Wall"? Across the edge of the new levee protection gates you will find French-speaking fishermen, Spanish-heritage Isleños, bayous and wetlands, shrimp and oyster boats. Fill up your gas tank and bring cash.

WALKING AROUND

One of my favorite things to do is put on a small 50mm or 40mm lens and walk the city—CBD, Tremé, or even the Riverbend—walking until I meet someone doing something, working, having lunch on the levee, and talk with them. The people of New Orleans are always quick to share a story and are genuinely interested in you. If you like to take portraits, here's your opportunity for a story and a photo. No better place to do it.

WHITNEY PLANTATION MUSEUM

An hour away in Edgard, La., 5099 LA-18, 225-265-3300; whitneyplantation.com

Between New Orleans and Baton Rouge, seventy miles of River Road wind along a tall grass levee, past dozens of antebellum mansions shaded in trees dripping Spanish moss like a tourist's dream. Most of the gorgeous mansions just host expensive weddings now and give tours that dwell on the opulent lives of former white plantation owners. Some of the tours might even mention the slaves that made it all possible.

But down the levee a bit as you near Wallace, Louisiana, you'll arrive at a vast sea of sugarcane that obscures the view of **Whitney Plantation**, America's first and still only museum dedicated exclusively to telling the story of slavery. Purchased almost twenty years ago by white New Orleans lawyer John Cummings, the stunning art exhibit that is Whitney was mostly put together by doctor of history Ibrahima Seck.

Across the Whitney's marshy landscape, visitors view in the distance a cage that once trapped slaves. Ceramic African children sit inside an old church, forever listening to some of the world's only taped interviews with slaves, many very young. A monument to the 1811 slave revolt features a row of spikes, each topped with a ceramic head and a plaque documenting each executed person's bravery. A garden of marble slabs lists randomly the names of hundreds of slaves for whom Dr. Seck has traced their previously missing lineages.

With no advertising but a lot of good press, the Whitney attracted 75,000 visitors in its first year and a half. Today you must call ahead for reservations: 225-265-3300.

Statues of enslaved children at the Whitney Plantation Museum.

Michael Patrick Welch

From **Tennessee Williams** to **William S. Burroughs** (whose house at 509 Wagner Street in Algiers across the river was visited by **Jack Kerouac** and company in *On the Road;* today it's inscribed with a plaque), from **William Faulkner** to **Truman Capote** to **Charles Bukowski** (whose first two books were published from an apartment on Royal Street), **Anne Rice**, **Walker Percy**, **Andrei Codrescu**, and poor old **John Kennedy Toole** (whose novel *A Confederacy of Dunces* was published and won a Pulitzer after Toole killed himself), New Orleans has always been a writer's mecca. If you're into books, read up:

LITERARY NEW ORLEANS

Maurice Ruffin, author of *We Cast a Shadow,* reads at M. Francis Gallery, which moved from Julia St. to Central City.

Tad Bartlett

NEW ORLEANS
BOOK FAIR

currently each December, but check the website for location; neworleansbookfair.com

One more reason to visit New Orleans in the wonderful winter weather is our great book fair, featuring big and small names in independent publishing, tons of local authors, plus anarchist literature, zines, and all types of singular, handmade pieces of art that happen to be books. New Orleans' book fair becomes a bit of a party that can get a little wild. If you come say hi to me there, I will pour you a free Bloody Mary or mimosa (my own book fair tradition).

NEW ORLEANS
BOOK FESTIVAL

Mid-City, City Park each November

A family festival each November, celebrating literature for all ages. Each year features a performance by the Louisiana Philharmonic Orchestra.

SAINTS AND SINNERS

Mid-May; sasfest.org

This Marigny literary festival features the top names in the gay and lesbian publishing/literary world. Saints and Sinners is curated in part by **Otis Fennell**, owner of **Faubourg Marigny Art and Books**, who also manages the literary angle of New Orleans' **Pride Festival** (June; gayprideneworleans.com) in Washington Square Park on Frenchmen Street.

TENNESSEE WILLIAMS/
NEW ORLEANS LITERARY
FESTIVAL

March, various locations; tennesseewilliams.net

For over a quarter century, the city's largest literary festival has welcomed writers, playwrights, poets, and scholars for a four-day, late celebration of **Blanche DuBois**'s creator, and other various wordsmiths who've made New Orleans home. In recent years the festival organizers have focused more on contemporary literature and diversity. The Tennessee Williams Festival can be fun if you like to mix your reading with your booze; several parties with liquor sponsors offer occasion to rub elbows with nationally known writers, French Quarter septuagenarians, and canny freeloaders. The Sunday afternoon Stella shouting contest in Jackson Square is world famous and worth experiencing, and be sure to hit **The People Say Project**'s annual late-night party, where young talent explores the weirder side of Tennessee Williams and his adopted hometown.

WORDS & MUSIC:
A LITERARY FEAST IN
NEW ORLEANS

French Quarter, 504-586-1609; wordsandmusic.org

Both new and established writers participate in this five-day multi-arts festival sponsored by the **Pirate's Alley Faulkner Society**. The festival evolved from a long weekend of festivities held each year around William Faulkner's birthday, September 24 (Faulkner wrote his first novel, **Soldiers' Pay**, in New Orleans).

NEIGHBORHOOD STORY PROJECT

neighborhoodstoryproject.org

The Best New Orleans Souvenirs You Could Possibly Buy

Abram Himelstein and **Rachel Breunlin** are two teachers who believe that New Orleans' story must be told by the people who live it. With that in mind, Abram and Rachel began the **Neighborhood Story Project**, which in 2008 opened its own office and writing workshop area in the Seventh Ward (corner of Miro and Lapeyrouse Streets). Anyone is welcome to pop in, tour the office, get free writing advice and guidance, and maybe even a book advance if you're local. NSP has published many well-received books born from the hearts and brains of regular New Orleanians—both adults and children—most documenting the nuanced struggles and celebrations of various neighborhoods, **Mardi Gras Indian** tribes, social aid and pleasure clubs, and other New Orleans phenomena of which the outer world knows little.

The NSP's books are among the best independent, grassroots sellers in the city. The 200-page, full-color tome *The House of Dance and Feathers: A Museum,* by Ronald Lewis, is based on the museum Lewis built in his backyard in the Lower Ninth Ward, on Tupelo Street (also see "Galleries and Art Museums"). Lewis takes readers through the social aid and pleasure club world and that of the **Northside Skull and Bones Gang**, and in the process maps the history of the Lower Ninth Ward.

If you can't make it down to the NSP's offices, all their books are sold at most New Orleans bookstores. You couldn't buy a better souvenir of your trip to the city.

Kids and other community members publish books about their lives and their surroundings with the Neighborhood Story Project.

Rachel Breunlin

LOCAL BOOKS ON MUSIC

The Definition of Bounce: Between Ups and Downs in New Orleans by 10th Ward Buck, Alison Fensterstock, and Lucky Johnson

Garrett County Press; gcpress.com

A coffee-table picture book on the beginnings of New Orleans' bounce rap craze, featuring narrative by charismatic rapper 10th Ward Buck, as told to *New Orleans Advocate* music writer Alison Fensterstock.

Ernie K-Doe: The R&B Emperor of New Orleans by Ben Sandmel

Historic New Orleans Collection; hnoc.org

The folklorist, drummer, and producer Ben Sandmel, author of *Zydeco!*, tells the world the dynamic story of New Orleans R&B underdog singer Ernie

"Mother-in-Law" K-Doe. Wild archival material reflects the one-of-a-kind subject.

The Gravy: In the Kitchen with New Orleans Musicians by Elsa Hahne

Independent

A compilation of awesome photographer **Elsa Hahne**'s long-running **OffBeat** magazine columns, which glean recipes from local musicians of all stripes. Features an introduction by **Dr. John**.

Groove Interrupted: Loss, Renewal, and the Music of New Orleans by Keith Spera

St. Martin's Press

The city's foremost newspaper music writer (now at the *Advocate*), Keith Spera chronicles **Aaron Neville** returning to New Orleans for the first time after Hurricane Katrina to bury his wife; **Fats Domino** promoting a post-Katrina tribute CD; **Alex Chilton** living forsaken in a cottage in Tremé; rapper **Mystikal** rekindling his career after six years in prison—and these are just the beginning.

The Kingdom of Zydeco
by Michael Tisserand

Arcade Publishing

Former *Gambit Weekly* editor Michael Tisserand studied the Alan Lomax archives in DC, worked with a genealogist, and lived in Lafayette for a year hunting down and spending time with zydeco legends at church dances and trail rides. Tisserand's newest is *Krazy,* an exhaustive and beautiful biography of New Orleans' *Krazy Kat* cartoonist, George Herriman. All of his books are great.

New Atlantis: Musicians Battle for the Survival of New Orleans
by John Swenson

Oxford University Press

In the wreckage of Katrina, widely published music journalist and author John Swenson followed the paths of **Dr. John**, **the Neville Brothers**, "**Trombone Shorty**," **Big Chief Monk Boudreaux**, and others, touching intimately on New Orleans music genres from jazz, R&B, and brass band to rock and hip-hop.

Roll with It: Brass Bands in the Streets of New Orleans
by Matt Sakakeeny

Duke University Press

A firsthand account of the precarious lives of musicians in the Rebirth, Soul Rebels, and Hot 8 brass bands, who despite their fame remain subject to the perils of poverty, racial marginalization, and urban violence that characterize life for many black Americans. Contributions by artist Willie Birch.

Secret New Orleans
by Chris Champagne

Jonglez Publishing

Chris Champagne is a local comedian, poet, and radio show host who does funny one-man shows like a Yat version of Spalding Gray. He's also lived in New Orleans much longer than I have, and knows way more about it. This book includes attractions like a beret that belonged to comedian Groucho Marx in a glass case at Antoine's restaurant, and a pair of ancient Egyptian mummies in a tiny room of Tulane University's Anthropology Department.

The World That Made New Orleans: From Spanish Silver to Congo Square
by Ned Sublette

Chicago Review Press

Musician, historian, and mad scribbler Ned Sublette gives a dense and entertaining lesson in how New Orleans slavery culture begat all music in America. The book is a must-read for all musicians and lovers of New Orleans music.

Writer and monologist Chris Champagne is a hilarious genius, and author of *Secret New Orleans*.

Chris Champagne

LOCAL PUBLISHERS

Looking for local poetry? New Orleans is fortunate to have several small presses with integrity, good taste, and smart editors.

BLACK WIDOW PRESS

blackwidowpress.com

The prolific, long-standing poetry imprint from **Crescent City Books** owner Joe Phillips.

GARRETT COUNTY PRESS

gcpress.com

Run by G. K. Darby of UNO Press, GC Press publishes all things high quality, from the poetry of **Andrei Codrescu** to reprints of travel books by world-famous hobo author **Leon Ray Livingston**, with an emphasis on newish New Orleans authors.

LAVENDER INK

lavenderink.org

Run by literary OG Bill Lavender, this press publishes veterans and upcoming voices on the local scene, including poetry anthologies, fiction, and a "Yat dictionary." Bill's network stretches from Scotland to Mexico, and the catalog is refreshingly experimental. Highly suggested: poet **Thaddeus Conti**. Lavender also runs the celebrated translations imprint Dialogos.

TREMBLING PILLOW PRESS

tremblingpillowpress.com

Publisher of **Bernadette Mayer**, **John Sinclair**, **Bill Lavender**, and other important writers, Trembling Pillow was founded in 1997. Current publisher **Megan Burns** continues to produce chapbooks, broadsides, postcards, and the *Solid Quarter* poetry magazine, as well as host the Blood Jet reading series each Wednesday night at **BJ's** bar (Bywater, 4301 Burgundy St.).

CHARLES BUKOWSKI

If not for New Orleans, Charles Bukowski may have amounted to nothing. This city played just as big a part in his career as it did in **Faulkner's**. In the documentary *The Outsiders of New Orleans: Loujon Press* (loujonpress.com), **Louise "Gypsy Lou" Webb**—now well into her nineties and currently living in the burbs of Slidell—tells how she and her husband **Jon Webb** published the avant-garde literary magazine *The Outsider* from a small apartment on the corner of Royal Street and Ursulines Avenue in the French Quarter in the early 1960s. *The Outsider* and Bukowski's first two books by **Loujon Press**—*It Catches My Heart in Its Hands* and *Crucifix in a Deathhand*—are now rare collectibles, along with two other handcrafted books by **Henry Miller**. Bukowski cavorted around the Quarter drinking and fighting with strangers while the Webbs labored over his work in their apartment. At some point he etched "Hank was here" in the cement outside of the **R Bar**

(1431 Royal St.). For the longest time, one of the guest rooms he rented upstairs from the R Bar was called the Bukowski Suite. Somehow that wasn't a big selling point, and the name was more recently changed.

Author Charles Bukowski

BOOKSTORES

ARCADIAN BOOKS & PRINTS

CBD, 714 Orleans Ave.,
504-523-4138

Known for its pulley system that keeps a large floor fan strapped above one of the aisles, this small bookshop is crammed with an incredible selection of used books in all genres, with a focus on local history, and books in French.

BECKHAM'S BOOKS

French Quarter, 228 Decatur St.,
504-522-9875;
beckhamsbookshop.com

Containing an estimated 50–60,000 books, Beckham's looks like a used bookstore in a movie about New Orleans. A rolling ladder helps you access upper shelves, where you might find a book of spells—though you're more likely to find classic literature. Near the front door is always a good selection of new local novels, cookbooks, and whatnot, and the upstairs is loaded with classical music LPs for sale, and more books. Truly a gorgeous place.

BLUE CYPRESS

Uptown, 8126 Oak St., 504-352-0096;
bluecypressbooks.com

Blue Cypress buys, trades, and sells classic and contemporary fiction and nonfiction, poetry, art and photography books, science fiction, mysteries, and antiquarian and collectible books.

Its claim to fame is the largest local secondhand collection of children's and young adult books. Check the website for a great schedule of author readings and other events.

CRESCENT CITY BOOKS

CBD, 124 Baronne St., 504-524-4997;
crescentcitybooks.com

This treasure trove of local, rare, used, and popular books—complete with couches upon which to read them—also doubles as a poetry hive, with frequent in-store readings. Shop owner **Joe Phillips** also curates the poetry imprint **Black Widow Press** and hosts many book releases.

CRESCENT CITY COMICS

Uptown, 4916 Freret St.,
504-891-3796; 3135 Calhoun St.,
504-309-2223;
crescentcitycomics.com

Both Crescent City Comics locations boast vast selections of independent and underground comics and graphic novels, your favorite superheroes, and a friendly staff.

DAUPHINE STREET BOOKS

French Quarter, 410 Dauphine St.,
504-529-2333

Cluttered but deceptively well-organized used bookstore, complete with cat.

FAUBOURG MARIGNY ART
AND BOOKS (FAB)

60 Frenchmen St., 504-947-3700; fabonfrenchmen.com

Otis Fennell of Faubourg
Marigny Art and Books (FAB)

Zack Smith

The gay and straight (and also, gay) bookstore **Faubourg Marigny Art and Books** (FAB) first opened in 1977. When in 2003 the original owner decided to call it a day, **Otis Fennell** bought the store, simply to save a cultural institution. "Now that Oscar Wilde's in Greenwich Village has closed," Otis says, "FAB might be the only bookstore of its type in the States. You'll go all over the country and not find anything like this."

FAB carries one of the city's best selections of both straight and gay New Orleans–bred literature, alongside a nice selection of new national releases and worn classics. Otis also hosts readings by nationally famous, mostly gay authors. Regardless of sexual orientation, you'll want to stop in and talk to Otis, who has lived in New Orleans for over fifty years. Since buying FAB, Otis has become the don of Frenchmen Street, standing beside the rainbow Napoleon statue outside his shop on the corner of Chartres every single day from noon to midnight. "I'm open late because the street is a late-night spot," he smiles, watching the crowds pass.

Under his reign, FAB has become essentially the only de facto art gallery on Frenchmen. "I also represent Frenchmen's musicians by selling their music in my store," says Otis. "Mainly the classic CDs and albums. I have a 30-year-old **Dr. John** LP, but I also have bands like **Why Are We Building Such a Big Ship?**—who, incidentally, got their start on the corner across the street. That corner continues to attract music all day and night."

FAB becomes more and more important as Frenchmen becomes more like the French Quarter. If Otis were to give up for some reason, Starbucks would surely pay stacks for such prime real estate. So please support FAB during your visit!

Otis also recommends visiting New Orleans in mid-May for the **Saints and Sinners** literary festival (sasfest.org), which he helps curate, featuring the top names in the gay and lesbian publishing/literary world, as well as the literary aspects of the **Pride Festival** (gaypridenewvorleans.com) in June, in Washington Square Park on Frenchmen Street.

FAULKNER HOUSE BOOKS

French Quarter, 624 Pirate's Alley,
504-524-2940; faulknerhouse.net

Funny to call this the most high profile bookstore in the city, since it is nonetheless small, quaint, and quiet. But located in the French Quarter's heart, Faulkner House is the force behind the **Pirate's Alley Faulkner Society**, the nationally recognized nonprofit arts organization that hosts **Words & Music: A Literary Feast in New Orleans**, as well as the **William Wisdom Creative Writing Competition**, among other achievements. It even has its own literary Mardi Gras krewe, the **Krewe of Libris**.

GARDEN DISTRICT BOOKS

Uptown, 2727 Prytania St.,
504-895-2266;
gardendistrictbookshop.com

Garden District Books is in a building converted from a nineteenth-century skating rink. The staff actually read the books they sell, making them very informed and eager to help. This shop may not have every indie title but will definitely carry your mainstream favorites.

KITCHEN WITCH

Mid-City, 1452 N. Broad St., Ste. C,
504-528-8382; kwcookbooks.com

Though specializing in rare, out-of-print, and preowned cookbooks, this odd and charming little store also seems to contain at least one copy of each book ever published about New Orleans.

LIBRAIRIE BOOK SHOP

French Quarter, 823 Chartres St.,
504-525-4837

Pick from a good selection of new and used New Orleans–centric books, then walk around the corner and sit and read in Jackson Square or on the river. This place is owned by the same awesome guys who own the incredible **Beckham's Books** on Decatur.

OCTAVIA BOOKS

Uptown, 513 Octavia St. (corner
of Laurel), 504-899-READ;
octaviabooks.com

As eclectic and "local" as anything in the French Quarter, but also a tad smarter and classier than your average bookstore. The staff works tirelessly keeping up with local titles and amazing books from national indie presses. At great readings featuring well-known and local authors, Octavia never forgets the wine and cheese. The shop is a wee bit tricky to find in what at first seems like too residential an area, but it's so worth the effort.

RANK & FILE BOOKS

Uptown, 5206 Magazine St.,
504-510-4379; sistersinchrist.space

A collection of radical literature and anarchist culture zines, located inside the great Sisters in Christ record store.

DOGFISH READING SERIES

St. Roch neighborhood (between Marigny and Bywater), 2448 N. Villere St., second Thursday of every month; dogfishneworleans.com

Even people who love hearing authors read their works aloud will tell you: readings have great potential to be super boring. But with the right talent, the right food, drinks, and intellectual company—i.e., the right community—a reading series can fill a real need. "In our case that means lots of food and lots of booze, and all of it is free," says teacher and Pushcart Prize–nominated fiction writer Jessica Kinnison, who started the Dogfish Reading Series in New Orleans in January of 2015. "I have a passion for reading series, where people have the chance to talk about great new work that's being made."

The first Dogfish Reading event consisted of Kinnison's fellow teachers at Loyola University's New Orleans Writing Institute. "We were just wanting our students to have courage to read in front of others, so we set this up for them," says Kinnison. "Eighty people showed up to that first event,"

The Dogfish Reading Series goes down in Bywater.

Taylor Murrow

LITERARY NEW ORLEANS

she says, still seeming surprised. "So we realized there was a need." The Dogfish Reading Series usually features just one or two main, reputable readers, followed by a well-curated open-mic of five to ten greener readers. "We try to get past the academic world," Kinnison promises.

Dogfish co-conspirator, local journalist, and writer Cate Root admits, "I can be kind of introverted and socially award. So the Dogfish space is really made for people like me; it's casual, and you can sit down and relax and know there's entertainment. People go out in the backyard for a while and mingle. It's also a warm room for the open mic. I go and read for five minutes and I get to share my work with people. It's nice to go somewhere every month and see how people react. . . . It's great if I've been working on this thing lately, and I want to see what people think of it."

12. THEATER, COMEDY, AND DANCE (INCLUDING BURLESQUE)

With all the day-to-day drama around the city, of course New Orleans would also possess a thriving theater scene. We've always been famous for our plays and our dancing (in whatever odd form it takes). Here, however, burlesque is taken as seriously as Shakespeare. As with all other events in New Orleans, the dance scene strives to, above all, entertain; almost every entertainer in the city, no matter how self-serious, puts the crowd's pleasure on par with his/her own. Meaning, even the most "arty" or "postmodern" dance or theater production here will likely be energetic, smart, and fun.

THEATER VENUES AND COMPANIES

ALLWAYS LOUNGE & THEATRE

Marigny, 2240 St. Claude Ave., 504-218-5778; theallwayslounge.net

There's no telling what to expect at the wildest, most colorful little club in the Marigny. A small professional theater exists in back for readings and intelligently bawdy plays.

ANTHONY BEAN COMMUNITY THEATER

Mid-City/Gentilly, 3738 Paris Ave., 504-862-PLAY; anthonybeantheater.com

Community theater in the truest sense. Those with theatrical ambitions come to light and shine in original produc-

tions tackling issues unique to the city. Not the flashiest thing to do on vacation, but you'll certainly get a glimpse into what New Orleans is really like.

ARTSPOT

Bywater, 609 St. Ferdinand St., 504-826-7783, 866-ART-SPOT; artspotproductions.org

New Orleans is not big on modernity, or on thinking too hard in general, but **Kathy Randels** is an exception. In 1995, Randels founded ArtSpot, an ensemble of artists dedicated to creating original, "meticulously LIVE theater" that blends and bends disciplines. Original multimedia works are codeveloped among the cast, music is written, and rehearsals are painstaking and physical. ArtSpot also bolsters the **LCIW Drama Club**, a theater company of inmates at the Louisiana Correctional Institute for Women in St. Gabriel, Louisiana.

ASHE CULTURAL ARTS CENTER

Uptown/Central City, 1712 Oretha Castle Haley Blvd., 504-569-9070; ashecac.org

Also a community gathering place and conference center, this performance space promotes African, Caribbean, and African American art and artists with frequent live concerts, dance recitals, movies, etc. Humble space but amazing programming.

BROAD THEATER

Mid-City, 636 N. Broad St., 504-218-1008; thebroadtheater.com

Mostly a cute, tiny movie house with good bar food and booze, showing new release movies and hosting small niche film festivals. But the space is flexible enough to sometimes host small theater and dance productions.

CONTEMPORARY ARTS CENTER (CAC)

CBD, 900 Camp St., 504-528-3805; cacno.org

In two separate auditoriums and a main multi-room gallery, the CAC hosts not only visual art but theater, local and national touring dance companies, and film festivals. There's always something big and interesting on the CAC's schedule.

CRIPPLE CREEK THEATRE COMPANY

Marigny, 2240 St. Claude Ave.; cripplecreektheatre.org

New Orleans today boasts a robust crop of inventive, ambitious groups like Cripple Creek Theatre Company, led by artistic director **Andrew Vaught**. CCTC has fostered an improvisational approach that has produced edgy if fragile productions of politically shaded works by Gogol, Wilder, Dario Fo, and others—many of which seem to shadow the events taking place in the city. Along the way, Vaught's own writing has evolved (his original country songs are terrific, too), as did the company's partnerships with other new groups like **Goat in the Road Productions**, the **NOLA Project**, **Mondo Bizzarro**, **Skin Horse Theater**, and **Keen Amity Productions**, as well as more established **Southern Rep** and **Tulane Dance**.

DRAMARAMA PERFORMING GROUP

CBD, Contemporary Arts Center, 900 Camp St., 504-528-3805

This group curates an open-call mini-festival of all things theatrical (entry forms on the website). For six hours each April, DramaRama fills every inch of the massive **Contemporary Arts Center** with new works of comedy, dance, and theater from nationally known artists plus most of New Orleans' local dance/theater companies. Its offshoot, **DramaRama Junior**, features new works by teenagers, while **DancerRama**, in March at the CAC, is a six-hour sampler platter of dancers from New Orleans and beyond.

Andy Vaught of Cripple Creek Theatre levitates.

Zack Smith

ACTOR MICHAEL MARTIN SUGGESTS LOCAL THEATER OPTIONS

Beloved local theater workhorse and spectacular drag queen Michael Martin has been an indispensible fixture of New Orleans' DIY theater scene since 2002. As an actor, writer, director, producer, and at the "help desk," Martin has powered a number of acclaimed theater and small film roles. Martin's beautifully craggy face is impossible to forget, and his New Orleans theater suggestions are to be taken as The Word:

Actor and local icon Michael Martin eats pie.

Michael Martin

ART KLUB

Bywater, 1941 Arts St., 504-583-8232; artklub.org

Reese Johanson's Art Klub is devoted to dance and performance art first and foremost. The young warehouse space has quickly developed a cozy, funky vibe. Reese's reach in the national performance scene is a big plus, with touring acts stopping by regularly for residencies, including classes. Art Klub scored a coup in 2017 by being invited to be part of Prospect.5, which broadened its audience.

Reese Johanson runs the Art Klub performance space, and performs there herself.

Chana Rose Rabinovitz

CRUNCHTOWN

neworleansairlift.org

Once every spring, Crunchtown creates an immense DIY pop-up "cult theater" performance event. Drawing on an unmatched network of New Orleans' most adventurous fringe artists, it selects the show, finds and edits the text, casts, builds costumes and sets, composes music, and secures the venue, all in only weeks for never more than one weekend of performances. 2017's *Marat/Sade* showcased almost 75 artists, amateurs, performers, teachers et al. How do you find them? You got me. I never know until the spring event is looming.

MUDLARK PUBLIC THEATRE

Marigny, 1200 Port St.

Although artistic director **Pandora Gastelum** is dedicated to the puppet arts above all else (as part of a national network of puppet troupes unique in New Orleans, many of whom perform at her awesomely evocative little space), she and her partner, **Andy Anderson**, regularly make time for local experimental and noise music plus semi-traditional theater events. Anybody wondering where "the scene" is hidden needs to stop at the Mudlark. (For those interested in puppetry, find also the work of **Harry Mayronne**.)

FAUX/REAL FESTIVAL

venues all around Bywater/Marigny,
504-941-3640

Evolved from the beloved **New Orleans Fringe Fest,** Faux/Real offers two weeks of top-tier theater and experimental performances, readings, plus liquor and wine tastings and other parties. Performers do their thing at theaters, cabarets, outdoor venues, warehouses, galleries, cafés, bars, and any other outlet that works.

INFRINGE FEST

venues all around the Bywater/
Marigny; infringefest.org

Our man **Michael Martin** serves as director of artist relations and **Ratty Scurvics** as technical director for this four-day weekend each November, bringing New Orleans a big sampling of mostly local, all challenging theater productions in small venues with low ticket prices ("art before commerce," reads the website).

LE PETIT THÉÂTRE DU VIEUX CARRÉ

French Quarter, 616 St. Peter St.,
504-522-2081; lepetittheatre.com

One of the nation's oldest continuously operating theaters. Meaning, it's beautiful but rather than envelope-pushing, expect schlocky musicals and lots of Tennessee Williams—much of the **Faulkner** and **Tennessee Williams** festivals are held at Le Petit.

LOUISIANA PHILHARMONIC ORCHESTRA (LPO)

offices at 1010 Common St., Ste.
2120, 504-523-6530; lpomusic.com

The LPO is a musician-owned and -operated symphony—meaning they can play their classical music and pops favorites wherever they choose, from New Orleans' small First Baptist Church, to the huge Morial Convention Center, to the annual Book Fest in City Park each November.

MAHALIA JACKSON THEATER OF THE PERFORMING ARTS

Tremé, 1419 Basin St., 504-287-0350;
mahaliajacksontheater.com

Located in **Louis Armstrong Park**, and named for the famous New Orleans–born gospel star, this beautiful theater is famous as a place to hear opera and the Louisiana Philharmonic. The theater also hosts mainstream Broadway fare like *Cats* and *The Color Purple,* plus a smattering of famous comedians and black theater productions.

MARIGNY OPERA HOUSE

Marigny, 725 St. Ferdinand St.,
504-948-9998;
marignyoperahouse.org

This gorgeous stone church was originally built in 1853 and then reopened in 2014 as a "nondenominational church of the arts." Home to the **Marigny Opera Ballet** (which performs the works of New Orleans–based choreographers and composers each October through March), the venue also hosts "Sunday Musical Meditations" as well as arts and religious events. Depeche Mode filmed its "Heaven" video here.

NEW ORLEANS CENTER FOR THE CREATIVE ARTS (NOCCA)

Marigny/Bywater, 2800 Chartres St., 504-940-2787; nocca.com

This school for creative high school students (which counts **Harry Connick Jr., Wynton** and **Branford Marsalis,** and **Terence Blanchard** as its graduates, among many others) hosts performances of all kinds from the school and from around the globe. Artists come to teach NOCCA students and give stage performances that are open to the public at very reasonable ticket prices.

NEW ORLEANS OPERA ASSOCIATION

CBD, 935 Gravier St., Ste. 1940, 504-529-3000; neworleansopera.org

The New Orleans Opera Association, founded as the **French Opera House,** is the oldest opera in North America. Performances are held at the Morial Convention Center and Tulane University's McAlister Auditorium.

NEW ORLEANS SHAKESPEARE FESTIVAL AT TULANE

Uptown, Lupin Theater, Tulane University, 504-865-5105; neworleansshakespeare.org

Shakespeare performances presented around the city in awesome park settings as well as on campus, May through July.

RUNNING WITH SCISSORS

norunningwithscissors.com

This kooky, well-loved troupe presents mainly farce and high-camp produc-

tions such as ***Grenadine McGunkle's Double-Wide Christmas!*** Performance locations vary from small theaters like **Le Chat Noir** to even bowling alleys, so check the website.

SOUTHERN REP THEATRE

Uptown, 6221 S. Claiborne Ave., #573, 504-522-6545; southernrep.com

Southern Rep presents both classic and modern American and regional drama, featuring experienced local thespians as well as Broadway and Hollywood performers.

VALIANT THEATRE & LOUNGE

Bywater, 6621 St. Claude Ave., 504-298-8676; valianttheatre.com

Home of the award-winning **Lex et Umbra** theater company, this venue hosts plays but also concerts and burlesque events. Refined but funky productions, featuring beloved neighborhood talent.

ZEITGEIST MULTI-DISCIPLINARY ARTS CENTER

Uptown/Central City, 1618 Oretha Castle Haley Blvd., 504-352-1150; zeitgeistnola.org

Famous for its "theater experiments," Zeitgeist is considered one of the premier alternative arts centers in the South. The space also presents modern film, video, performance and visual art, as well as literary events up to six nights a week, year-round, plus many small festival-type events in between. Support this amazing place!

THE THEATERS OF DOWNTOWN NEW ORLEANS

Imagine a time in New Orleans history when one could walk the French Quarter streets at night taking one, two, three theater shows, sometimes more. All clustered within walking distance, several of New Orleans' most historic theaters still offer dramatic productions and concerts alike:

THE CIVIC

510 O'Keefe Ave., 504-272-0865; civicnola.com

A newly refurbished, giant theater now used for big movie premiers, rock concerts, and comedians big enough to draw just over 1,000 fans.

JOY THEATER

1200 Canal Street, 504-528-9569; thejoytheater.com

One of four original postwar movie theaters in downtown New Orleans, the 8,500-square-foot Joy is now a state-of-the-art venue for live music, theatrical performances, comedy, and other special events. Lounge on the mezzanine while looking down upon 2 Chainz.

ORPHEUM

129 Roosevelt Way, 504-274-4870; orpheumnola.com

First opened in 1918 (some say 1921), the visually ornate Orpheum now shows films, and hosts everything from big traveling theater events to violin concertos to Herbie Hancock.

SAENGER THEATRE

1111 Canal St., 504-287-0351; saengernola.com

Built in 1927, its interior was designed to look like an eighteenth-century Italian courtyard with gardens and columns, even a dome sky of twinkling fake stars. Destroyed after Katrina, the Saenger came back strong in 2013 and now hosts Broadway theater, concerts (both David Bowie and Prince have played the Saenger), and comedians on the level of Dave Chappelle and Amy Schumer.

STATE PALACE THEATER

1108 Canal St.

This theater opened playing silent movies in 1926 and later became the beating heart of New Orleans' rave scene in the '90s (shout-out to **Disco Donnie**). It has sat more or less lifeless since Katrina.

DANCING GROUNDS

*Bywater, 3705 St. Claude Ave.,
504-535-5791; dancingrounds.org*

This nonprofit organization brings high-quality, inclusive, and accessible dance education programs to New Orleans residents of all ages and backgrounds. They host some performances, but mostly offer affordable classes (20 adult classes per week and Saturday, plus youth programs) with interesting teachers from all around New Orleans' dance community.

HAPPENSDANCE

*offices at 129 University Pl.,
504-523-6530*

Founded by **Louisiana Philharmonic** cellist **Jeanne Jaubert**, a postmodern, experimental, but fun dance troupe.

MARIGNY OPERA HOUSE

*Marigny, 725 St. Ferdinand St.,
504-948-9998, marignyoperahouse.org*

This gorgeous stone church was originally built in 1853 and then reopened in 2014 as a "nondenominational church of the arts." Home to the **Marigny Opera Ballet** (which performs the works of New Orleans–based choreographers and composers October through March), the venue also hosts "Sunday Musical Meditations" as well as arts and religious events.

The Marigny Opera House is home to its own ballet troupe.

Marigny Opera House Foundation

NEW ORLEANS BALLET ASSOCIATION (NOBA) MAIN STAGE AND EDUCATION PROGRAMS

performances and classes at various venues, check website; nobadance.com

In addition to hosting several performances a year by an array of world-class companies, NOBA offers an extensive education program. The NOBA dance institute is the largest dance classroom on the Gulf Coast, providing thousands of recitals, concerts, lectures, workshops, and classes, many of them free. Check website for schedule.

NEW ORLEANS BALLET THEATRE

various venues, 504-826-0646; neworleansballettheatre.com

This company's founders, **Gregory Schramel** and wife **Marjorie Hardwick**, danced in Miami, Cincinnati, Atlanta, and Dallas before returning to their hometown to open this theater. They claim as influences George Balanchine, Maurice Béjart, and Twyla Tharp. Recent programs include the comedy *Yes Virginia* and *Thick as Thieves,* with music by U2.

NEW ORLEANS DANCE NETWORK

504-298-8591; noladancenetwork.org

Really a website built to connect the local dance community and disseminate information about performances and training resources, NODN also hosts real-life community and networking events plus some performances in unique locations around the city. Its Dance Week each June offers thirteen days of performances, classes, a dance social, a second-line parade, and a flash mob.

TSUNAMI DANCE COMPANY

1107 Cambronne St., 504-865-8810; tsunamidance.com

Since 2002, this New Orleans–based modern/multimedia dance company has incorporated athletic, innovative movement with a dynamic contemporary style. In fall 2008, Tsunami created an edgy take on **Bruno Schulz** imagery and philosophy for *Street of Crocodiles.* They can be seen at most of the events detailed in this section.

TRIXIE MINX AND NEW ORLEANS' BURLESQUE TRADITION

Fifty or sixty years ago, Bourbon was populated with swankier nightclubs where well-dressed couples hit the town to hear music and watch burlesque dancers such as **Blaze Starr**, **Lilly Christine the Cat Girl**, **Tajmah, the Jewel of the Orient**, and exotic, green-haired **Evangeline the Oyster Girl**. New Orleans' renaissance burlesque scene was nurtured in the late '90s at club **Shim Sham** on Toulouse, now **One Eyed Jacks**. Today, several revivalist troupes exist in New Orleans and perform fairly frequently.

Trixie Minx and her Fleur de Tease troupe provide the nucleus of New Orleans' new-school burlesque scene.

Zack Smith

173

But there is no one in town like the mighty **Fleur de Tease** (fleurdetease.com). A ballet dancer before moving to New Orleans in 2001, Fleur de Tease's leader **Trixie Minx** didn't realize she wanted to dance burlesque until she evacuated for Hurricane Katrina and began to fear she might never get the chance. "I remember in my big heavy evacuation backpack," says Trixie, "I had no real change of underwear or clothes, just my pictures and journals and a pair of pasties that I was given, to learn how to twirl with." When finally allowed back into her city, Trixie founded Fleur de Tease burlesque variety show, which rocks one Sunday night a month at One Eyed Jacks. "Our themes are well-rounded," Trixie explains. "We are more of a vaudeville variety show, meaning not just girls getting naked but equal amounts fire, aerial acrobatics, hula-hooping, music, and magic. And all of our girls are power players in the New Orleans burlesque community. Almost all of them have their own solo shows."

Fleur de Tease member **Roxie LeRouge** also hosts the revolving monthly **A Night at the Roxie**. **Natasha Fiore** and **Madame Mystere** run the **Storyville Starlettes** troupe, while aerialists **Sarah Bobcat**, **Niki Frisky**, and **Ooops the Clown** guide the **Mystic Pony Aerial Troupe**. Fleur de Tease's former kinkiest member, **Bella Blue**, founded the **New Orleans School of Burlesque** at **Crescent Lotus Dance Studio** (3143 Calhoun St., 504-382-5199), while her more seasoned students perform in the Burlesque 101 Showcase series at **All-Ways Lounge**. This venue also plays host to Bella's **Dirty Dime Peep Show,** which, Trixie adds, "is way more naked than any other show in town, way more alternative."

Trixie herself (or, if she's on tour, a sexy stand-in) can be seen, backed by a live band, each Friday at midnight for free in the cast of **Irvin Mayfield's Burlesque Ballroom** (French Quarter, Royal Sonesta, 300 Bourbon St.). "The weekly Ballroom show is a modern take on a classic show, and a very good introduction to burlesque, with live jazz from musicians such as **Meschiya Lake**, **Linnzi Zaorski,** or **Gerald French**."

COMEDY

Among the many changes in our city in the years since Katrina, New Orleans has since become a mecca of comedy, from improvisation classes to traditional stand-up events seven nights a week. As a testament, ultra-popular comedians Louis C.K. and Hannibal Buress famously chose our newly comedy-rich environment to work out new material for their respective stand-up specials.

One of the more consistent and tenacious purveyors of open-mic comedy of late has been British ex-pat, author, travel journalist, and comic **Paul Oswell**, who began visiting New Orleans regularly starting in 2001 for work. "I couldn't get booked on many shows," admits Oswell, "because I wasn't well known. So, starting my own comedy night seemed like a good way to get booked." The result was Oswell's **Local Uproar** comedy event (Saturdays at **AllWays Lounge**, Marigny), and also **Night Church** (Thursdays at **Sidney's**, Tremé), both of which offer free ice cream to garnish the laughs.

Paul Oswell is a comedian. He also facilitates other comedians at two weekly comedy nights, with free ice cream.

Josh Vine

Paul was kind enough to compile this list of where you can see comedy in New Orleans every single night of the week (for even more comedy events, visit nocomedy.com):

12 MILE LIMIT

*Mid-City, 500 S. Telemachus St.,
504-488-8114*

Bear with Me is a Mid-City open mic hosted by **Julie Mitchell** and **Laura Sanders.** Sign-up is at 8:30 p.m., with a 9 p.m. show. Free entry and free food!

SIBERIA LOUNGE

*Marigny, 2227 St. Claude Ave.,
504-265-8855; siberialounge.com*

Comic Strip is a slightly weird mix of comedy and burlesque that maybe shouldn't work, but it does, largely thanks to hosts **Corey Mack** and **Chris Lane (**brilliant MC of Fleur de Tease burlesque troupe). 9:30 p.m. show.

HOWLIN' WOLF DEN

*CBD, corner of St. Joseph and
S. Peters St., 504-529-5844;
thehowlinwolf.com/the-den.html*

Comedy Beast at 8:30 p.m. draws lots of pro comics touring our region.

LOST LOVE LOUNGE

*Marigny, 2529 Dauphine St.,
504-949-2009; lostlovelounge.com*

Every Tuesday night for years, **Cassidy Henehan** and **Scottland Green** have hosted **Comedy Catastrophe**, which usually starts late, 10:30 p.m. at the earliest.

CARROLLTON STATION

*Uptown, 8140 Willow St.,
504-865-9190; carrolltonstation.com*

Every Wednesday at 8 p.m. for seven-plus years, **Mike Henehan** and **Scotland Green** have hosted **"Think You're Funny?"** a high-quality comedy open-mic night. Packed audiences. Cheap drinks. Free entry.

DRAGON'S DEN

*Marigny, 435 Esplanade Ave.,
504-940-4446; dragonsdennola.com*

In what is normally a small, two-story electronic music club, comedian **Mark Caesar** (shout-out to **Team Piss Yo Pants**) hosts **Groove Therapy**, a do-what-you-like open-mic weekly.

Beloved local comedian Mark Caesar is often on the road these days.

Mark Caesar

THURSDAY

HOWLIN' WOLF DEN

CBD, corner of St. Joseph and S. Peters St., 504-529-5844; thehowlinwolf.com/the-den.html

Every Thursday, comedian **Red Bean** hosts **Comedy Gumbeaux**. This comedy night with an urban edge features the best in the city, plus the occasional national star. 8 p.m.

SIDNEY'S SALOON

Tremé, 1200 St. Bernard Ave., 504-224-2672; sidneyssaloon.com

Night Church comedy hour not only has free ice cream but is a great intimate comedy showcase that has seen its share of famous comics in its relatively short existence. 8.30 p.m.

FRIDAY

DRAGON'S DEN

Marigny, 435 Esplanade Ave., 504-940-4446; dragonsdennola.com

Weekends are weirdly quiet in the absence of a comedy club in the city, but **Comedy F**k Yeah** at the **Dragon's Den** is a fine way to kick-start your night—hosted by **Vincent Zambon** from 8.30 p.m.

SATURDAY

ALLWAYS LOUNGE & THEATRE

Marigny, 2240 St. Claude Ave., 504-218-5778; theallwayslounge.net

The weekend's most consistent showcase takes place at 8 p.m. **Local Uproar** also has free ice cream and a wealth of comedic talent passing through on the regular. The lounge setting makes for a great atmosphere, too.

BULLET'S SPORTS BAR

Tremé, 2441 A. P. Tureaud Ave., 504-948-4003

Permanent Damage is a Seventh Ward showcase hosted by **Tony Frederick**. 8 p.m. show, $3 at the door.

SUNDAY

HI-HO LOUNGE

Marigny, 2239 St. Claude Ave., 504-945-4446; hiholounge.net

The **NOLA Comedy Hour** weekly Sunday showcase is the most respected open mic in town, featuring up-and-coming locals and a live band. Any famous comics in town will be on that stage.

13. MARDI GRAS AND OTHER FESTIVALS

New Orleans is an economically challenging place to live some-times, especially during this post-Katrina housing bubble/crisis. That is why I keep a side job giving tours of **Mardi Gras World**, the art studio (or "den") that creates the props and floats for 18 of the city's 55 Carnival season parades. That means the den is employed by 18 Carnival krewes—a krewe is like a sorority or fraternity that you can join for one year. Your membership fee gets you a sprinkling of social activities throughout the year; then during Carnival season you'll ride in your krewe's parade and attend its annual Mardi Gras ball. For just 18 parades, Mardi Gras World decorates between 400 and 500 floats every year.

Locals who've lived through many Mardi Gras might turn their noses up at the idea of touring Mardi Gras World. But even for those who do know the history of the holiday stretching back to the eighteenth-century French founding of Louisiana, it's always an amazing experience to stand surrounded by hundreds of huge, colorful props and floats, some of which have ridden in parades for decades. Though touristy, a tour of Mardi Gras World is worth the $20 ticket. Comes with a free slice of **king cake**!

When giving tours to people who haven't attended Carnival, I explain to them how Mardi Gras is not an event; it's a holiday. The holiday begins each year on January 6 (aka 12th Night, aka the Epiphany) and stretches for weeks. It peaks the night before Fat Tuesday, which is called Lundi Gras, and ends on Mardi Gras Day, aka Fat Tuesday, which is always 47 days before Easter—a date that jumps around on the calendar, meaning Carnival season can last just a few weeks, or else close to two daunting months long!

Whatever you imagine goes on during Mardi Gras surely does go on, but so do a million other celebratory rituals of which you've never dreamed. Sure, you can lick hurricane drink off a stranger's chest on Bourbon Street, but you can also enjoy a crawfish picnic with your kids (New Orleans kids get ten days off school for Carnival season) while listening to a traditional brass band, if that's your scene. A shy, sober person will have as much fun as an effusive drunk will, and your kids, especially, will have a blast.

Mardi Gras day itself is an all-city lovefest, where we walk and bike around in creative costumes, with the simple objective of finding and hugging our also costumed, drunken friends. Mardi Gras provides a break from reality. Mardi Gras resembles Christmas without the capitalist pressure. Mardi Gras is quite possibly the most fun thing ever.

The Secret Society of St. Anne parade on Mardi Gras day; notice the lack of observers, only participants.

Jonathan Traviesa

MARDI GRAS TIMELINE

Though the greatest Mardi Gras experiences often begin without clear direction, here are some of our suggestions anyway, presented as a timeline running throughout the weeks of Carnival season:

JANUARY 6

JOAN OF ARC PARADE

French Quarter; joanofarcparade.org

A medieval-themed walking parade in a theatrical procession celebrating St. Joan of Arc's birthday and her liberation of the citizens of Orléans, France, from a British siege in 1429—resulting in her moniker "The Maid of Orléans." The parade begins at the golden French Quarter statue of Joan that was given as a gift from France in the 1950s. Grab a candle and join one of the only parades that winds through the French Quarter.

SOME SATURDAY A FEW WEEKS LATER

KREWE DU VIEUX PARADE

Marigny, check website for date; kreweduvieux.org

For many locals, this low-budget parade of crude sex jokes is the unofficial kickoff of Carnival season. Krewe du Vieux (as in Vieux Carré, the French name for the French Quarter) is a satirical parade in nineteenth-century Carnival style, featuring mostly walking krewes interspersed with small floats drawn by krewe members and mules. Someone fun always reigns as KdV's king or queen, often a musician such as **Big Freedia** or **Dr. John.**

After Krewe du Vieux night, you will be able to catch a parade somewhere around New Orleans almost every night—definitely every weekend night. Krewes generally parade bundled in nights of three or four, with each krewe rolling roughly three dozen floats apiece. As Fat Tuesday approaches, parades fill both days and nights. All Mardi Gras parades are fun, but here are a few we especially love, or that you might not hear of on your own:

THE VERY NEXT SATURDAY!

'TIT REX

Marigny, daytime; titrexparade.com

You really have to lean in for the city's only "micro-krewe." 'Tit Rex rolls shoebox-sized floats crafted by some of the city's most eccentric and curmudgeonly personalities. Instead of big strands of beads, the throws are handcrafted and very tiny. The "parade" takes ample time stopping at great local bars.

You have to get up close to see the curmudgeonly 'Tit Rex parade.

Jonathan Traviesa

CHEWBACCHUS

Marigny, nighttime; chewbacchus.org

The intergalactic **Krewe of Chewbacchus** walks the perimeter of the Marigny on Saturday night before Mardi Gras. That means hordes of Wookiees, R2-D2s, and other contraptions. This massive and oddly controversial krewe, which calls itself "the Revel Alliance," welcomes one and all to join their nerd orgy.

THE NEXT DAY (SUNDAY!)

BARKUS PARADE

French Quarter, early afternoon; barkus.org

Featuring hundreds of hilariously costumed dogs (and also some cats, and maybe a goat or two), this group gath-

ers at around 10 a.m. at Armstrong Park on Rampart Street before the parade begins at 2 p.m., heading down St. Ann. The day culminates in an animal costume contest and a Barkus Ball (humans only, sorry!).

THE FOLLOWING WEDNESDAY

MYSTIK KREWE OF NYX

CBD to Uptown; kreweofnyx.org

The female krewes are the best krewes. From **Cleopatra** to Muses, the ladies are simply more creative and fun and generous with their throws (the male krewes often don't seem to see male spectators, or even children, as they scan the crowd for nubile young ladies), and Nyx is no exception. Catch lipstick and purses and other items all imprinted with the Nyx name.

Dance troupes like the Gris Gris Strut are not uncommon during Mardi Gras.

Zack Smith

PINK SLIP

Mardi Gras's first-ever rock band, featuring the famous **Susan Cowsill** and **Sue Ford.** Once an all-woman group that now includes Sue's husband, drummer **Jimmy Ford**, Pink Slip got their foot in the door via the all-female **Krewe of Muses**, who wanted a band of all-female musicians, and not the typical jazz and blues. Every year now, the Fords invite a new cast of char-

acters aboard their small float to play classic rock and disco standards, plus originals like the heavy tune "I Wanna Die in New Orleans." White Zombie's **Sean Yseult** sometimes plays keyboards for Pink Slip, along with guitarist **Dave Catching** of Eagles of Death Metal. The same band plays nightclub stages locally and all over America as **DiNOLA**.

Pink Slip (aka DiNOLA) was the first rock 'n' roll band to perform in traditional Mardi Gras parades. This guy, in the hat, is bassist Eddie.

Michael Patrick Welch

Quintron's Ninth Ward Marching Band features celebrity grand marshals such as dirty New York rapper Peaches, pictured here.

THE NEXT NIGHT, THURSDAY

KREWE OF MUSES

CBD to Uptown; kreweofmuses.org

The first all-female breakout krewe. Muses tosses the absolute best throws, and boasts the most dynamic array of nontraditional floats and live bands from brass to rock. Again, whereas traditionally the pretty girls always end up receiving the most throws, the all-female krewes spread the loot among everyone. People go crazy trying to catch Muses' signature throw, a hand-decorated high-heel shoe.

NINTH WARD MARCHING BAND

Founded by one-man band **Mr. Quintron**, this team of thirty-plus artists and oddballs in clean, pressed red-and-white uniforms emblazoned with sparkly 9s began in the late '90s, inspired by the musicianship, choreography, and showmanship of the high school marching bands. Because the Ninth Ward is largely considered a black neighborhood, some locals roll their eyes at the nearly all-Caucasian band. Still, they've proven themselves with a fun dance team, cheerleaders, a gun squad, and flag girls—the whole (ahem) nine yards. The team has recently been welcomed by the mainstream and can be seen in several big "official" Mardi Gras parades, including **Muses** and **Bacchus**.

FRIDAY

KREWE OF ORPHEUS

kreweoforpheus.com

This "superkrewe," founded by Harry Connick Jr. among other "famous" locals, charges a membership fee of $1,500 a year. Around 1,500 people join every year. All of that money essentially goes toward creating super-elaborate art (miles and miles of giant cardboard flowers) for their coed parade.

Markus Davis of Naughty Palace is also the driving force behind DrumCart, which provides big-ass beats for wild walking parades.

Jonathan Traviesa

KREWE OF VAPORWAVE

check website for time and date of livestream; kreweofvaporwave.com

New Orleans' first virtual parade krewe—named after the sadly nihilistic loop-based "music" genre from YouTube—is best experienced at home, alone, in the dark. Actually, it's a humorous and clever-enough way for cyber introverts to express their love for the mighty Mardi Gras. Each float is a free-standing Vaporwave music video that scrolls from left to right on your screen as the parade moves. Vaporwave artists from Argentina, Los Angeles, and Austin participate each year.

SATURDAY BEFORE MARDI GRAS

NEW ORLEANS' MOST TALKED OF CLUB (NOMTOC)

Zulu gets all the shine, but NOMTOC is Orleans Parish's other famous African American krewe. One of the last true neighborhood parades, NOM-

TOC—formed in the 1950s but denied a parading permit until the early '70s—continues to roll in Algiers even after all the other West Bank krewes have given up and succumbed to the lure of St. Charles Ave.

SUNDAY BEFORE MARDI GRAS

BACCHUS

Uptown around Toledano and St. Charles Ave.; kreweofbacchus.org

Since 1969, the mainstream but still wild Krewe of Bacchus has rolled with many small alternative krewes in tow, including the ever-entertaining **Box of Wine** krewe, who celebrate the Roman god of wine by randomly pouring the magic elixir down the gullets of those in attendance. Open wide! This krewe's floats are also among the most creative, funny, and eye-catching.

THE NOISICIAN COALITION

Bacchus Sunday, also Lundi Gras midnight; noisiciancoalition.org

With an array of self-styled instruments including tubas made from drainpipes, saxophones melded with bullhorns, and guitar-pedal-accordion contraptions, this ragtag krewe dressed in red and black split the sartorial difference between steampunk, pirate, and scary clown. Begun as an expression of **Mattvaughn Black**'s love of strange noises, the Noisicians love confusing spectators waiting for the **Bacchus** parade, before their annual midnight march on Lundi Gras night (technically the first parade of Mardi Gras day).

NOLA MOMENT

COSTUME SHOPS

The author and his partner dressed as squids for Mardi Gras 2003.

Michael Patrick Welch

We interrupt your Mardi Gras timeline for this important advice. Again, it's up to you how you party, but don't go out to the parades without a costume (same goes for New Orleans Halloween!). Ideally, Mardi Gras is all participants, no observers. Here is a quick list of places to grab a great costume before you dive in:

BOUTIQUE DU VAMPYRE

*French Quarter, 709 St. Ann St.,
504-561-8267; feelthebite.com*

A real-deal gothwear, jewelry, and accessories store that also sells creepy dolls.

FUN ROCK'N/POP CITY

*French Quarter, 940 and 1125
Decatur St., 504-528-8559;
Uptown, 3109 and 3118 Magazine
St., 504-304-7744; popcitynola.com*

Usually a store for fun knickknacks, party supplies, and pop culture paraphernalia, this shop transforms into the premier store for masks and other costume supplies during Mardi Gras season.

JEFFERSON VARIETY STORES

*Jefferson, La., 239 Iris Ave.,
504-834-5222; jeffersonvariety.com*

You say there's no reason you can think of to visit a fabric store on vacation? Apparently, you've never been to New Orleans, where parties, parades, festivals, and other various and sundry occasions demand a costume. And Jefferson Variety, with its rainbows of costume satin, yards of shimmering taffeta, and what look like endless miles of strips of braided sequins, rhinestones, and multicolored fringe, will make you want to find a reason. It's also where, they claim, Mardi Gras Indians buy their feathers, and big-time Carnival krewes buy the elaborate sequined appliqués and fake stones that give their royal robes sparkle.

MARDI GRAS SPOT

*Uptown, 2812 Toulouse St.,
504-482-0000; mardigrasspot.com*

Krewe members riding floats must purchase their own beads, cups, doubloons, and toys to throw, and this is where they buy them. Though mainly a store selling bulk trinkets of all kinds (it's worth visiting even if you're not buying anything), masks are in abundance alongside lots of other ways to scrape together a wild costume.

MISS CLAUDIA'S VINTAGE CLOTHING & COSTUMES

*Uptown, 4204 Magazine St.,
504-897-6310; missclaudias.com*

Though more of a fun vintage boutique, Miss Claudia always keeps a well-curated mess of costumes during New Orleans holidays.

NEW ORLEANS PARTY & COSTUME

*CBD, 705 Camp St., 504-525-4744;
partyandcostume.com*

Nice, spacious, well-organized two-story costume shop with everything you could possibly need.

UPTOWN COSTUME AND DANCEWEAR

*Uptown, 4326 Magazine St.,
504-895-7969*

This comprehensive costume hub is the busiest shop in town during Mardi Gras and Halloween, just packed with college kids—which is actually really fun and helps you get in the spirit! Worth checking out even if you have to stand in line outside.

Now back to your Mardi Gras timeline . . .

MONDAY (LUNDI GRAS)

LUNDI GRAS FESTIVAL

Tremé, all day, free;
lundigrasfestival.com

The **Zulu Social Aid & Pleasure Club** throws this festival in **Woldenberg Riverfront Park**, where Zulu's king greets Rex, the king of Carnival, at 6 p.m. Zulu also introduces its royalty and characters to the public (including Big Shot, Witch Doctor, and the Zulu Mayor) and presents live music on several stages—expect brass bands, bounce rap DJs, Mardi Gras Indians, and maybe even some zydeco.

KREWE DU POUX

Bywater, nighttime

A satire of the satirical Krewe du Vieux parade (described above) put on by bike-punks, fauxbeaux, and other colorful snowbirds and Bywater/Marigny cretins. After the parade and coronation (**Ratty Scurvics** and **Ooops the Clown** of **Fleur de Tease** have served as king and queen multiple times), the krewe meets in an alley near Franklin Street in Marigny for its annual demolition derby of creatively altered shopping carts. The carts crash and bash until only the champion is left standing—that is, if the cops don't come and break it up first. Check the Krewe du Poux YouTube documentary.

QUINTRON & MISS PUSSYCAT, LIVE!

usually at One Eyed Jacks,
but check local listings;
quintronandmisspussycat.com

Lundi Gras is the best night of the year to go see New Orleans' beloved, eccentric, dynamic duo. Quintron is a one-man-dance-party-band playing organ and light-sensitive analog synths, backed by his wife who sings backup and opens each concert with a hilarious psychedelic puppet show. You've never danced more in your life.

FAT TUESDAY AKA MARDI GRAS

NORTHSIDE SKULL AND BONES GANG

Tremé, early morning

Dressed in black, with papier-mâché skull masks and other spooky attire, this long-standing Creole krewe (established in the early nineteenth century) delivers an early morning wake-up call to the Tremé neighborhood and "brings the spirits to the streets on Mardi Gras morning," says **Bruce "Sunpie" Barnes**, the gang's second chief.

SECRET SOCIETY OF ST. ANNE

Bywater, a house on Clouet St.,
sunrise; kreweofsaintanne.org

The now not-as-secret Society of St. Anne amasses early Mardi Gras morning on Clouet Street and marches into the French Quarter (to Canal Street for the big **Rex** parade, before doubling back into the Quarter) wearing some of the best, most elaborate costumes Carnival has to offer.

ZULU PARADE

CBD, Canal St. down St. Charles; kreweofzulu.com

This African American–founded krewe, dating back to the early 1900s, is active all year at their popular clubhouse on Broad St. in Mid-City. Zulu's parade consists of black people wearing blackface, making fun of the white idea that blacks are "savages." Wearing grass skirts, lard-can hats, and banana-stalk scepters, the krewe hands out much-coveted Zulu coconuts. Zulu's extremely dense and fascinating history and calendar of yearly events can be accessed on the krewe's website.

BABY DOLLS

A group of African American women (and some men) strutting through the streets in satin and lace baby doll get-ups (that look more like French maid costumes with short satin skirts, bloomers, and garters), continuing a black female tradition with Jim Crow roots. Before her recent death, **Miss Antoinette K-Doe** had resurrected the dormant baby doll tradition to great success. The Baby Dolls can be seen in the Zulu parade.

KREWE OF REX PARADE

rexorganization.com

This parade considers itself "King of Carnival," with its own annual king, coronated before all of his "subjects" on St. Charles Avenue on Mardi Gras day around noon. Rex gave Mardi Gras its official colors of purple (for justice), green (for faith), and gold (for power).

KREWE OF KOSMIC DEBRIS

begins at noon on Frenchmen St., Mardi Gras day

Formed in 1977, this now 200-plus-person French Quarter pub crawl parade on Mardi Gras morn invites all comers in costume to join in and jam on Dixieland standards—whether or not you know how to play an instrument.

NOLA MOMENT

MARDI GRAS INDIANS

Mardi Gras Indians, resplendent in their intricately hand-beaded suits and headdresses weighed down with thousands of brightly colored feathers, are ubiquitous images in New Orleans' tourist materials. They're hired to parade through **Jazz Fest** to create ambiance, and since Katrina, nonprofits have subsidized Indian "practices" that are open to the public. These friendly presentations can contribute to a public image of the stalwart tradition bearers as sort of happy, colorful feathered friends. That has not always been the case.

Locals say that the Indians—African American groups divided into tribes that identify as either Uptown or downtown-based—have been around since the nineteenth century. Tribal hierarchies include a Big Chief, a Big Queen, and sometimes second and third chiefs and queens, plus the "spy boys," "flag boys," and "wild men." The tradition is interesting for combining aggressive, territorial hyper-masculinity with the domestic act of sewing; each man works all year to sew delicate, intricate patterns into a suit he will show off once or twice, before destroying it and starting over for next year. Indians don't parade so much as roam their neighborhoods, looking for other tribes for showdowns. Spy boys (you know the song) wander out ahead of the Big Chief to spot other tribes. These days, the contest is about who has the prettiest suit, but back in the day the battles were violent. As recently as the '90s, one Indian was allegedly nearly murdered by another looking to settle a score with him by a hatchet to the head. Some locals whisper that secret Indian council meetings still have the power to decide life or death.

In the early '70s, members of the **Wild Magnolias** tribe, along with **Willie Tee**, recorded the first album of Indian songs ever put on wax (self-titled, but later put out with extra songs as *They Call Us Wild*), a deliciously raw and dirty slice of funk—one of the finest and most unique artifacts of genuine American music in existence—with the clattering tambourine and drum percussions the Indians use on actual runs.

On Mardi Gras day and Super Sunday, neighborhood bars near Claiborne Ave. or under the Claiborne overpass (e.g., the **Mother-in-Law Lounge**), or Second and Dryades Streets, Bayou St. John, and Tremé, are all great vantage points to catch the Indians' awesome spectacle. Or else all year round, you can visit the **House of Dance and Feathers** or the **Backstreet Cultural Museum** (see "Galleries and Art Museums") to learn more about Mardi Gras Indian history and custom.

Mardi Gras Indians

Zack Smith

MARDI GRAS ADVICE FROM GEOFF DOUVILLE OF EGG YOLK JUBILEE

Geoff Douville

Geoff Douville of Egg Yolk Jubilee.

Wanna know what Mardi Gras is like for your average New Orleans musician? Just before Mardi Gras 2008, we randomly ran into **Geoff Douville**, a native New Orleanian, local filmmaker, guitarist, educator, and banjo player in much-loved, genre-defying brassish band **Egg Yolk Jubilee**. Geoff is a shining example of a local artist and neighbor.

Geoff was sitting outside of **Café Rose Nicaud** on Frenchmen Street catching his breath (which admittedly smelled of a couple drinks), sweating in formalwear like he'd just come from a job—because he had just come from a job. With his shiny banjo case at his feet he told me, "I was playing at this crazy wedding with the marching band version of Egg Yolk. We play another party tonight, and had some time to kill in between, so we all took our instruments and decided let's go to the **Alpine Bar** off Jackson Square for a Bloody Mary. While we're in there the owner says, 'Hey, play for us, I'll buy a round, play a couple tunes!' So we end up drinking a few more!"

On the way to his next gig, Geoff gave us some factoids about New Orleans, and his Mardi Gras suggestions for you (drop a tip in Geoff's bucket!):

DOUBLOONS

"As far as the stuff they throw off of floats, people only more recently switched over to wanting beads. Beads used to be small, but the demand for bare breasts drove up the size of beads. Then ten or fifteen years ago people were crazy about cups, whereas people don't even pay attention now when cups are thrown. I am on a one-man crusade to bring the doubloons back: the gold coins. Doubloons used to be the big thing when I was little. I have even been given the black doubloon: it's covered in black enamel, very treasured, the rarest, carried only by the black-hooded marshal KKK-looking creepy guy on the horse that leads the parades. If you get that, it means you've been chosen."

HIGH SCHOOL MARCHING BANDS

"I am a connoisseur of New Orleans high school marching bands. They are the heart and soul of any parade, and of New Orleans itself. And their sound is honed by the frequency of Mardi Gras, and the fact that band directors have been participating in Mardi Gras for years and years. I really support that Roots of Music

Foundation (therootsofmusic.org) started by **Derrick Tabb** of **Rebirth Brass Band,** that buses kids out to learn marching band music when middle-school programs are cut."

LEE CIRCLE (SOON TO BE RENAMED)

"Watch the parades under the **Calliope** overpass at Lee Circle. There is this reverb under that bridge, and the high school marching bands always play at that moment. They do their best routine, to hear it in that monstrous reverb. Plus since it's a circle, you get the chance to see the bands twice."

WHICH PARADES?

"I always go to **Endymion** in Mid-City. I usually go to the **Krewe of Mid-City,** which has been moved to Uptown; they have unique floats made of tinfoil, tinfoil decorations, it's totally unique, plus they are the marching band parade. I always love playing in **Krewe du Vieux** with the **Ninth Ward Marching Band.** And this year I played in the 'Tit Rex parade, where the floats are miniature, shoebox sized. So they asked me to dress up like a giant."

OTHER NEW ORLEANS FESTIVALS

New Orleans literally has a festival for everything.

MARCH

BUKU MUSIC AND ARTS FEST

*Uptown on the river, near
1380 Port of New Orleans Pl.;
thebukuproject.com*

For one weekend in March you can hear the thump of techno bass from most of the city's neighborhoods. This truly progressive festival of EDM and other youth music sprinkles in an interesting dose of intelligent hip-hop legends like Public Enemy and Run the Jewels, plus famous DJs of popular genres past.

CONGO SQUARE RHYTHMS FESTIVAL

*Tremé, Armstrong Park,
701 N. Rampart St., 504-558-6100;
jazzandheritage.org/congo-square*

Cuban, African, and New Orleans brass and gospel music. Also featuring the **Class Got Brass** competition for Louisiana middle and high school students. Free.

FÊTE FRANÇAISE

*Uptown, Ecole Bilingue de la
Nouvelle-Orléans, 821 General
Pershing St., 504-896-4500;
fetefrancaise.com*

A great occasion to speak French, plus partake of French food, art, music, children's activities, and demonstrations. Free.

ITALIAN-AMERICAN ST. JOSEPH SOCIETY PARADE

*French Quarter, starts at Canal and
Chartres Streets, 504-561-1006;
iamcnola.org*

New Orleans even makes a big deal out of St. Joseph's Day each March 19! Not only can you barhop and check out dozens of elaborate St. Joe altars (with free cookies, cakes, breads, and beans), but this parade features sixteen floats, nine marching bands, and hundreds of members marching in tuxedos and giving women roses in exchange for a kiss. Parade starts at 9 p.m.

LOUISIANA CRAWFISH FESTIVAL

*Chalmette, La. (nine miles east of
N.O.); louisianacrawfishfestival.com*

St. Bernard Parish, home of the Battle of New Orleans site overlooking the Mississippi River, also hosts the Crawfish Fest (est. 1975). Crawfish (aka. crayfish, crawdads, mudbugs) are pretty much poor man's shrimp. They take a li'l more work to peel, but are totally worth it—not to mention, crawfish bring people together, creating a whole other party scene during the winter festival season. Aside from your basic boiled crawfish, this fest offers crawfish bread, crawfish pasta, crawfish pies, crawfish rice, crawfish jambalaya—infinite crawfish options, all of them good. You'll also enjoy big carnival rides, regional arts and crafts, crawfish racing competitions, and live Louisiana music. Four nights' worth of "Cajun entertainment" builds up finally to the coronation of the Crawfish Queen. In 2012, they were exhibiting a taxidermied two-headed albino cobra, but we're not sure it was real.

SOUL FEST

Uptown, Audubon Zoo,
6500 Magazine St., 504-861-2537;
auduboninstitute.org/soul-fest

This event celebrates African American jazz, gospel, and R&B, with dancers, Mardi Gras Indians, soul food, and kids' activities.

ST. PATRICK'S DAY PARADE

Uptown; irishchannelno.org

The Irish Channel St. Patrick's Day Club holds its annual mass drinking celebration every March 15, beginning at noon at St. Mary's Assumption Church (corner of Constance and Josephine Streets), followed by a huge parade with generous throws that starts at the corner of Felicity and Magazine at 1 p.m. Parade goers are pelted with traditional Irish vegetables—cabbages, potatoes, carrots, etc.—from atop floats, as men in formal attire walk in drunken groups, collecting kisses in exchange for flowers.

APRIL

BUNARCHY (PUB CRAWL AND BALL)

A surprisingly popular bar crawl where everyone dresses up as sex bunnies, mostly on the S&M tip. The bunnies crawl (or hop, I suppose) each April on a route that stops at **Marie's** bar and **Mimi's in the Marigny** among other great bars (a percentage of sales going to benefit the Louisiana SPCA). The krewe also hosts a popular live band dance party ball each year during the summer, the Bunarchy Ball. Check the Bunarchy Facebook page for deets.

S&M gear is the norm at the annual Bunarchy pub crawl.

Eli Mergel

FESTIVAL INTERNATIONAL DE LOUISIANE

Lafayette, La. (about 135 miles west of N.O.); festivalinternational.org

If you want to escape **Jazz Fest**, the last weekend in the Festival International is the free, Francophile alternative, featuring global stars like **Femi Kuti** and **Steel Pulse**. Food booths offer every type of alligator- and crawfish-based delicacy, and the music is outstanding. We recommend an overnight stay any time of year to get a suitable taste of this capital of Acadiana, where ample music venues and the distinctive Cajun lifestyle offer countless adventures.

FRENCH QUARTER FEST

French Quarter, along the Mississippi; fqfi.org/frenchquarterfest

Still considered by some locals to be an "alternative" to the big festival, FQF

A buzzed tourist frustratedly searches for his patch of lawn chairs at Strawberry Fest.

Jonathan Traviesa

offers over 500 musicians on 23 stages. There's barely room to walk along the river, and lines for food and drinks can get huge at French Quarter Fest—because the music lineup is so damned good. FQF lacks the cheesy national headliners of Jazz Fest, and is certainly more local (and free!); the musicians often overdo the "entertain the tourists" shtick since they're playing in the Quarter. Still, worth the trouble.

NEW ORLEANS GIANT PUPPET FESTIVAL

Marigny, Marigny Opera House, 725 St. Ferdinand St., 504-948-9998, and Mudlark Public Theatre, 1200 Port St.; marignyoperahouse.org

Puppetry in a variety of styles and sizes: over ten puppet companies performing in two venues. Check to make sure which shows are for kids, and which are for adults only.

PONCHATOULA STRAWBERRY FESTIVAL

Memorial Park, downtown Ponchatoula, La. (about 50 miles northwest of N.O.); lastrawberryfestival.com

This festival celebrating that sweet, lusty berry features rides, games (egg toss, sack race), bands, a cat judging contest, a strawberry ball and coronation, a baking contest, talent show, and a 10-K "Strawberry Strut" competitive run. During almost no time does the live Louisiana music stop. Also, there are strawberries.

ASIAN HERITAGE FESTIVAL

Uptown, Audubon Zoo,
6500 Magazine St., 504-861-2537;
auduboninstitute.org

The Asian/Pacific American Society and Audubon Zoo present this celebration of Asian culture with traditional song and dance and arts and crafts from China, Japan, Thailand, Vietnam, India, Taiwan, and the Philippines.

BAYOU BOOGALOO

Mid-City, at Bayou St. John;
thebayouboogaloo.com

This laid-back, family-friendly fest was first organized as a morale booster for the flooded Mid-City neighborhood around Bayou St. John. The Boogaloo takes place on the bayou's banks for two days on three stages, with a mixture of excellent marquee-name and neighborhood-favorite zydeco, funk, rock, and Latin music. In 2009, the festival went 100 percent green, with solar-powered stages, biodiesel generators, and organic snacks.

CHAZFEST

Bywater, Wednesday between
the two weekends of Jazz Fest;
check website for location;
chazfestival.com

Conceived as a balm for the egos of a group of downtown musicians who weren't booked at Jazz Fest, Chazfest is the Bywater's companion piece to the monster fest. Named in honor of the prolific, quirky bluesman **Washboard**

Chaz, Chazfest is organized by Chaz's sideman, singer and guitarist **Alex McMurray**. The fest features groups like the **Happy Talk Band**, brass bands, side projects like McMurray's sea-shanty outfit the **Valparaiso Men's Chorus**, and of course, Chaz himself. Admission is usually $25–$35 (about half the cost of actual Jazz Fest). Great food and drinks are reasonably priced. For those averse to huge crowds, and who want to socialize and drink with some of the city's best musicians rather than stare at them from afar, Chazfest is a wonderful alternative.

CRAWFISH MAMBO

Uptown, University of New Orleans
campus, 2000 Lakeshore Dr.,
The Cove on Founders Road,
504-280-2586; crawfishmambo.com

Reap the benefits of a mudbug cook-off with all-you-can-eat boiled crawfish and live local music. The event supports professional development programs at UNO. People go crazy for free crawfish, so come early or risk an empty stomach.

GREEK FESTIVAL NEW ORLEANS

Lakeview, Holy Trinity Cathedral
grounds, 1200 Robert E. Lee Blvd.,
504-282-0259; gfno.com

For over forty years this fest has showcased Greek food, music, and culture. Features children's activities plus traditional Greek dancers and music.

Keith "Deacon Johnson" Moore founded NOizeFest. The author hosts NOizeFest every year in May on the last Sunday of Jazz Fest.

NOizeFest

locations vary, last day of Jazz Fest

Keith "Deacon Johnson" Moore was the son of **Deacon John**, the famous R&B singer who played guitar on almost every famous New Orleans record ever. NOizeFest blossomed out of Keith's anger at Jazz Fest for ignoring all the nontraditional/experimental/original music that is nonetheless part of the lifeblood of the city. After Keith was shot and killed uptown in 2005, his friends continued the fest in Michael Patrick Welch's backyard behind **Bacchanal** wine shop, which was big enough to accommodate simultaneous multiple performers, but comfy enough to create serious sonic overlap. NOizeFest's anti-"band" lineup still runs the gamut from DJs to tape manipulators to an all-noise marching band to well-known acts like **Mr. Quintron**, doing everything but his usual dance-rock.

Recently some classical musicians have braved the fest's noisy waters, taking it to a new level. But in true New Orleans fashion, all ten hours of the NOizeFest promise unpretentious, giddy fun.

JUNE

CAJUN ZYDECO FESTIVAL

Tremé, Louis Armstrong Park, 701 N. Rampart St.; jazzandheritage.org/cajun-zydeco

Two days of authentic, free zydeco from the likes of Grammy winner **Chubby Carrier**, **Geno Delafose**, the **Lost Bayou Ramblers**, and **Dwayne Dopsie**. Food vendors sell Italian ice, popsicles, ice cream, and other summertime treats inside a large arts market that provides handmade wares and activities for kids plus lots of misting fans to keep everyone cool.

CREOLE TOMATO FESTIVAL

French Quarter, French Market,
1008 N. Peters St., 504-636-6400;
frenchmarket.org

Food booths offer creole tomato favorites like fried green tomatoes, creole tomato Bloody Marys, stuffed shrimp with grilled creole tomatoes, creole tomato–cream crawfish pies, blooming onion on a bed of creole tomato—plus cooking demonstrations, music, and dancing throughout the weekend.

NEW ORLEANS OYSTER FESTIVAL

French Quarter, Woldenberg
Riverfront Park, 1 Canal St.,
504-835-6410;
neworleansoysterfestival.org

Over twenty restaurants offering oyster dishes, music, an oyster shucking and eating competition, and a largest-oyster contest. Proceeds help to support the Louisiana oyster industry, plus security for the NOPD's 8th District. Free.

NOLA CARIBBEAN FESTIVAL

Central City, 1201 S. Rampart St.;
nolacaribbeanfestival.com

A whole weekend of Caribbean cuisine, music, dance, and culture highlighting New Orleans' deeply rooted cultural connections as the Caribbean's northernmost city. The fest is replete with a kids' corner, a salsa dancing tent, African drum lessons, and New Orleans' first-ever dancehall vs. bounce dance competition. General admission: $10.

JULY

CAJUN MUSIC AND FOOD FESTIVAL

Lake Charles, La. (about 200 miles
west of N.O.), Burton Coliseum,
7001 Gulf Hwy., 337-794-2541;
cfmalakecharles.com/festival

This Cajun culture festival is worth the drive; includes Cajun dance contests, a live auction, a French mass on Sunday, and other activities.

ESSENCE MUSIC FESTIVAL

Superdome and various nearby
locations; essence.com/festival

The annual hyper-corporate, four-day music festival features national and local acts on eight stages at the Superdome, plus African American speakers and authors at the Morial Convention Center. Tickets range from $130.50 to $2,700 to see a rotation of artists from Mary J. Blige to Kendrick Lamar to Beyoncé—and also Frankie Beverly and Maze, every year.

MECHACON

CBD, Hyatt Regency Hotel;
mechacon.com

A three-day anime festival focusing on Japanese animation, Japanese culture, and Transformers. The fest is now the largest, longest-running anime convention in Louisiana, growing in ten years from 1,500 attendees to 15,000.

NOLA TIME FEST

Metairie, La., Jefferson Orleans North facility, 2600 Edenborn Ave.; kreweduwho.com

Presented by **Krewe du Who** and the **Consortium of Genius**, this festival celebrates time travel as experienced via the TV show *Dr. Who*. Expect lots of Dr. Who nerds, speakers, and activities (like the annual Dr. Who pinball tournament), plus crazy sci-fi themed bands like The Tomb of Nick Cage.

SAN FERMIN IN NUEVA ORLEANS, AKA RUNNING OF THE BULLS

various locations; nolabulls.com

The ladies of **Big Easy Rollergirls** play the part of bulls in a traditional running of the bulls ceremony, aping those in Pamplona, Spain, except on roller skates. The attending festival includes other traditional San Fermin parties, events, and great live Latin music.

TALES OF THE COCKTAIL

various locations, 504-948-0511; talesofthecocktail.com

Cocktail heaven or a hipster yuppie hell? Every bartender and liquor enthusiast in the country turns out for Tales' dozens of seminars, tasting rooms, competitions, awards, and concerts celebrating American drink culture. Admission runs from $40 to $695.

AUGUST

DIRTY LINEN NIGHT

French Quarter, second Saturday, Royal St.

Similar to White Linen Night, but celebrating the galleries of the (less interesting) Royal Street art district in the French Quarter. Participating galleries and shops give away dirty martinis and dirty rice—Cajun seasoned rice—just look for the laundry baskets outside the galleries.

MID-SUMMER MARDI GRAS

Uptown, begins at Maple Leaf Bar, 8316 Oak St.

Another event in the *all participants/ no observers* file: For more than twenty years, the **Krewe of O.A.K.** (acronym for "outrageous and kinky," they claim, but the parade also starts on Oak St.) has celebrated a faux Mardi Gras with this glorified pub crawl, six months after the actual Fat Tuesday. Floats in this "parade" are generally decorated golf carts, rolling between brass bands and a sweating, drunk, dancing crowd. The heat keeps the mandatory costumes skin-oriented.

SATCHMO SUMMER FEST

four days at the end of July and beginning of August; Marigny/French Quarter; fqfi.org/satchmosummerfest

A family-oriented, fat weekend of jazz music, food, and historians from around the world celebrating the life of **Louis Armstrong**. The music is traditional, but most of it is free, and New

Orleans mellows out in late summer, making Satchmo all around less stressful (and cheaper!) than your average fest.

WHITE LINEN NIGHT

CBD, Julia Street Arts District and the Contemporary Arts Center, 504-528-3805; cacno.org

The first Saturday in August is hot as hell, so everyone wears white linen as they stroll around sipping wine, checking out art, and socializing. Food is served, hand fans are flappin', and bands play on the street.

SEPTEMBER

BOGALUSA BLUES AND HERITAGE FESTIVAL

Bogalusa, La. (about 75 miles north of N.O.), 625 Willis Ave., 985-205-1075; bogalusablues.com

With a surprising dearth of blues music in the city proper, it might be worth driving an hour away for a day of celebrating the blues and other local music. Features a juried art show, food, and more.

FRIED CHICKEN FESTIVAL

French Quarter, Woldenberg Riverfront Park, 1 Canal St.; friedchickenfestival.com

Two days equals hundreds of different fried chicken recipes, a tenders eating contest, and, ultimately, the Best Fried Chicken award. Two stages of surprisingly hip, high-quality music, plus a third cooking demo stage.

LOUISIANA SHRIMP AND PETROLEUM FESTIVAL

downtown Morgan City, La. (roughly 85 miles southwest of N.O.), 985-385-0703; shrimp-petrofest.org

Ah, what a delicious-sounding combination: shrimp and petroleum. This celebration of the products that keep the Gulf Coast economically afloat features rides, crafts, food, a "Blessing of the Fleet" ceremony, and a water parade.

NEW ORLEANS HORROR FILM FEST

nolahorrorfilmfest.com

A four-day movie festival created by and for indie horror filmmakers, featuring full-length movies, "gore shorts," plus other programs dedicated to different horror sub-genres.

SOUTHERN DECADENCE

French Quarter, Bourbon St., Labor Day weekend; southerndecadence.net

For many, many years this gay outdoor sex party was extreme enough to make Mardi Gras blush—until some religious group pointed out to the city that public sex was against the law, and made the taxpayers spend hundreds of thousands on security for an event at which no one had ever previously been arrested. Decadence still goes off every year, but is now much mellower, at least on its surface—one must assume fun still cooks behind all those tall French Quarter gates. Sunday is still alive with ultra-flamboyant cross-dressers and leather studs, all

Blake Miller of the Revelers performs at the Blackpot Festival, which is worth the drive out of town.

culminating in an excellent drag parade that's fun for everyone (kid friendly, if you aren't a prude!).

SUGAR CANE FESTIVAL

New Iberia, La. (130-odd miles west of N.O.), 337-369-9323; hisugar.org

An example of the Louisiana tendency to push all parties to the max: This 70-year-old free festival celebrating Louisiana's sugar growers (attendees are encouraged to "dress in farmer's attire") includes four days of giant rides and fair games, plus square-dancing presentations, a flower show, a boat parade, fireworks, a special southern mass and authentic blessing of the crop, and of course, "sugar artistry." Numerous Cajun bands are on hand to honor whoever is crowned **King and Queen Sucrose**. And you'll be blessed with the most dynamic, crazy taste of authentic Louisiana jazz and other music.

OCTOBER

BLACKPOT FESTIVAL

Lafayette, La. (about 135 miles west of N.O.), 300 Fisher Rd., 337-233-4077; blackpotfestival.com

Very different than any other festival in the world, Blackpot is officially just a two-day camping festival, but for the entire week beforehand it features not only the basic music and food, but also music lessons for attendees with mega-famous Louisiana musicians, plus cooking lessons and a cook-off of dishes that can be prepared in a black iron pot.

BLUES & BBQ FESTIVAL

CBD, Lafayette Square Park, 540 St. Charles Ave., 504-558-6100; jazzandheritage.org/blues-fest

Outside of the blues tent once a year at **Jazz Fest**, this free, two-day festival is the city's best blues music fix:

big-name blues artists playing all styles from acoustic to electric, plus the city's usual top-shelf festival food.

CARNAVAL LATINO

parade through the French Quarter; carnavalatinola.com

New Orleans has deep Latin roots, and Latin culture has again begun to flourish here ever since Latinos rebuilt the flooded city. Many of them decided to stick around, reenlivening this now twenty-year-old festival that boasts Latin music and food galore—we suggest trying the Honduran *baleada:* like naan (Indian bread), flakey and buttery, topped with beans, eggs, and cheese.

GRETNA HERITAGE FESTIVAL

downtown Gretna (West Bank); gretnafest.com

This three-day West Bank get-down features seven stages of music and over one hundred food choices plus an Italian village, German beer garden, and carnival rides. Recent years have seen headlining sets by ZZ Top, Kiss, and the B52s.

JAPAN FESTIVAL

Mid-City, New Orleans Museum of Art, One Collins C. Diboll Circle, City Park, 504-658-4100

A day full of energizing performances on the steps of one of the city's most gorgeous museums. Kaminari Taiko drummers and other demonstrations punctuate art-making activities and Asian art tours throughout the museum.

LOUISIANA SEAFOOD FESTIVAL

French Quarter, Woldenberg Riverfront Park, 1 Canal St.; louisianaseafoodfestival.com

For three days, local chefs show off their seafood chops. Also features two stages of music, an arts-and-crafts village, cooking demonstrations, and a children's pavilion. Bring your appetite.

PONDEROSA STOMP

ponderosastomp.com

Highlighting the largely unsung architects of rock 'n' roll, this fest began as Stomp creator **Ira "Dr. Ike" Padnos**'s elaborate wedding party, which morphed into a wild bowling alley getdown, and then an ambitious nonprofit organization. Each year, Dr. Ike scrapes the far corners of his musical mind and his rolodex, and digs up obscure old rock, soul, and blues artists and puts them on stage.

ST. TAMMANY PARISH FAIR

Covington, La. (about 40 miles north of N.O.), St. Tammany Parish Fairgrounds, 1304 Columbia St.; sttammanyparishfair.info

Rides, a beauty pageant, animal exhibits, contests, food, a Friday parade, dance team competitions, live music, and even a rodeo.

NEW ORLEANS FILM FESTIVAL

neworleansfilmsociety.org

Kim Welsh

The movie *Flood Streets* premiered at the New Orleans Film Festival in 2008.

Even before the film industry exploded in Louisiana, the New Orleans Film Festival was an impressive, week-long event of screenings, parties, and panels. Celebrating its twenty-eighth anniversary in 2018, the festival continues to showcase more local films than ever.

Although the festival does not specifically seek out local film submissions, there is so much grassroots film activity here that many New Orleans–made features, documentaries, and shorts are getting into this highly selective festival. The organizers have even added an "I Love Louisiana Day" to celebrate this trend.

The **New Orleans Film Society**, which organizes the festival, schedules other film-related events throughout the year, including panels, special screenings, and drive-up "theaters" at abandoned parking lots across town.

The author performs in his band the White Beach at Voodoo Fest.

Michael Patrick Welch

VOODOO MUSIC & ARTS EXPERIENCE

Mid-City, City Park, corner of Esplanade and Carrollton Aves., Halloween weekend; voodoofestival.com

New Orleans' only festival of nationally famous alternative rock bands, the Voodoo Music Experience in City Park makes Halloween weekend in New Orleans just that much more of an event. From **TV on the Radio** to **Nine Inch Nails** to **R.E.M.** to **Kiss** . . . there's even a small **Preservation Hall** tent if you just gotta hear the standards. Voodoo's best quality, though, may be its location in City Park; whereas Jazz Fest puts you in direct contact with the sun for long hours with barely any shelter, much of City Park is shaded by giant oak trees, which also serve to break up the Voodoo crowd and dilute that claustrophobic festival feeling.

FAUX/REAL FESTIVAL

venues all around Bywater/Marigny, 504-941-3640

Evolved from the beloved **New Orleans Fringe Fest,** Faux/Real offers two weeks of top-tier theater and experimental performances, readings, plus liquor and wine tastings and other parties. Performers do their thing at theaters, cabarets, outdoor venues, warehouses, galleries, cafés, bars, and any other outlet that works.

OAK STREET PO-BOY FESTIVAL

Uptown, 8100–8800 Oak St., 504-228-3349; poboyfest.com

A seven-block party in celebration of the mammoth sandwich of French bread and fried seafood or roast beef.

Of course you'll find many more dynamic variations on the cultural staple at this fest, which also hosts two stages of music, over sixty artists, a children's section with games, a po'boy photo booth, and panel discussions covering the po'boy's history.

THANKSGIVING AT FAIR GROUNDS RACE COURSE & SLOTS

Gentilly, 1751 Gentilly Blvd., 504-944-5515; fairgroundsracecourse.com

On many special occasions throughout the year in New Orleans, black people dress to the nines and go out in public. But the one time of the year when a lot of white folks get equally gussied up for the express purpose of showing off is the opening day of horse racing at New Orleans' Fair Grounds (the site of our annual **Jazz & Heritage Festival**). The food is amazing, the drinks are strong, everything's pretty cheap (entry is free!), and every sector of New Orleans humanity is represented. Friendship and holiday love hang thick in the air. Dress mad stylish, and do not forget a special hat of some sort.

TREMÉ CREOLE GUMBO FESTIVAL

Tremé, Armstrong Park, 701 N. Rampart St., 504-558-6100; jazzandheritage.org/treme-gumbo

New Orleans brass band music is the other main dish at this fest (ten brass bands over the course of two days!), while food vendors offer various takes on gumbo, both traditional and brave.

CELEBRATION IN THE OAKS

Mid-City, City Park, 1 Palm Dr., 504-483-9415; neworleanscitypark.com

City Park is one of New Orleans' crown jewels—especially during the holidays. Massive oak trees stand dressed in hundreds of thousands of twinkling lights and displays scattered all throughout City Park's twenty-five acres, including its botanical garden, the **Storyland** park of fairy tale characters, the **Carousel Gardens Amusement Park**, even the putt-putt golf course!

CHRISTMAS BONFIRE PARTY

Vacherie, La. (about 50 miles west of N.O.), Oak Alley Plantation, 3645 Hwy. 18, 225-265-2151; oakalleyplantation.com

Cajun and Creole food, an open bar, dance, and a band-led procession to the levee for bonfire lighting are all included in this event's $125 ticket price.

CHRISTMAS EVE BONFIRES ON THE LEVEE

top of the levee in Lutcher and Gramercy, La. (about 45 miles west of N.O.)

Like a Christmas version of Burning Man: Artists build large wooden structures on the levee, only to later set them ablaze as a sort of lighthouse for the Cajun Santa Claus, Papa Noël. There are designated lots for parking along LA 641, with a short walk to the levee. Synchronized lighting at 7 p.m.; arrive early. Free.

NOLA CHRISTMAS FEST

CBD, Morial Convention Center; NOLAChristmasFest.com

The only time you'll see an ice skating rink (52′ by 140′) in New Orleans. This festival also features rides and inflatables like the Kringle Carousel, Winter Whirl, Amazing Funhouse Maze, and the Snowy Summit Climbing Wall.

WORDS & MUSIC: A LITERARY FEAST IN NEW ORLEANS

French Quarter, 504-586-1609; wordsandmusic.org

Both new and established writers participate in this five-day multi-arts festival sponsored by the **Pirate's Alley Faulkner Society.** The festival evolved from a long weekend of festivities held each year around William Faulkner's birthday, September 24 (Faulkner wrote his first novel, **Soldiers' Pay**, in New Orleans).

NOLA MOMENT

WHERE TO GET NAKED

BIG DICK'S HOUSE OF BIG BOOBS

Marigny/Bywater, Mudlark Public Theatre or else AllWays Lounge, check listings

Intermittently there is also the "DIY strip club" experience at **Big Dick's House of Big Boobs**, which purports to feature "Gender-bending bouncers, auto-fellating performance artists, dozens of glorious glory holes, and the longest C-section scars in the city GUARANTEED!" Guests are encouraged to "bring an act, take off all your clothes, or just watch teenage runaways perform feats of lewd, crude entertainment in a sexual jamboree that would make R. Kelly blush." Genital Portraits, Cuntfessional Booth, Free Sex Advice, and Tarot and Nipple Readings are available, plus special fun hosts and DJs. BDHoBB usually goes down at the **Mudlark Public Theatre** or else **AllWays Lounge**. Don't forget to bring singles!

DRIFTER HOTEL POOL

Mid-City, 3522 Tulane Ave., 504-605-4644; thedrifterhotel.com

This newish hipster hotel is clothing optional above the waist. Drifter also hosts concerts and other events by its pool—live shows here are sporadic, from bands to DJs to fashion shows to the occasional kooky water ballet. The Drifter also provides specialty coffees, fresh frozen cocktails, Japanese beers and sakes, and local wines.

No matter where you go, from San Francisco to Spain, the guide-books always make it seem like consuming goods in a strange new place is one of life's more important cultural experiences. Luckily New Orleans has music. But we also do have scads of shopping options to scratch your capitalist itch.

MAGAZINE STREET HAS EVERYTHING

Just a tiny fraction of the shop signs on Magazine St.

Jonathan Traviesa

There are a few lovely and highly walkable strips of shops here, of which Magazine Street uptown is the most notable—for clothes, antiques, cool odds and ends, not to mention food. The businesses are almost exclusively owned by New Orleanians. Magazine Street is several miles long and shops stand shoulder to shoulder, making for a safe and pretty stroll through the Garden District, with its sprawling mansions and lush foliage. On the Saturday before Mother's Day in May, Magazine Street's shops all stay open till 9 p.m. for a champagne stroll. The rest of the time, all day every day, you'll find the following record stores, thrift stores, T-shirt shops, and tattoo parlors, plus places that offer haircuts, food, and drink:

MAGAZINE ST. RECORD STORES

MUSICA LATINA

1522 Magazine St., 504-299-4227

This jam-packed, one-room shop sells all things Latin, from the musical traditions of Cuba to Argentina to mambo greats, plus mariachi and salsa artists.

PEACHES RECORDS

4318 Magazine St., 504-282-3322; peachesrecordsandtapes.com

Store owner **Shirani Rea** was instrumental in the New Orleans rap and hip-hop scene beginning in 1975 when she opened her original Peaches record store (once a branch of the now-defunct national chain; the Nola outpost, which keeps the original sign, is now indie and, as far as we know, the only one left). Apart from a store, Peaches functioned almost as an office and community center for everyone from **Soulja Slim** to the **Cash Money Crew**. The '90s queen of **No Limit Records**,

Mia X, was supposedly discovered while working at Peaches. Definitely not the cheapest place, but always worth a visit.

SISTERS IN CHRIST

5206 Magazine St., 504-510-4379; sistersinchrist.space

A punk rock, noise, metal, ambient, etc., record store owned by lead singer of Thou **Bryan Funk**, who hires the best local DJs and other music scene denizens to work behind the counter.

MAGAZINE ST. THRIFT STORES

FUNKY MONKEY

3127 Magazine St., 504-899-5587; funkymonkeynola.com

The funnest and hippest used clothing boutique devotes a large space to costumes several times per year. Divided into men's and women's sides, Funky Monkey sells gently used cool clothes and accessories of mostly recent vintage, plus some new pieces, sunglasses, and costume jewelry. The men's side also prints T-shirts to order or with logos of deceased local businesses like **K&B** and **Hubig's Pies**.

MISS CLAUDIA'S VINTAGE CLOTHING & COSTUMES

4204 Magazine St., 504-897-6310; missclaudias.com

Gorgeous, high-quality used dresses, shoes, and boots, plus costumes right when you need them.

NO FLEAS

4228 Magazine St., 504-900-1446; www.la-spca.org/nofleas

This resale shop raises funds for the Louisiana SPCA by selling everything from books to furniture to antiques.

TRASHY DIVA

2048 Magazine St., 504-299-8777; French Quarter, 537 and 712 Royal St., 504-522-4233; trashydiva.com

Begun as a vintage shop in the French Quarter in the mid '90s, Trashy Diva is now the showcase for owner **Candice Gwinn**'s lovely, retro-inspired, original dresses. Done in silk and cotton in a variety of midcentury-style prints, the designs are brand-new versions of the amazing 1940s- and '50s-era styles that are now impossible to find, or cost a grand on eBay. There's also jewelry and a carefully curated selection of bags and shoes (Trashy is the only Frye shoe retailer in town). The French Quarter store also has a boutique dedicated to lingerie and corsets.

MAGAZINE ST. T-SHIRT SHOPS

DEFEND NEW ORLEANS

1101 First St. at Magazine St., 504-941-7010; defendneworleans.com

Prior to the flood, Defend New Orleans was just a tongue-in-cheek logo. But imbued with a new, stronger meaning post-flood, Defend New Orleans garnered mad success, and now hundreds of bathroom mirrors, walls, and cop cars all bear the appropriated Mohawk skull graphic. Defend New Orleans clothing can be purchased at various locations around town in addition to its own store. DNO's website doubles as a community sounding board, hipster video blog, music and events calendar, and ongoing documentary of the same types of local culture featured in this guidebook.

DIRTY COAST

5631 Magazine St.; Marigny, 713 Royal St., 504-324-3745; dirtycoast.com

Founded in 2004, Dirty Coast is the premier brand for clever New Orleans in-jokes printed on T-shirts and stickers sold at many local stores, including Rouses groceries and two different Dirty Coast shops. The company's print styles are reminiscent of Urban Outfitters but depict jokes about beignets, absinthe, and the West Bank. Dirty Coast's products serve as simple billboards of New Orleans pride, encouraging locals and visitors alike to "Be a New Orleanian wherever you are."

Several clever, New Orleans–themed T-shirt shops reside on Magazine St.

Zack Smith

FLEURTY GIRL

632 St. Peter St. and 3117 Magazine St.; fleurtygirl.net

A cute, feminine version of Dirty Coast, with expanded New Orleans inventory beyond T-shirts, including original "Bywater rainboots" graced with fleur de lis, and galvanized buckets adorned with our city's memorable sewerage and water board meter logo. The brand's various locations also offer New Orleans music, books, and other souvenirs.

MAGAZINE ST. TATTOO PARLORS

HELL OR HIGH WATER TATTOO SHOP

2035 Magazine St., 504-309-5411

Veteran guitarist **Tony Barton**, late of psych-rap act **MC Trachiotomy** and downtown R&B group the **Special Men**, opened **Hell or High Water Tattoo Shop** in September 2009. "Mine is more of an old-style New Orleans street shop," says Barton, a Louisiana native. "We do appointments but also walk-ins." His artists vary in style. "We cover all the bases, from neo-traditional, to realistic portraits, to straight, traditional old-school like it came from the '50s, with simple shading and bold outlines."

TATTOOAGOGO

4421 Magazine St., 504-899-8229; tattooagogo.com

This art-focused custom shop draws designs for each client. The school-educated artists vary in style from traditional to Americana to Japanese.

Aidan Gill is the best legal place in town where men can pay for pampering.

IF YOU WANT A HAIRCUT

AIDAN GILL

2026 Magazine St., 504-587-9090;
aidangillformen.com

A sort of manly beauty shop for the refined gentleman, Aidan Gill is a haven for men to repair to while their lady friends shop the block. The barber-shop in the rear offers haircuts and hot-towel shaves with a gratis Scotch on the rocks. The boutique in the front sells high-end shaving products like bone-handled brushes and razors, plus cologne, cuff links, ties, and small books on etiquette and other masculine pursuits.

GOLDEN SHEARS

6008 Magazine St., 504-895-9269

The oldest barbershop currently operating in New Orleans features classic buzz cuts, straight razor shaves, and shoe shines.

STARDUST SALON

1904 Magazine St., 504-525-7777; stardustsalon.com

Almost twenty young, hip stylists to choose from, including owner **Jerry Miller**, who ten years ago walked away from a management position at a clothing store to open his dream salon. Stardust hosts events and sells Bumble and Bumble hair products.

MAGAZINE ST. RESTAURANTS

CASAMENTO'S

4330 Magazine St., 504-895-9761; casamentosrestaurant.com

This old man's oyster bar is only open for lunch, so get down there early for your raw oyster fix. The Big Easy Platter, which feeds 4–6, combines over a dozen fried oysters, a pound of crab claws, a dozen pieces of fish, three dozen shrimp, plus French fries, all for $85.

JUAN'S FLYING BURRITO

2018 Magazine St., 504-569-0000; also 4724 S. Carrollton Ave., 504-486-9950; juansflyingburrito.com

This punk-rock burrito shop stuffs huge California-style burritos for cheap with loud rock 'n' roll in the background and

local art on the walls. There's a branch on Carrollton Avenue in Mid-City that lacks some of the hipster appeal of the original, but the chips and salsa and margaritas remain tremendous.

LILETTE

3637 Magazine St., 504-895-1636; liletterestaurant.com

Simultaneously fancy and casual French bistro. Huge selection of unique and adventurous gourmet options. Open for lunch.

TEE EVA'S

5201 Magazine St., 504-899-8350; tee-evapralines.com

Local culinary icon Tee Eva passed away in 2018 (in the same week as Anthony Bourdain), but her name and her goodies live on. Good snowballs and tasty pies and praline candy. Try the miniature pies—pecan, sweet potato, or creole cream cheese, all just enough for a snack.

MAGAZINE ST. DRINKS

HEY! CAFÉ

4332 Magazine St., 504-891-8682; heycafe.biz

Home base for **Community Records**, this is a great spot for getting news on indie shows, reading in relative peace, or watching the bustling traffic. The servers all help roast the coffee beans so are passionate and knowledgeable, and the in-house stereo is always eclectic and killer.

LE BON TEMPS ROULÉ

*4801 Magazine St., 504-895-8117;
lbtrnola.com*

Amazing music at a li'l hole in the wall, plus a menu that includes basic bar food. Le Bon Temps still hosts **Soul Rebels Brass Band** every Thursday night, and organ player **Joe Krown** every Friday with free oysters on the back patio!

MS. MAE'S

4336 Magazine St., 504-218-8035

Ms. Mae's is not only open 24 hours but was, until recently, famous for $1 drinks and beers *at all times.* Prices have gone up only slightly. Ms. Mae's "Wall of Shame" features photos of people who have fallen victim to the bar's dangerously low-priced drink specials.

NOLA MOMENT

Our dearly departed Veronica Russell knew what was up with thrift stores. We love you, V.

Scott Stuntz

THRIFT SHOPPING WITH ACTRESS VERONICA RUSSELL

Veronica Russell has been an active member of New Orleans' theater and performance community since 1990-something, winning numerous awards for acting and costume design. She performed burlesque and variety under the alias **VeVe laRoux** and was a founding member of both the **Noisician Coalition** and the **Big Easy Rollergirls**. Veronica passed away suddenly of cancer in 2014, leaving us all heartbroken. We have kept and updated the section of this book she once curated. She needed a lot of different clothes for all of those jobs mentioned above, so we asked her where you should go thrift shopping while in town:

STRAIGHT-UP THRIFT STORES

You never know what you will get. But in New Orleans, your basic thrift store is always interesting and funny.

BLOOMIN' DEALS

Uptown, 4645 Freret St., 504-891-1289; bloomindeals.org

Twice-annual "bag sales" where $10 buys you a garbage bag full of whatever fits inside!

BRIDGE HOUSE

Uptown/Hollygrove, 4243 Earhart Blvd., 504-821-2479; bridgehouse.org

New Orleans' most important gendered recovery center is also its best thrift store.

RED, WHITE, AND BLUE

30 minutes away in Harahan, La., 5728 Jefferson Hwy., 504-733-8066; redwhiteandbluethriftstore.com

A little far afield, but the biggest and best on the East Bank of the river. Worth the drive!

CONSIGNMENT

A last-minute evening-gown emergency is more common than you think during Carnival season! These will be more expensive than thrift stores or vintage/costume shops like **Funky Monkey** and **Miss Claudia's**, but still good spots for scoring discount designer duds offa Uptown debs and their moms.

PRIMA DONNA'S CLOSET

Uptown, 1206–1212 St. Charles Ave., 504-522-3327; primadonnascloset.com

Now with a "lagniappe" shop for men!

SWAP

Uptown, 7716 Maple St., 504-304-6025; swapboutique.com

Upscale, featuring many brand-name labels.

BARGAIN CENTER

Bywater, 3200 Dauphine St., 504-948-0007

Bargain Center is one of the coolest junk shops you'll ever visit. Everything from nice clothes to slightly damaged musical equipment to a comprehensive collection of Mardi Gras costumes and paraphernalia.

FIFI MAHONY'S

French Quarter, 934 Royal St., 504-525-4343; fifimahonys.com

Owned by **One Eyed Jacks** club owner **Ryan Hesseling** and his wife **Marcy**, Fifi's is a temple to all things glamorously over-the-top. Need a rhinestone ring the size of a doorknob? Perhaps a bubblegum-pink wig covered in glitter, done up in a three-foot bouffant?

Pancake makeup that'll cover your five o'clock shadow? A favorite of burlesque dancers, drag queens, and Carnival revelers of all stripes, Fifi's is your spot.

LE GARAGE

French Quarter, 1234 Decatur St., 504-522-6639

On the funky strip of lower Decatur, there are also several intriguing antique and junk shops of which Le Garage— so named because of its garage door that yawns open like Aladdin's cave—is one of the longest standing. It has a large stock of Carnival costumes and odd military surplus, plus various quirky objects including movie posters, ceramics, and other treasures and relics.

SHOPPING

PIETY STREET MARKET

Bywater, second Saturday of every month, 11 a.m. to 4 p.m., 612 Piety St., 504-782-2569; 612piety.com/piety-street-market

Located at **Old Ironworks**, home of **Piety Street Sno-Balls**, the market features 40-plus vendors in an expansive indoor/outdoor setting with live acoustic music and great local food. Vendors include creative artists, crafters, vintage and flea market dealers, mix-and-match booths, and sellers of handmade art and garage sale finds. The family-friendly market hosts a lively kids' activity area beneath a shady tree in the

Clothing designer and Piety Street Market maven Cree McCree dresses up noise guitarist Rob Cambre for Mardi Gras.

Cree McCree

courtyard, where a miniature train built by Old Ironworks owner **Gilbert Buras** enchants shoppers of all ages. The market is currently run by **Cree McCree** (Uptown, 504-269-3982), who became a professional flea in 1975 and has taken her cheap but wearable assemblage art, using found objects, garage sale items, and vintage hats, around the country. Author of the how-to guide *Flea Market America: The Complete Guide to Flea Enterprise* (available on Amazon), Cree several times a year opens her home to sell her own line of Halloween cocktail couture (bat bustiers, skeleton bras, and vintage hats festooned with bats, spiders, ravens, and snakes), plus fabulous Mardi Gras headpieces. Otherwise, her wares can be found at **Freret Street Market**, **Broad Street Flea Market & Bazaar**, **Blue Nile Boo-tique** (Sunday before Halloween), and the Blue Nile Mardi Gras Costume Sale (Sunday before Mardi Gras).

MUSICAL INSTRUMENTS

The best-case scenario for you on vacation would be having such a good time that you drink a large daiquiri and end up impulsively buying a new guitar to take home. Visiting musicians, please patronize these independent music shops:

INTERNATIONAL VINTAGE GUITARS

CBD, 1430 Baronne St., 504-442-0696; internationalvintageguitars.com

You won't find many deals here, but there's a lot of gear to drool over, all of it well maintained. Deep cuts as far as both guitars and amps.

Mountain of Wizard guitarist Paul Webb fixing someone else's guitar at his Bywater Music shop.

Jonathan Traviesa

DOWNTOWN MUSIC/UPTOWN MUSIC EXCHANGE

Downtown, 527 Dumaine St., 504-358-3100; Uptown, 739 Octavia St., 2nd Floor, 504-891-7670; dmnola.com

This locally owned shop buys, sells, trades, and consigns musical instruments. Who knows what famous local musician's axe you might find on offer? Also offering lessons.

WEBB'S BYWATER MUSIC

Bywater, 3217 Burgundy St., 504-304-5965

The first music store in recent mind to take up residence in the musicians' haven that is Bywater. **Paul Webb**—of metal bands **Spickle**, **Hawg Jaw**, **Mountain of Wizard**, and **Classhole**—worked for many years at the New Orleans Music Exchange, which didn't fix guitars. Now at his own shop, Webb will do anything for any musician. We have a distinct memory of Webb, one Mardi Gras, dressed as Jesus, carrying an electric guitar he'd built, shaped like a raw wood crucifix—so, surely he could do whatever simple thing you needed. Open at noon.

Guitarist Tony Barton, owner of Hell or High Water Tattoos on Magazine St.

Zack Smith

TATTOO PARLORS

ELECTRIC LADYLAND

Marigny, 610 Frenchmen St.,
504-947-8286;
electricladylandtattoo.com

Located among Frenchmen's many awesome music clubs, this is a real clean, laid-back den of talented people, named "Best Place to Get a Tattoo" ten times by *Gambit Weekly.*

UPTOWN TATTOOS

Uptown, 575 S. Carrollton Ave.,
504-866-3859

Near the university, this place is old-style traditional. Worth a visit just to see the attached machine shop, which creates fancy, handcrafted, custom-built tattoo machines.

HAIR SALONS

SHOPPING

BOUFFANT BEAUTY

Uptown, 802 Nashville Ave.,
504-894-8099

Fair prices, good conversation, precision haircuts, custom color, event styling, texture management, and barbering.

IN THE MASTER'S HANDS SALON AND SPA

Gentilly, 3810 Elysian Fields Ave.,
504-943-8873;
inthemastershands.com

A popular multicultural neighborhood hair salon for thirty-five years.

ROCKET SCIENCE BEAUTY BAR

Marigny, 640 Elysian Fields Ave.,
504-218-8982; rocketsciencenola.com

If you want to treat yourself, this funky, hip Marigny shop offers every service imaginable for both men and women.

SAVAGE BEAUTY

Bywater, 3212 Burgundy St.,
504-729-7334;
savagebeautysalon.com

In the early 2000s, **Jo Starnes** learned hair and makeup working at **Fifi Mahony's** in the Quarter before training at a high-end Manhattan salon. Feeling that New Orleans street fashion provided a better home for her individual voice, she moved back to cut hair at **R Bar** (1431 Royal St.) and **Pal's Lounge** (949 N. Rendon St.) before breaking off on her own in 2010. Starnes offers personalized and affordable hair coloring, texture-changing processes, and manicures. Women's cuts are $60, men's $30.

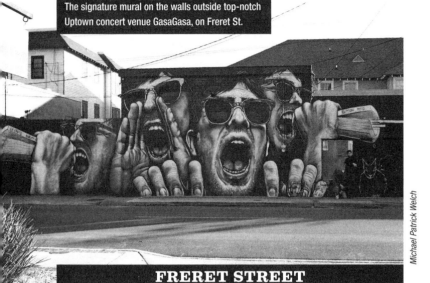

The signature mural on the walls outside top-notch Uptown concert venue GasaGasa, on Freret St.

Michael Patrick Welch

FRERET STREET

thenewfreret.com

In recent years, the commercial corridor of **Freret Street** has experienced a renaissance of small businesses and new food options. After some promised post-flood aid money failed to materialize, entrepreneurs in the area decided to rebuild their community themselves. Zoning as an arts-and-entertainment district allowed locals to start a monthly market that quickly brought a lot of positive attention to the area, along with a slew of independent, locally owned restaurants, bars, and other shops. A walk from Jefferson Avenue to Napoleon now offers snowballs, garden supplies, haircuts, auto repair, coffee, cocktails, and two types of pizza. Couched in a diverse Uptown neighborhood, Freret continues to evolve. **Freret Market** of crafts, food, and bands happens on the first Saturday of the month, while the all-day **Freret Street Festival** (first Saturday in April) that began in the 1990s still hosts food and beer vendors, puppet shows, kids' activities, and local music. Today there's still something essentially soulful and a little bit Caribbean about these blocks, even if Tulane and Loyola kids are ever-present.

Here are a just a few of Freret Street's great shops:

CRESCENT CITY COMICS

*4916 Freret St., 504-891-3796; also
3135 Calhoun St., 504-309-2223;
crescentcitycomics.com*

Without a doubt, the best selection of comics and graphic novels in the city.

CURE

*4905 Freret St., 504-302-2357;
curenola.com*

Pricey little craft-cocktail lounge for mixology fans and celebrity spotters.

GASA GASA

*4920 Freret St., 504-338-3567;
gasagasa.com*

A main player in the revamping of Freret Street into a low-key entertainment district, Gasa Gasa is the city's nicest small club, hosting mostly touring rock, electronic, out jazz, and experimental music.

MIDWAY PIZZA

*4725 Freret St., 504-322-2815;
midwaypizzanola.com*

Specializing in deep-dish, Midway is the rare noncorporate pizza joint with a lunch buffet. Open till midnight.

SARITA'S GRILL

4520 Freret St., 504-324-3562

The owners are Cuban, but the menu tackles all foods Latin from tacos to rice bowls to pressed sandwiches.

15. PARKS, SPORTS, AND OTHER FAMILY FUN

Do we recommend you bring your kids to New Orleans? Yes, if 1) you've already been here at least once before to enjoy it as an adult; 2) you're okay with not getting as drunk as you did that time; and 3) the only time you flash folks is when you're breast-feeding. If you meet these requirements, then, yes, your kids can get as much of a kick out of this beautiful, crazy place as you do. That is, if your trip is tightly curated. Here's a head start:

PARKS

Some of New Orleans' parks are very elaborate and fun (and sell booze), while others are simple places to lie in the grass and chill (and drink booze). Or else ride horses, paddle canoes, and other forms of relaxing play.

Armstrong Park (named after Louie) sits just across from the French Quarter in the Tremé.

Jonathan Traviesa

AUDUBON PARK

Uptown, 6500 Magazine St.,
1-866-ITS-AZOO;
auduboninstitute.org

Designed by the same fellow who did Central Park, this bird-oriented jogging park (where people ride horses!) leads you around a beautiful moat full of giant white egrets, ibis, and other feathered species. Or if captive animals are more your thing, there's a zoo, and **Cascade Stables**, where the kids can take a riding lesson or just gawk at the show ponies.

BAYOU SAUVAGE NATIONAL WILDLIFE REFUGE

New Orleans East;
fws.gov/bayousauvage/

Fifteen minutes from the Quarter, you can take a stroll along a boardwalk that carries you into the bayou. Yes, there are gators and wild boar lurking, but mostly you get the feeling of life in the odd world of Louisiana swamps. Birders and kids love it, and the road there carries you past **Versailles**, the Vietnamese village that offers great bakeries and banh mi joints.

CITY PARK

Mid-City, 1 Palm Dr. (corner of
Esplanade and Carrollton),
504-482-4888;
neworleanscitypark.com

This grand old park, which houses the **New Orleans Museum of Art** (and its amazing sculpture garden) is also home to many remarkably gigantic oak trees.

Also on the vast shady grounds: tennis courts, an old but operating minitrain, and the kiddie park **Storyland**, with its antique merry-go-round and miniature roller coaster, among other rides (plus low-key to-go beers and drinks for the parents).

THE FLY

Uptown, Riverview Dr.,
Audubon Park

In back of **Audubon Park**, this uptown river levee, known as The Fly, hosts a series of picnic areas and sports fields where, on nice days, hordes of college students and girls in bikinis play Frisbee, sunbathe, drink, and smoke weed. During mellower times it's one of the city's nicest breezy places (New Orleans doesn't get many breezes) to view the Mississippi, sip wine, and watch the giant barges float by.

LAFAYETTE SQUARE PARK

CBD, 500 St. Charles Ave.

A beautiful patch of foliage and public art amid New Orleans' tallest buildings. This is where the free **Concert in the Park** series is held Thursdays in the spring, as well as the **Harvest the Music** free concert series each Thursday in the fall. Both series cater to more touristy notions of New Orleans music (you will almost surely hear "When the Saints Go Marching In"), even though most concert attendees are locals just getting off work. If you're visiting, however, it may be the best part of your and your kids' trip.

FAMILY FUN

WASHINGTON PARK

Marigny, corner of Frenchmen St. and Royal St.

This "no dogs allowed" park functions as the Marigny's official dog park. Go figure. Along with some intermittent small annual events (**Saints and Sin-** ners literary fest in May, **Pride Fest** in June) and truly interesting public art (including **Marcus Brown**'s interactive sound sculpture, HUMs), one can also witness fauxbeaux practicing juggling, hula-hoop tricks, and other mild acrobatics.

LOCAL SPORTS

Teams you can watch (while possibly drinking beer):

BABY CAKES BASEBALL

Metairie, La., 6000 Airline Dr., 504-734-5155; milb.com

Since this book's last edition, our baseball team the Zephyrs changed their name and logo to the Baby Cakes. From April to August, witness the Baby Cakes' truly creepy giant baby mascot and a not half-bad baseball team. The stadium resides in the not-far-away burbs of Metairie. Zephyr tickets are cheap, with lots of special deals and giveaways and live bands, plus fireworks after every game.

FRIDAY NIGHT FIGHTS GYM (BOXING)

Central City, 1632 Oretha Castle Haley Blvd., 504-895-1859

Mike Tata has trained fighters around the globe and carries the swagger of a man unafraid to set up shop and put on a spectacle. His Friday Night Fights series take place monthly with ring girls, live bands, and beer (which you bring yourself)—with lots of show biz surrounding the above-average amateur bouts. Tata's running banter from the DJ table is well worth the ticket price.

NEW ORLEANS LADIES ARM WRESTLING (NOLAW)

check website for club (often 12 Mile Limit); nolaw.org

NOLAW hosts tournaments every other month that combine WWE-style entourages, costumed performers who try to tear their opponents' arms off, and serious post-match dance parties. Wild half-time shows and celebrity judges round out your full night of matriarchal mayhem. Best two out of three matches wins. All proceeds benefit worthy women-focused causes in the metropolitan area.

NEW ORLEANS PELICANS

CBD, New Orleans Arena, 1501 Girod St., 504-525-4667; nba.com/pelicans

October through April, watch New Orleans' own NBA team, the Pelicans (formerly the Hornets), shoot hoops at the New Orleans Arena. Tickets range from $15 to $1,700.

NOLAW: New Orleans Ladies Arm Wrestling

Katrina Arnold

BIG EASY ROLLERGIRLS

Lakefront, 6801 Franklin Ave.; bigeasyrollergirls.com

The Big Easy Rollergirls roll it up.

Scott Stuntz

New Orleans' highly popular contribution to the now well established national trend of that extreme girlie sport. The players escribe their brand of flat-track roller derby racing as "burlesque meets the X Games meets WWE." The league consists of three teams: the **Confederacy of Punches**, the **Crescent Wenches**, and the **Storyvillains**. They even have their own pinup calendar of big leggy blondes in short shorts crashing against petite redheaded schoolgirls, and every other foxy female archetype on eight wheels.

Roller derby is not unlike being in a band—except way more work, with less drinking. The girls' intensely athletic practices occur early on weekend mornings, meaning the skaters can't really party much. If they miss practice, they're canned. On the days bouts occur, the ladies spend entire mornings and afternoons decorating the venue and laying down their own special track. Several hundred New Orleanians fill the bleachers at the girls' brawls. A top-quality local rock band begins every event, and also provides entertainment for halftime, when most of the audience is drunk and howling for chick blood.

They skate and fight at top energy for a couple of hours, and then when the huge crowd finally leaves, having been totally rocked, the girls remove their skates to load everything back into the truck.

All this to say: in no way is roller derby for wimps. Sit in the front row and maybe you'll get some of their hard-earned sweat on you. Season runs almost all year round. Bouts take place at the University of New Orleans' Human Performance Center, by Lake Pontchartrain, on the corner of Leon C. Simon Drive and Elysian Fields Avenue.

NEW ORLEANS SAINTS

CBD, 1500 Sugar Bowl Dr., 504-587-3663; neworleanssaints.com

Win or lose, New Orleanians love dem Saints, our beleaguered boys in black and gold. Even if you dislike sports, Saints games are a great excuse to party NOLA. Outside of the completely refurbished Superdome, you'll be swept up in a parade of football-frenzied fans, some in elaborate costumes, almost all toting beer and daiquiris. Inside, you'll be treated to impromptu performances by jazz bands that roam the stands and a crowd that so completely understands what it means to lose that its ability to celebrate victory is unparalleled. Add in a ticket price below the NFL average and you win, whether or not the Saints do.

WILDKAT WRESTLING

Various suburban high school gyms. Check the website for times and locations: wildkatwrestling.com

In the '80s and '90s, the WWE pretty much killed off our otherwise healthy network of independent southern pro wrestling. Lately, that local phenomenon has returned, helmed by big and professional Wildkat Wrestling. Proprietor and touring wrestler **Luke Hawx** is the real deal and totally looks the part. He busts his ass not only putting on hilarious, thrilling local events, but in developing wrestlers at his Wildkat Gym. Hawx books his wrestlers gigs in other states, where they meet outside wrestlers who then travel to New Orleans to fight at WildKat matches. So, it's not unfair to say that Hawx has singlehandedly brought back independent American wrestling, even on a touring level. All his matches are PG (though Hawx sometimes hosts a rare XXX night in a bar, with blood).

MORE FAMILY FUN

AQUARIUM OF THE AMERICAS

French Quarter, 1 Canal St., 504-861-2537; auduboninstitute.org/aquarium

Not a very New Orleansy thing to do on your trip to New Orleans, since every city has an aquarium now. Still, ours is pretty nice, with a focus on Gulf Coast wildlife—you can't argue with albino alligators and big sharks. To Mom and/or Dad, we recommend hitting the downstairs IMAX snackbar at the start of your aquarium tour, so you'll have a daiquiri to sip while walking around.

AUDUBON INSECTARIUM

CBD, 423 Canal St., 504-861-2537; auduboninstitute.org/insectarium

This insect attraction opened in 2008 and has been heartily embraced by New Orleans parents. Along with learning about bugs, you can touch some, walk among them in a butterfly garden, even eat crispy Cajun crickets and grasshopper chutney in the **Crit-**

ter Café. Just don't lead off with, "Hey kids! Wanna go eat bugs?" Closed on Mondays.

CELEBRATION IN THE OAKS

December; Mid-City, City Park, 1 Palm Dr., 504-482-4888; neworleanscitypark.com

During the holidays, the already gorgeous City Park is thoroughly decked out with acres of illuminated Christmas tableaux (some with hilarious Cajun themes), various school displays, and sporadic live music. **Storyland** and the **Carousel Gardens Amusement Park** are both open at night featuring rides and food, with the addition of hot buttered rum and wine for moms and dads.

FAUBOURG MARIGNY HOME TOUR

Mid-May; starts at Washington Square Park, 700 Elysian Fields Ave., 888-312-0812; faubourgmarigny.org

This big, fun self-guided walking tour lets you into the Marigny neighborhood's most magnificent historic and post-Katrina renovated homes and gardens. The event starts at 10 a.m. with a kids' activity area (kids under 12 tour free) and an art market showcasing local art, photography, jewelry, home furnishings, and more. The tour now also stops in the **Den of Muses**, where visitors can see colorful and bawdy floats being made and painted. Tickets are $15 in advance.

FRERET MARKET

Uptown, intersection of Freret St. and Napoleon Ave.; freretmarket.org

On the first Saturday of each month (except June, July, and August). If the petting zoo in the elaborate Kid Zone isn't enough, the Humane Society also brings dozens of cute dogs and cats. Somewhere in there is usually some free roller derby as well! Two hundred local vendors and restaurants are represented, plus four stages of local music like **Big Sam's Funky Nation**, **Tin Men**, **Debauche**, and **Free Agents Brass Band**.

LOUISIANA CHILDREN'S MUSEUM

CBD, 420 Julia St., 504-523-1357; lcm.org

Smack in the middle of the **Julia Street Arts District**, this 30,000-square-foot playground for kids' bodies and minds is an essential part of any child's visit to New Orleans. Among a million other things, LCM offers a kids' spelunking wall, astronomy demonstrations, a miniature New Orleans grocery store, live kids' music, plus continuous art and music classes and other special events such as Winnie the Pooh's birthday, done New Orleans–style.

MARDI GRAS WORLD

CBD, 1380 Port of New Orleans Pl., 504-475-2056; mardigrasworld.com

Many of Carnival's mainstream floats are built at the incredibly colorful, outsized studio of **Blaine Kern**, the world's leading makers of float sculp-

Michael Patrick Welch

The author's daughter, Cleopatra, plays outside the Old Point Bar (but not all the time!).

tures and props. Giant grinning heads, giant mythological beings, giant crabs and crawfish—everything GIANT. As close as a kid may come to Charlie's Chocolate Factory. Plus, visitors get to try some king cake—all year round!

MUSIC BOX VILLAGE

Bywater, 4557 N. Rampart St.; musicboxvillage.com

A collection of twelve interactive "musical houses," the Music Box is like a steam-punk version of a children's museum. Guests stomp on loud, creaky floors, bang on percussive walls, and tweak soundwaves that carry across the property. Parents will love the small but sweet assortment of wine, beer, and cocktails always available, with proceeds going to support New Orleans Airlift. Tickets are very cheap, but the weekly Saturday market gives you and the kids a free chance to check out the Music Box as well as dozens

of visual artists, artisans, clothing makers, and the like. Though you will be tempted to let the kids run free, the Music Box is definitely not intended as a playground, and they do require a minimum of one adult per three children. The Music Box and New Orleans Airlift also provide lots of adventurous education opportunities for local school kids and are worthy causes for donations.

NOMA EGG HUNT

March; Mid-City, City Park, Sculpture Garden at the New Orleans Museum of Art, One Collins C. Diboll Circle, 504-658-4100; noma.org

The **Sydney and Walda Besthoff Sculpture Garden** at NOMA should be on your list anyway, but in March the garden's Easter egg hunt draws hundreds of friendly local families to its petting zoo, spacewalks, face-painting booths, and other arts and crafts activities.

RUSSIAN FESTIVAL FOR CHILDREN

April; Kenner, Rivertown Theaters for the Performing Arts, 325 Minor St., 504-461-9475; rivertowntheaters.com

Little princesses will love this event's **Jefferson Ballet Theatre** performance of the 1938 version of *Cinderella,* by Russian writer Evgeny Shvarts.

ZOO TO DO FOR KIDS

April; Uptown, Audubon Zoo, 6500 Magazine St., 504-581-4629; auduboninstitute.org

You wouldn't think kids would need even more to do while at the zoo, but when the weather is nice in April, Audubon Zoo spends a couple days transformed into a giant playland with face painters, live music, inflatable structures, crafts, and a video game center.

NOLA MOMENT

A NEW ORLEANS DADDY DAY WITH HISTORICAL GEOGRAPHER RICHARD CAMPANELLA

Circuitous Crescent City Perambulations to Keep Toddlers Active, Edified, and Entertained

Along with being a celebrated author and local historian, Richard Campanella is an active dad of a six-year-old boy. Below, Campanella has mapped out for you a circuit of low-key neighborhood spots on a continuous stroll of interesting scenes. Or as he puts it "rambling routes for peripatetic parents and their rambunctious progeny":

The Downtown Playground Crawl (4 miles, 4 hours):
   Start at the **French Market**—always lots to see there. Make your way down to the **Old U.S. Mint** (400 Esplanade Avenue); the exhibits are free, as is the air conditioning, and the clean, empty restrooms are the French Quarter's best-kept secret. Surrounding this historic building are grassy lawns and benchlike walls, all kid-friendly and toy-condu-

Richard Campanella's son Jason maps out a day with his dad in the Crescent City.

cive, and at least once every few months, there's a festival on these grounds.

Cross North Peters Street and make your way to **Crescent Park**, by means of an elevator or steep staircase over the **Public Belt Railroad**. You'll get great views of the French Quarter and Faubourg Marigny as well as the Mississippi River, while junior will marvel at the choo-choo trains below.

Descend to the covered **Mandeville Street Wharf,** where on select weekends you may come upon farmer's markets or other events. Make your way along Crescent Park, which as of 2017 extends nearly two miles downriver. At the **Piety Street Wharf**, walk out over the river and see ships, wakes, interesting bankside stuff, and what my son calls "the broken choo-choo tracks"––old collapsing wharves where yard engines once serviced cargo ships arriving from Central American banana plantations. If your timing's right, you'll see the steamboat **Natchez**, various oceangoing freighters, and, if it's late afternoon on a Saturday or Sunday, one of the gigantic cruise ships making its way to Cozumel.

At this point, you can either cross over the aptly nicknamed "Rusty Rainbow" pedestrian bridge into the neighborhood of Bywater (you'll find a couple of eateries and a Saturday morning flea market on the other side), or continue for another half-mile along Crescent Park. I recommend the latter.

Exit Crescent Park and loop back along either Chartres or Royal. Note the circa-1826 **Lombard Plantation House** on Chartres, the last antebellum plantation house on the Mississippi River within the East Bank of Orleans Parish. There are some lunch spots in the vicinity, including **The Joint** BBQ restaurant (701 Mazant St.), and you may want to stop at the neighborhood Alvar Library (913 Alvar St.).

From there make your way toward **Markey Park** on Royal, which has the first of the three playgrounds on our excursion. The neighborhood kids make for friendly playmates. Afterwards, you can walk over to **Pizza Delicious** (617 Piety St.) and get lunch.

Now head over to Dauphine Street, where you will find a couple of weird bric-a-brac stores and sneering hipsters (tell junior to sneer right back at them) at **Frady's** corner store or the **Satsuma Café** (3218 Dauphine St.), where you can use the restroom and order nothing. Continue up Dauphine and explore **Clouet Gardens** (710 Clouet St.), a "tactical urbanism" intervention on the part of local meliorists, and the circa-1865 **Blessed Francis Xavier Seelos Catholic Church**, which is sometimes open and has a pleasant fountain and grotto.

Continue across the Press Street railroad tracks—great train spotting—and on the other side check out some weekend markets and urban gardens associated with **NOCCA**, which also runs an eatery (**Press Street Station**) and art gallery there.

Continue up any street toward Elysian Fields Ave. and **American Aquatic Gardens** (621 Elysian Fields Ave.), a private garden store that feels like a botanical garden. Else, head across Elysian Fields to **Washington Park**, where you will find the second of our three playgrounds. Relax here on the shady benches, among shady characters, and you can find coffee and snacks on nearby Frenchmen Street.

Continue up Royal Street across Esplanade into the quiet residential end of the Quarter; on weekend afternoons, it's a wonderful place to be. Make a right at Barracks and walk two blocks toward Dauphine Street, where you'll find the third playground—**Cabrini Park**. Be sure to enjoy the gardens, some of which appear right out of a French village. Also walk past the remarkable **Ossorno House** (913 Governor Nicholls St.), which was originally built as a rural plantation house along Bayou St. John until it was disassembled and moved into city limits in the 1780s.

There's lots more to do from here: perhaps there's a festival at nearby **Armstrong Park** and **Congo Square**, five blocks up North Rampart Street, or you might want to work your way back to Royal, Chartres, or Decatur Street, known for its curio shops and gutterpunks.

This will take you to famous **Jackson Square**, where it's always fun to hear musicians or chase pigeons and look at art. By this time, junior might be ready for a nap on a park bench, and you might be too.

FAMILY FUN

16. HOTELS AND LEGITIMATE BED & BREAKFASTS

Since we live here, we had to do a lot of research and make many calls in order to find you some nice places to stay that aren't too expensive—and in the summer, you need a pool! We've also included a few fancier, special places to lay your head. The prices of all New Orleans B&Bs fluctuate depending on festivals and other holidays (except at certain places like **Annabelle's House**), with the lowest prices during the summer. We've rated these vaguely, between **$** and **$$$**.

NOLA MOMENT

LOCAL WRITER JULES BENTLEY ON THE PROBLEM OF SHORT-TERM RENTALS IN NEW ORLEANS

When one visits New Orleans, there is of course the question of where to stay. Short-term rentals are attractive for a number of reasons, but by choosing one you make yourself an actor in a tragic, ongoing, and deeply racist pattern of mass displacement.

Short-term rentals are killing our city. Because New Orleanians are mostly quite poor and New Orleans is a tourist economy, renting a home to tourists a few days a month is more profitable than renting it long-term to a New Orleanian. This means that short-term rentals are replacing homes, and displacing New Orleanians—overwhelmingly, the same New Orleanians who made New Orleans what it is.

Have you heard of the Tremé? It was for centuries the heart of black New Orleans and New Orleans music. Now that its former homes are short-term rentals, a vital creative line stretching back through generations has been severed. The links are broken, the lineage sundered, and the legacy lost.

All the elements that draw tourists to New Orleans are products of black labor—but black folks are disproportionately among those displaced from New Orleans by floods, $2.09 hourly tourist-economy wages, and short-term rentals' sinister "disruption" of housing availability. Notice, as you browse the short-term rental websites, the complexions of the hosts in this historically black city. They're overwhelmingly white. These vultures pimp out (promised) access to our culture while actively destroying it; they are a driving force in the disenfranchisement and displacement of New Orleans' culture creators.

The situation is increasingly desperate. We're in the final throes of a terminal housing crisis; whole blocks of the Marigny and Bywater are already Airbnb ghost towns. If you rent an Airbnb, especially from a white host, you are choosing to participate in this unfolding crime.

Consumer choices will never undo capitalism's cruelty, but when something we claim to love is dying, mightn't we at least refrain from disporting in its blood? Mightn't we at least resist deliberately wetting our hands in the gore and daubing our faces as a component of a fun vacation? If you care at all about New Orleans, I would ask you to prove it by patronizing one of our many superb guesthouses or hotels, not a short-term rental.

HOTELS

1870 BANANA COURTYARD

French Quarter, 1422 N. Rampart St., 504-947-4475/800-842-4748; bananacourtyard.com

Each antique-appointed room has its own name in this 1870s house a half-block from the Quarter. The back relaxation area is tropical, and the veranda hosts a hammock and a porch swing—stoop-sitting being a big New Orleans pastime. **$$**

ACE HOTEL NEW ORLEANS

600 Carondelet Street, 504-900-1180; acehotel.com

Sleek, clean modern rooms above a rocking little progressive live music club downstairs (far enough downstairs you won't hear bass in your sleep). Choose from several different menus (Seaworthy serves salty raw oysters) and several different bars (including the poolside, rooftop bar, Alto), all in one beautiful, modern building. **$$$**

ANNABELLE'S HOUSE BED AND BREAKFAST

Uptown, 1716 Milan St.,
504-344-0938

This 52-room Victorian mansion has three guest rooms. Continental breakfast includes fresh waffles. **$$**

AULD SWEET OLIVE BED AND BREAKFAST

Marigny, 2460 N. Rampart St.,
877-470-5323; sweetolive.com

The former owner, an artist who worked in set design on many famous movies shot in New Orleans, transformed the Sweet Olive into a work of live-in art. The website brags, "Around each corner is another visual treat." New owners now thoughtfully curate the former owner's works. **$$**

AVENUE INN BED AND BREAKFAST

Uptown, 4125 St. Charles Ave.,
1-800-490-8542; avenueinnbb.com

This 1891 Thomas Sully mansion is located in the shopping district that Magazine Street has become. It's steps from the streetcar line and just off Lee Circle, home of the **Circle Bar**, one of the best (and smallest) clubs in the city. **$$**

B&W COURTYARDS BED AND BREAKFAST

Marigny, 2425 Chartres St.,
800-585-5731; bandwcourtyards.com

This award-winning restoration job consists of three nineteenth-century buildings connected by courtyards, and features a Jacuzzi, massages if you need them, and a continental breakfast. **$$**

BALCONY GUEST HOUSE

Marigny, 2483 Royal St.,
504-810-8667;
balconyguesthouse.com

This B&B is located above Silk Road restaurant and wine bar (formerly Schiro's), serving unique Indian-Asian-Creole cuisine. The rooms are homey, not fancy. The real plus here is location: a laundromat next door, two great coffee shops nearby, a half-dozen great nighttime hangouts (some with live music). So much entertainment, you may forget about Frenchmen Street and the Quarter just blocks away. **$$**

FRENCH QUARTER MANSION BOUTIQUE HOTEL

French Quarter, 730 Dumaine St.,
504-525-9949;
frenchquartermansion.com

The former "Biscuit Palace" in the heart of the Quarter has very reasonable rates and can't be beat for its geographic centrality. It's located inside a historic Creole mansion with a fading, ancient ad for Uneeda biscuits painted on the side. Rooms are still old-style New Orleans Storyville swank, and some have wrought-iron balconies overlooking Dumaine Street. **$$**

BURGUNDY
BED AND BREAKFAST

*Bywater, 2513 Burgundy St.,
504-261-9477; theburgundy.com*

The Burgundy welcomes straight folks, but it is definitely gayish. It is nice, and clean, with fascinating southern antiques, and though you can't smoke inside, outside you are welcome to sunbathe nude—an option that really should appeal to anyone. **$$**

BYWATER BED & BREAKFAST

Bywater, 1026 Clouet St., 504-944-8438; bywaterbnb.com

This rose-colored double shotgun offers, among the usual amenities, a library of books about New Orleans and a CD collection of Louisiana music, plus a sweet back patio with ceiling fan—perfect for reading whilst drinking. **$$**

CATAHOULA HOTEL

CBD, 914 Union St., 504-603-2442; catahoulahotel.com

This Peruvian-themed, 35-room boutique downtown hotel keeps it casual, cozy, and human. The hotel lounge doubles as a coffee shop and a pisco bar, celebrating Peruvian cocktail culture. There is also Peruvian cuisine like ceviche and lomo saltado (stir-fried beef) to be eaten while enjoying rooftop terrace views of both the French Quarter and the Superdome. **$$$**

CHEZ PALMIERS
BED AND BREAKFAST

*Marigny, 1744 N. Rampart St.,
504-324-4059; chezpalmiers.com*

Just two blocks from the French Quarter and four blocks from Frenchmen Street, Palmiers is like staying with friends. Meaning, you make your own bed. Breakfast is included, but otherwise you're left to your privacy. **$$**

CHIMES BED
AND BREAKFAST

Uptown/Garden District, 1146 Constantinople St., 504-899-2621; chimesneworleans.com

Each room boasts a private entrance, a private bath, and grand French doors opening onto a tropical courtyard. Following a continental breakfast of freshly baked local pastries, walk two blocks and hop the St. Charles streetcar, or grab the Magazine Street bus line through the shopping district and directly to the French Quarter. **$$$**

A CREOLE COTTAGE

*Marigny, 1827 Dauphine St.,
504-495-8970; acreolecottage.com*

This circa-1810 Creole cottage sits just one block from Bourbon Street and two blocks from Frenchmen. The one rental unit boasts a living room, bedroom, bathroom, and kitchen with a refrigerator for all the leftovers you will inevitably have after visiting our gluttonous restaurants. **$$**

The Drifter isn't ideally located (unless you like isolation, in which case it is), but it does have a great coffee shop and bar, and a topless-optional pool that hosts bands, DJs, and other entertainment.

Nicole Franzen for Design Hotels™

CREOLE GARDENS AND GUESTHOUSE BED & BREAKFAST

CBD, 1415 Prytania St., 866-569-8700; creolegardens.com

More like a hotel, with 24 guest rooms; large enough to host weddings. Located a block from the streetcar, and dog friendly with a dog park around the corner. Creole Gardens also provides a full southern breakfast. **$$**

CREOLE INN

Marigny, 2471 Dauphine St., 504-941-0243; creoleinn.com

In this unassuming little Marigny cottage, the double suites all have two private bedrooms, rather than just one room with two beds like a hotel. No breakfast, but the beds are memory foam. Oooh. "Quiet hour" after 9:30. **$$**

CRESCENT CITY GUEST HOUSE

Marigny, 612 Marigny St., 877-281-2680; crescentcitygh.com

This pet-friendly guesthouse is sweetly located in the Marigny, so close to the Quarter you can hear the calliope playing on the Mississippi from your hot tub (actually, you can hear that thing's drunken hoot from almost anywhere in the city). Also features an enclosed sunbathing area, and gated off-street parking. **$$**

DAUPHINE HOUSE

Marigny, 1830 Dauphine St., 504-940-0943; dauphinehouse.com

Not the most bohemian of places, just your basic, excellently restored two-story pre–Civil War house with 12-foot ceilings and hardwood floors. Rooms each feature a private bath, small refrigerator, microwave, wireless internet, etc. Continental breakfast is left in your room. **$$**

THE DRIFTER

Mid-City, 3522 Tulane Ave.,
504-605-4644; thedrifterhotel.com

This newish hipster hotel hosts concerts and other events by its pool—enough said! In the mornings, the Drifter provides specialty coffees before transitioning into fresh frozen cocktails, Japanese beers and sakes, and local wines. Rooms are sleek and basic. **$$$**

EMPRESS HOTEL

Tremé, 1317 Ursulines Ave.,
504-529-4100;
empresshotelneworleans.com

The bare minimum (see the works of Bukowski for similar boardinghouses). But all 36 rooms are just a very short (and slightly sketchy) two-block walk from the French Quarter. This may be your place, if you enjoy unseemly adventure. **$**

FAIRCHILD HOUSE BED AND BREAKFAST

Uptown, 1518 Prytania St.,
504-524-0154/800-256-8096;
fairchildhouse.com

Courtyard for small weddings, with a minister available if you get that drunk during your visit. Walking distance to the streetcar, which will take you right to the Quarter. Proprietor speaks Portuguese, English, French, Italian, and Spanish. **$$**

FRENCHMEN HOTEL

Marigny, 417 Frenchmen St.,
504-945-5453; frenchmenhotel.com

Lay your head "30 steps from 14 live music venues" as the website reads, not to mention all the restaurants and shopping you could want. The rooms and suites feature period and contemporary furnishings, some with private balconies. A little pool and deck out back are perfect for sipping cocktails while meeting your temporary neighbors. **$$$**

GREEN HOUSE INN

Uptown/Lower Garden District,
1212 Magazine St.,
504-525-1333/800-966-1303;
thegreenhouseinn.com

Tropical gardens surround a heated saltwater swimming pool and a huge Jacuzzi hot tub. Clothing optional, so adults only. Three blocks from streetcar. **$$**.

HENRY HOWARD

Uptown, 2041 Prytania St.,
504-313-1577;
henryhowardhotel.com

Small enough you could rent out the entire mansion, the Henry Howard (named after the famous Louisiana Irish architect) strives to be a calm Garden District oasis. Its handsome, stylish, and spacious rooms mix vintage and custom furniture with local original artwork. The parlor features a nice bar, and there's a breezy front porch. **$$$**

HOTEL STORYVILLE

Tremé, 1261 Esplanade Ave.,
504-948-4800; hotelstoryville.net

Nine rooms boast colorful, almost Floridian décor. Each has a private dining area. The grand backyard garden features a lighted bamboo patio bar and a reflecting pool. Or else chill and drink and people-watch on the front porch facing gorgeous Esplanade Avenue. Efficiencies now available for single travelers. **$$$**

INDIA HOUSE HOSTEL

Mid-City, 124 S. Lopez St.,
504-821-1904;
indiahousehostel.com

Only American students and foreign travelers are allowed to stay in this amazing big yellow house with its seasonal crawfish boils and "Indian Ocean" swimming pool. Communal rooms and private "Voodoo" and "Bayou" Cajun cabins that sleep two (with communal bathrooms) are super cheap, as are double rooms. **$**

INN ON ST. PETER

French Quarter, 1005 St. Peter St.,
504-524-9232/800-535-7815;
frenchquarterguesthouses.com

Aside from its nicer-than-average price, this tropical brick courtyard with broad iron-lace balconies is exactly what one would expect of a French Quarter hotel. Continental breakfast included. **$$**

LA DAUPHINE BED AND BREAKFAST, RÉSIDENCE DES ARTISTES

Marigny, 2316 Dauphine St.,
504-948-2217; ladauphine.com

La Dauphine's Alec Baldwin Suite features the Louisiana cypress four-poster bed in which Alec made love to Kelly Lynch in the movie *Heaven's Prisoners,* filmed locally. The innkeepers speak Danish, Norwegian, Swedish, Spanish, English, French, and German, and yet state on their website, "We steer clear of the formal, pretentious crowd. We love to host nice, relaxed people who can 'go with the flow.'" Couples or singles only, no children or pets, and a three-night minimum stay is required. **$$**

LAMOTHE HOUSE

Marigny, 621 Esplanade St.,
504-947-1161; lamothehouse.com

This architectural wonder built in 1839 now has a heated Jacuzzi and pool and serves a continental breakfast. 24-hour front desk. **$$$**

LIONS INN

Marigny, 2517 Chartres St.,
800-485-6846; lionsinn.com

Your basic pool, hot tub, and breakfast kitchen, but with a communal piano, "wine hour" every afternoon, and best of all: free use of house bicycles to pedal around town. Between the wine and the bikes, we fully endorse Lion's Inn. **$$**

LOOKOUT INN

Bywater, 833 Poland Ave.,
504-947-8188;
lookoutneworleans.com

Located by the Naval Annex, Lookout Inn is named for its tower, where the Navy/lady boys would keep lookout on the Mississippi during World War II. Choose from the Mission Suite, the Elvis Suite, the Mardi Gras Suite, or the Bollywood Suite, all 500 square feet. Lookout also has an awesome little saltwater pool and Jacuzzi. Though you're deep in the neighborhood, it's a great spot for killer restaurants (**The Joint BBQ, Jack Dempsey's** fried seafood) and dive bars like **BJ's** and the inimitable **Vaughan's**. Closed from June to September (the best months for having a pool). **$$**

MAISON DE MACARTY GUESTHOUSE

Bywater, 3820 Burgundy St.,
504-267-1564; maisonmacarty.com

One of Bywater's few guesthouses, this historic Victorian-style building across the street from the country's first World War I monument was once part of the Chevalier de Macarty plantation. In January 2012, new owners added a 1,000-square-foot deck and stage. A full sit-down breakfast is included in your stay. Unregistered guests are not allowed to join you for a swim in the sweet little pool, nor are children under ten. **$$$**

MARIGNY MANOR HOUSE

Marigny, 2125 N. Rampart St.,
504-943-7826;
marignymanorhouse.com

An affordable, quaint, restored 1840s Greek revival house located very close to Frenchmen Street's music clubs and restaurants (as well as **Gene's Po-Boys and Daiquiris**, the bright pink building on Elysian Fields). **$$**

MARQUETTE HOUSE

Uptown, 2249 Carondelet St.,
504-523-3014

A bare-bones, grungy hostel with $25 beds. But it also has a bar, and is near other bars such as Igor's, and after a Bloody Mary or two, it's fun to stumble out into the street and onto the streetcar and relax on a long slow ride through half of the city. **$**

NEW ORLEANS GUEST HOUSE

Tremé, 1118 Ursulines Ave.,
800-562-1177;
neworleansguest.house

This salacious pink building on the Tremé side of Rampart St. just across from the Quarter is an 1848 gable-sided Creole cottage with a tiny, funky-quaint garden. Its insides are less funky than its outside, with nicer-than-you-might-expect rooms. **$$**

DJ Otto commands a gorgeous view of the CBD from the NOPSI hotel rooftop pool.

NOPSI

CBD, 317 Baronne St.,
844-439-1463; nopsihotel.com

Pricey, but a great place to hang, especially when DJs like Otto select perfect music at NOPSI's rooftop pool. On Fridays and Saturdays, **DJ Otto** collaborates with live musicians on the level of keyboardist David Torkanowsky, and trumpeters Khris Royal and Benny Bloom. Pet-friendly accommodations are available. **$$$**

PONTCHARTRAIN LANDING

Southern side of Lake Pontchartrain,
6001 France Rd., 504-286-8157;
pontchartrainlanding.com

A waterfront RV park, marina, and boat launch that also rents out bungalows and floating villas that can house several people for **around $400.** The bar, restaurant, and pool are special enough to have attracted a regular local crowd who hang out, watch Saints games, swim, and party. **$$$**

RATHBONE MANSIONS

Mid-City, 1244 Esplanade Ave.,
504-309-4479;
rathbonemansions.com

These two mansions across the street from each other on gorgeous Esplanade Avenue border the French Quarter. One mansion features a pool and Jacuzzi, the other a lush courtyard for chillin'. Rooms are extra cheap during the summer, and a courtyard suite with kitchenette and three beds (sleeps six) is very affordable even during Mardi Gras. **$$**

ROYAL BARRACKS
GUEST HOUSE

French Quarter, 717 Barracks St.,
504-529-7269; rbgh.com

The bunk room, garden room, gothic room, and peacock room with ten-foot chandelier were each designed by a different local artist. The pool is open most of the time, but the courtyard wet bar remains always in service. **$$$**

ST. VINCENT'S GUEST HOUSE

Uptown, 1507 Magazine St., 504-302-9606; stvguesthouse.com

This 70-room hotel boasts an onsite restaurant, bike rental (all New Orleans hotels and B&Bs should loan bikes to their clientele!), and private rooms, plus male, female, and coed dormitories featuring three to six beds. **$**

THE TROUBADOUR

CBD, 1111 Gravier St., 504-518-5800; tapestrycollection3.hilton.com/tc/troubadour-new-orleans

The stylish, eclectic rooms sit above Petit Lion, a restaurant serving casual and contemporary French food, while upstairs the Monkey Board offers up "food-truck eats, liquid treats and live DJ beats against surreal sunsets and the scenic skyline of the Big Easy." **$$$**

NOLA MOMENT

ROYAL STREET INN AND ITS ROCKSTAR PROPRIETOR, GREG DULLI

Marigny, 1431 Royal St., 504-948-7499; royalstreetinn.com

Zack Smith

Greg Dulli of the Royal Street Inn

This place is more of a "bed and beverage," owing to the **R Bar** downstairs—a place essential to any New Orleans visit anyway, with its intermittent free shrimp and crawfish boils, and DJs spinning everything from old New Orleans R&B and garage rock to weird ancient country to whatever rock is cool in Brooklyn. On Monday nights, $10 will get you a shot, a beer, and a haircut by a semiprofessional stylist.

The inn and bar are owned these days by Afghan Whigs frontman (and former Twilight Singer and Gutter Twin) **Greg Dulli** and partners including **Bailey Smith** of beloved drunk-rock band the **Morning 40 Federation**. The bar has always given off a rock 'n' roll aura with its impeccable jukebox, but even more so under Dulli's ownership.

Upstairs the rooms are decorated for maximum "sleazy luxury." One room was formerly named the Bukowski Suite for the author who stayed there and etched "Hank was here" in the cement outside the R Bar's door. The room's name was changed after the inn was refurbished (I guess referencing the alcoholic author didn't flatter the Royal Street Inn's well-appointed bohemian suites), but it's still one of the cooler places you can stay, just blocks from the French Quarter.

17. BIKES AND PUBLIC TRANSPORTATION

BIKES

New Orleans' public transportation is just okay. Choose to rent a car and drive yourself, and parking can be nightmarish. Rely only on your feet, and risk missing chunks of the Quarter. A nicer way to put this would be: rent a bike. On a beach cruiser, you can pedal from one end of the remarkably flat city's heart to the opposite end, in about an hour if you hustle. On a bike you'll cover the most ground, see the most sights, and always find parking. **Nolacycles.com** provides great information on New Orleans' bike culture (not sports-oriented "bike culture," more like bikes with cupholders on the handlebars, Mardi Gras beads, and fake flowers), with listings of bicycling events and downloadable city biking maps. The following local shops are also fighting the good two-wheeled fight—they'll rent you a bike:

ARTS DISTRICT BIKE RENTAL

Uptown, 1121 Margaret Pl.,
504-521-6390;
artsdistrictbikerental.com

Maybe the cheapest bike rentals in the city: $20 per day, plus $15 colorful light-up bikes at night.

BICYCLE MICHAEL'S

Marigny, 622 Frenchmen St.,
504-945-9505;
bicyclemichaels.com

As far as legitimate professional (but still a tad funky) bike shops go, Michael's has a monopoly over the Mari-gny/Bywater. They're kinda pricey on some things, and sometimes the staff's kind of gruff, but they do set aside a gate outside of their shop for bands to post flyers. Bike rental is around $25 a day.

BIG EASY BIKE TOURS

Bywater, 3017 Chartres St.;
504-377-0973; bigeasybiketours.com

This company hosts the Esplanade Avenue of the Creoles tour, and the American Sector tour of the Garden District. Or, if you prefer a longer ride that might seem like exercise, BEBT hosts a 20-mile trip around the city.

BIKE EASY

*Marigny, 1024 Elysian Fields Ave.,
504-861-4022; bikeeasy.org*

Bike advocacy and safe bike route maps.

BULLFROG BIKE TOURS

*French Quarter, 214 Decatur St.,
1-877-734-8687;
neworleans.bullfrogbiketours.com*

Real live New Orleans musicians take you on two-wheeled music history tours, or on walking tours in the Quarter and around Frenchmen Street's live jazz scene.

BUZZ NOLA BIKE TOURS & RENTALS

*Uptown, 214 Magazine St.,
504-533-9688; buzznola.com*

Basic rentals and tours with the addition of electric bicycle options. Located a very short distance from the French Quarter.

NOLA MOMENT

CONFEDERACY OF CRUISERS BIKE TOURS AND A BICYCLE NAMED DESIRE RENTALS

Marigny, 634 Elysian Fields Ave., 504-400-5468; confederacyofcruisers.com

Some lucky visitors to New Orleans plop down on a random barstool and happen to sit beside a drinking, parading, gumbo-cooking historian who wants to spend the next three hours talking about the city they love. Confederacy of Cruisers Bike Tours and A Bicycle Named Desire Rentals aspire to give you that same funky educational experience, but while riding comfy cruisers (often equipped with drink holders).

Tours for those who don't usually take tours, CoC's excursions are easy riding through quiet, flat streets. The guides are the owner's friends and drinkin' buddies, who all share an obsession for the city's history. The stories they tell—both historical and what they did the night before—paint a great picture of how New Orleans remains apart from America to this day. CoC offers tours of the Creole side of New Orleans, neighborhood eating tours, the history of drinking tours (with bar stops), and a Ninth Ward tour that focuses on the

Zack Smith

The kind and sincere staff at Confederacy of Cruisers give some of the most fun and personable bike tours in town, with drinks and stories included!

importance of the neighborhood's culture, and why rebuilding is still so important.

Confederacy of Cruisers partners with A Bicycle Named Desire Rentals (abicyclenameddesire.com, office located at an address used in *A Streetcar Named Desire*) to provide rental bikes, maps, and ideas for those who'd rather set out on their own. Comfortable beach cruisers rent for $25 a day, including free delivery and pickup, plus helmet, lock, and basket.

Biking is the most efficient and exciting way to see the Quarter, for sure. The crew at CoC also suggests you check out these related businesses:

KAYAK-ITI-YAT

Mid-City, kayak tours begin on bank of Bayou St. John, 985-778-5034 or 512-964-9499; kayakitiyat.com

OK, no bikes but . . . paddle the Bayou St. John in a kayak near City Park, through the middle of a community filled with neighborhood parks, great food, fun bars, and sometimes music festivals or Mardi Gras Indians.

RUBARB

Bywater, 2239 Piety St.; rubarbike.org

Its name an acronym for Rusted Up Beyond All Recognition Bikes, this is a community bike shop where you can learn to build or repair a bike, obtain a bike through work, trade, or a small donation, or just volunteer. They even host field trips! Rubarb does offer some rentals during major New Orleans holidays, with all donations going back into the shop to purchase tools as well as art supplies (because your bike has to costume on Mardi Gras too!).

GERKEN'S BIKE SHOP

Bywater, 2803 St. Claude Ave., 504-373-6924; gerkensbikeshop.com

A down-home, cheap bike shop across the railroad tracks from the **Green Project** (an architectural salvage spot that's a junk collector's dream), Gerken's caters to the neighborhood boho bike crowd. They're not afraid to utilize used parts, and they'll fix stuff for you. Gerken's doesn't directly rent bikes, but call them and they'll figure something out for you.

MIKE THE BIKE GUY

Uptown, 4411 Magazine St., 504-899-1344; mikethebikeguy.com

This particular Mike worked fixing bikes for others for twenty years before opening his own place. Bikes rent for $30 a day, $120 for a week, but once one of the bikes has been used for a week, Mike sells them for around $180.

CANAL ST./ALGIERS FERRY

French Quarter, at the foot of Canal St. next to the Aquarium

Since 1827, the Algiers ferry has conveyed folks across the Mississippi to Algiers Point, a quiet but fun neighborhood of beautiful New Orleans architecture sans wild nightlife (aside from the great **Old Point Bar** and **Crown & Anchor Pub**) or relatively much crime. This 15-minute scenic budget cruise on the river features a panoramic view of the city. Cost is $2 each way per person, for bikers and pedestrians. Closed to cars.

CITY BUSES (RTA)

504-248-3900; norta.com

After flying into the Lil Wayne International Airport, you can take the $1.25 city bus into town, rather than wasting $30-plus on a cab ($30 can mean a lotta drinks in New Orleans' better dive bars!). Once you're in town, though, you'd only choose a bus over bike for A/C, or to dodge rain, or when shopping on Magazine Street, where they run straight and efficiently up and down miles of shops and cafés. Otherwise, our city buses are mostly only reliable for meeting interesting local characters. (From the airport, for $15 you can also get the airport shuttle, which will drop you at any hotel or guesthouse.)

GREYHOUND BUSES

CBD, 1001 Loyola Ave., 504-525-6075; greyhound.com

When you need to flee New Orleans at a moment's notice, Greyhound provides economic getaways for lawless fugitives, and for fauxbeaux utilizing Mom's gold card for an air-conditioned break from train-hopping.

MULE BUGGIES

French Quarter, 504-943-8820; neworleanscarriages.com

Especially during the hell-hot summer, these poor animals don't want to drag you around the French Quarter. All summer the poor things sweat, their tongues twisting and writhing trying to spit the bits from their mouths. No matter how well the mules are supposedly treated, they'd surely be much happier if you just rode a bike.

STREETCAR

504-248-3900; norta.com

Same as our city buses: $1.25, every fifteen minutes, though you can often, on foot, out-pace the streetcar to your destination. Of course that's not the point. Ride slow and long through the CBD, staring out the window at all the poor suckers working, before snaking around Lee Circle, through the Garden District and into the big trees and mansions of Uptown. The streetcar ain't meant for reaching important destinations on time, but then you might realistically end up sharing a streetcar with

The Krewe of Muses pokes fun at Uber for attempting to destroy traditional cab driving as a profitable New Orleans occupation. Call United Cabs instead!

Michael Patrick Welch

a brass band practicing on their way to a gig (the only time they might otherwise practice). New Orleans recently installed two new streetcar lines: one in the CBD between the French Quarter and the Superdome (locals call this one "the streetcar to nowhere") and another on St. Claude Ave., ending in the Marigny. Runs 5 a.m. to roughly 2 a.m.

TAXIS

United Cab, 504-522-9771; unitedcabs.com

In New Orleans you'll need to phone for a cab unless you're on Frenchmen Street, Esplanade, Decatur, or Canal, where you can maybe flag one down. United is the local favorite.

UBER

There are many reasons to hail a cab instead of an Uber while visiting New Orleans. First, Uber is a megacorporation that has helped dismantle cab driving across the nation, and turn it into a part-time hustle when once it was an occupation on which one could raise a family and build a business and become wealthy. Second, our city government only recently reamed the regular cabbies with tons of costly upgrades (including in-cab computer screens that blast ads in your face when you should be looking out the window, admiring our gorgeous city). Then that same government let Uber come in with almost no rules and take over. While in New Orleans, please use a local cab company.

PEDICABS

nolapedicabs.com; needaridenola.com; neworleansbiketaxi.com

In 2011, three pedicab companies won city council approval and took to the streets. Today you can stand on most corners in the Quarter and hop aboard within minutes. We have a fondness for local taxi drivers, but they're not always necessary or available, particularly below Canal Street. The supple legs of youth are your best bet, typically charging $1 per block and running late into the evening. Tips are welcome and rates seem, well, negotiable. Drivers are mostly young and willing to talk while they pump pedals. If you need to get from, say, Café Du Monde to the Superdome, pedicabs are quicker and easier than fighting French Quarter motor traffic.

Of course, if you want to know more about city politics, take a regular cab, mention pedicabs, and prepare for a treatise. (*Note:* The young pedicab drivers put up with a lot of drunken harassment. Don't be that guy).

TRANSPORTATION

18. HELPFUL LOCAL PUBLICATIONS AND WEBSITES

PRINT MAGAZINES AND WEBSITES

ANTIGRAVITY

antigravitymagazine.com

If you like this guidebook, you'll dig *Antigravity,* which covers the same underground local musicians you probably won't see at **Jazz Fest**. Printed in black and white, tabloid-sized *AG* gives a street-level view of NOLA's alternate musical universe of punk, metal, indie, and other sounds, plus a recent bent toward local politics, gardening, child-rearing, and other grownup topics.

GAMBIT WEEKLY

bestofneworleans.com

Gambit focuses on local politics, bar and restaurant guides, and A&E coverage, giving almost equal space to both traditional and edgy happenings both in its print publication and at its blog, bestofneworleans.com. We are still a little sore at *Gambit* for getting rid of its entire music section after Katrina, but the cover stories are usually pretty good.

NEW ORLEANS ADVOCATE

After our famous daily newspaper, the *Times-Picayune,* cut circulation to just a few days a week, this Baton Rouge paper swooped in and set up a newsroom in NOLA to deliver printed newspapers seven days a week. It's a little conservative and boring but, especially since it hired the *Picayune*'s discarded music writers **Alison Fensterstock** and **Keith Spera,** the *Advocate* is definitely the more thorough paper.

OFFBEAT

offbeat.com

This almost 30-year-old music magazine doesn't always have its ear to the streets, but *OffBeat* extensively covers Jazz Fest and other mainstream local events and artists. It reviews almost every Louisiana CD released, and at times can take you deeper into Louisiana roots music than any other publication. Look for the wildly opinionated columns of publisher and local hellraiser **Jan Ramsey**.

TIMES-PICAYUNE

nola.com

Besides having a truly great name, the *Times-Picayune* newspaper is a Pulitzer-winning paper that unfortunately now publishes only three days a week. Though the *Pic* axed its music writers a few years back, its Friday's Lagniappe pullout features the mainstream arts, music, and culture picks for the week ahead. The website features real-time breaking news and live-blog coverage of crimes and music festivals. Click for the articles, but stay for the most heinous comment boards in the known universe.

WHERE Y'AT?

whereyat.com

A slim little tabloid full of ads, bar guides, ads, some music coverage, and some ads, *Where Y'at?* (local slang for "hello, friend") is great reading for when you're at a bar and your date goes to use the bathroom and is there a long time.

OTHER LOCAL WEBSITES

Here are informative and fun websites you can check for New Orleans entertainment and culture news.

AMERICAN ZOMBIE

theamericanzombie.com

Blogger **Jason Brad Berry** was an essential truth-seeker after the storm, with particular dedication to corruption in public contracts. When the feds indicted former mayor **Ray Nagin**, local media credited American Zombie for digging up key dirt.

ARTS COUNCIL OF NEW ORLEANS

artsneworleans.org

This site keeps a strong calendar of events, as well as profiles of venues and cultural organizations.

DEFEND NEW ORLEANS

defendneworleans.com

Maker of now-iconic shirts and throwers of parties, Defend New Orleans' site features blog entries and videos of hipster antics, such as what happens when a bounce rapper plays a debutante party.

GONER RECORDS

goner-records.com

A Memphis record label with a serious crush on our city. The New Orleans section of its lively message board is great for garage and punk show listings and entertaining scene gossip.

HOME OF THE GROOVE

homeofthegroove.blogspot.com

Dan Phillips, a DJ for Lafayette's **KRVS** (88.7 FM), exhaustively catalogs live recordings of Louisiana musical acts, among other music history–oriented writing and other projects. Great place to find nearly forgotten New Orleans R&B, funk, and rock 'n' roll.

THE LENS

thelensnola.org

This nonprofit site started by preservationists and led by former *Times-Picayune* editors is dedicated to investigative journalism in the region, breaking big stories about local government, preservation issues, and the ongoing upheaval of public school education. A small venture that covers the issues other newsrooms pass up.

LIBRARY CHRONICLES

librarychronicles.blogspot.com

Begun as a vent for frustrated Katrina thoughts, this still-cantankerous blog will keep you cynically abreast of local flooding, drama with the Saints, city government's soft war on live music, dumb things New York magazine are writing about New Orleans, and other hot button local topics.

MY SPILT MILK

myspiltmilk.com

Editor **Alex Rawls** offers a source of interviews and think pieces dedicated as much to touring indie bands with upcoming New Orleans gigs as it is to local music. Alex hosts lots of free ticket contests.

NEW ORLEANS & ME

neworleans.me

Good creator of NOLA-related content, with updates on events, shows, and festivals. Same crew that designs the **Dirty Coast** T-shirts.

NOLA UNDERGROUND

nolaunderground.wordpress.com

"The true core scene of the South." Focusing mainly on the hard, loud, and/or fast, this blog was, in its words, "created as a tool for understanding the truth and reality of the best music scene spawned from the pits of NOLA." They also put on the **Raise the Dead Festival**.

PELICAN BOMB

pelicanbomb.com

Art site that runs features, portfolios from local artists, and gallery listings.

UPTOWN MESSENGER / MID-CITY MESSENGER

uptownmessenger.com / midcitymessenger.com

Robert Morris and company regularly break stories on crime, zoning, and school issues in several precise areas of the city. An unsung hero of local newsgathering.

WWOZ (90.7 FM)

wwoz.org

Incredible streaming real-time audio from the station—always especially great during Mardi Gras, or just after a famous New Orleans musician has passed away—plus DJ blogs, playlists, and community news.

WORTHY OF SUPPORT

The author and his telecaster get a checkup at the New Orleans Musicians' Clinic, which, funded through donations, treats local musicians and other artists for free. Donate!

Jonathan Traviesa

The following groups have specifically helped New Orleans and/ or our musicians in one form or another, and all of them are worthy of your donations:

HANDSON NEW ORLEANS

handsonneworleans.org

This volunteer aggregator partners eager volunteers with needy causes in New Orleans. Since Katrina, they've mobilized tens of thousands of volunteers.

NEW ORLEANS MUSICIANS' CLINIC (NOMC)

3700 St. Charles Ave., 504-412-1366; neworleansmusiciansclinic.org

Musicians are broke because you forgot to tip them, then went and downloaded their music for free. Though relied upon by New Orleans to help generate tourist dollars, musicians were woefully lacking a health safety net until, in 1995, the New Orleans Musicians' Clinic began offering comprehensive health services to the city's musicians and others of nonconventional employment, providing affordable medical care, mostly via LSU's medical school.

Today, the Musicians' Clinic is an American anomaly, and possibly the only thing in New Orleans that makes sense.

ROOTS OF MUSIC

therootsofmusic.org

Founded by **Rebirth Brass Band** drummer **Derrick Tabb** to fill a void in local music education, Roots of Music teaches students from all over the city the basics of marching band music while focusing on academic achievement. Some of the city's best brass band musicians lead the after-school classes, which have marched in the Rose Bowl Parade and **Jazz Fest**.

WEBSITES

Bassist Bru Bruiser of bands Gov't Majik and Gravity A (among others) holds out hope.

Zack Smith

For closing in on twenty years, journalist/musician/fisherman **Michael Patrick Welch** has covered New Orleans and its music. He has published cover stories in every major New Orleans publication, and his work has appeared in *The Guardian, Vice, Vox, Columbia Journalism Review, Oxford American, Newsweek, National Geographic, McSweeney's,* and many other fine publications.

On the side, Welch teaches a rap class in New Orleans schools. He's currently helping develop a movie about the fate of prisoners during Hurricane Katrina.

Welch lives on the sleepy side of the river in Algiers, in William Burroughs' old hood, with his partner, artist Morgana King, their two daughters Cleopatra and Xyla, and a herd of pygmy goats.

Follow him on Twitter @MPatrickWelch, or email him and he will take you fishing: michaelpatrickwelch@gmail.com

Brian Boyles is vice president of content at the Louisiana Endowment for the Humanities, where he serves as publisher of *Louisiana Cultural Vistas* magazine and directs public programs at the Louisiana Humanities Center. His work has been featured in *Oxford American, OffBeat,* the *Lens,* the *Brooklyn Rail, NOLA-Fugees, SLAM, Gathering of the Tribes* online magazine, and *Louisiana Cultural Vistas.* Follow him @brianwboyles.

Zack Smith is a lifestyle-branding and commercial photographer who has been involved in the social, musical, and cultural landscapes of Louisiana for the past twenty years. As a musician, artist, and storyteller, Smith believes that the world gets smaller as we celebrate our similarities and connect through our traditions and stories. As a producer and photographer, Zack has helped create powerful photography-branding campaigns for Brand USA, New Orleans Tourism and Marketing, the New Orleans Convention and Visitors Bureau, Canal Place, CHASE Bank, LSU Health, and many more. He recently opened a photography studio on Magazine Street, where he does commercial photography and teaches photography workshops year-round.

Jonathan Traviesa has been photographing in New Orleans since 1997. In 2009 the Ogden Museum of Southern Art exhibited a solo show of his work in conjunction with the publication of his book *Portraits: Photographs in New Orleans, 1998–2009.* His prints are collected privately around the United States and publicly in New Orleans by the Ogden and the New Orleans Museum of Art. Traviesa is a founding member of The Front, a contemporary art gallery in New Orleans, and his editorial work has been published in news and fashion magazines around the world. He also owns the world's most memorable hair.